CRITICAL APPROACHES TO RUBÉN DARÍO

Rubén Darío (1867-1916) of Nicaragua was the leader of the important Latin American literary movement known as Modernism. He is considered by many to be the greatest poet in Latin American literature, and the volume of writings devoted to his work since 1884 is perhaps greater than that on any other writer in the history of Spanish American literature. The celebration in 1967 of the centenary of his birth gave rise to a formidable number of new analyses, increasing the need for the classification and assessment of the many studies.

In this book Professor Ellis examines and evaluates the wide range of methods and perspectives available to the reader of Darío's works. He considers the biographical approach, social and political questions, influences and sources, structural analysis (providing three structural studies of his own), and, in an appendix, Darío's own concept of the role of the literary critic. His book is comprehensive both in time and in range, and includes an up-to-date bibliography.

This is the first systematic study of the critical works on a Spanish American writer. It is significant not only in its treatment of the work on an individual author, but also as a reflection on and an indication of the trends, methods, and preoccupations of modern appraisals of Latin American writing.

University of Toronto Romance Series 28

KEITH ELLIS is Associate Professor in the Department of Italian and Hispanic Studies at the University of Toronto. He has also written *El arte narrativo de Francisco Ayala*.

Critical Approaches to
Rubén Darío

KEITH ELLIS

UNIVERSITY OF TORONTO PRESS

© University of Toronto Press 1974

Toronto and Buffalo

Reprinted in paperback 2017

ISBN 978-0-8020-5309-1 (cloth)

ISBN 978-1-4875-9835-8 (paper)

LC 73-93235

University of Toronto Romance Series 28

TO ZILPHA AND CARMEN

Contents

Introduction

Literary criticism on Rubén Darío's work first appeared in 1884 when he was seventeen years old. Since that time the volume of writings devoted to his work has probably become greater than that dealing with any other figure in the history of Spanish American literature. The celebration in 1967 of the centenary of his birth provided the occasion for an impressive number of new studies of his work. Now that nearly all the special publications announced for that occasion have appeared, the time may not be unsuitable for a critical examination of the trends indicated by some of the significant studies in this body of critical work. I shall not attempt the Herculean task of accounting for the whole bibliography of works published on Darío. I aim rather to represent the range of methods employed by a selection of critics, to categorize these methods in the light of generally recognized concepts of criticism, to indicate some specific findings with regard to Darío's life and works, and to gauge the extent to which the methods are useful in elucidating his literary production. Consequently, the critical works studied are usually to be viewed as examples of certain perspectives. Nevertheless, I shall attempt to deal with a substantial number of works and particularly with those books and articles that establish or are foremost in sustaining trends.

In the first of the broad categories that I perceive, the biographical, the works devoted to the story of Darío's life and that treat the relationship between his biography and his work are discussed. Writings on Darío's view of social and political questions are dealt with in the second chapter, while studies of influences and sources are explored in Chapter 3. Chapter

4 deals with critical studies that treat internal aspects of Darío's work but which are not concerned, except incidentally, with the way in which these aspects cohere with others in individual works to form harmonious compositions. Studies that do have the latter orientation find their place in Chapter 5. In Chapter 6 studies assessing Darío's lasting contribution to literature are considered. The Appendix offers a brief essay on Darío as a literary critic, and is followed by a bibliography of the works mentioned in this study.

The placing of studies into categories is a necessary convenience which carries with it the difficulty posed by works not easily bound by any one category. Where this difficulty is particularly obtrusive I have tried to discuss the work in question in such a way that its multiple relationships are made evident; and I make reference to the work in other chapters.

The critical work done on Darío is so significant that its examination inevitably casts some reflection on the trends, methods, and preoccupations that characterize the literary criticism done on Spanish American writers in general. While the need remains clear for an even greater increase in the attention paid to the wider subject of Spanish American literary criticism than has occurred in recent years, I must limit my explicit aim here to an examination of critical approaches to Rubén Darío.

This book has been published with the help of a grant from the Humanities Research Council of Canada, using funds provided by the Canada Council, and a grant from the Andrew W. Mellon Foundation to the University of Toronto Press.

CRITICAL APPROACHES TO RUBÉN DARÍO

CHAPTER ONE

The Biographical
Approach

Biography, which had produced impressive achievements in the eighteenth century in Europe – Boswell's *Life of Samuel Johnson* (1791) being the outstanding example of that century – became more widespread in the nineteenth. In our own century such biographers as André Maurois, Lytton Strachey, and Stephan Zweig have continued, in Boswell's way, the art of telling the story of the lives of famous literary and historical personages. They have tended to regard biography as, in Strachey's words, 'the most delicate and humane of all the branches of the art of writing,'[1] involving a process of re-creating the spirit and likeness of a figure from a body of materials and impressions surviving his passage through life. Sainte-Beuve's persistent use of biography in the assessment of literary works and their authors lent another facet to the practice of biography, that of establishing it as a method of literary criticism. To discover biographical facts concerning a writer, to portray his personality and character, and to integrate these steps in an assessment of his literary work formed the basis of this method. Sainte-Beuve was to express his principal critical concepts in his *Nouveaux lundis* as follows:

> Literature, the literary product, is for me indistinguishable from the whole organization of the man. I can enjoy the work itself, but I find it difficult to judge this work without taking into account the man himself. I say without hesitation: *Like tree, like fruit*. Literary study thus brings me naturally to the study of morals ... One has to ask oneself a certain number of questions about an author, and give answers to them (even

though not out loud – and even though the questions may seem quite irrelevant to the nature of the works to be studied). Only after such questions can one be sure about the problems one faces. What did the author think about religion? In what way was he impressed by the contemplation of nature? How did he handle himself in the matter of women? How in the matter of money? Was he rich? Was he poor? What rules of living did he follow? What was his daily routine? And so on. – To sum it up: what was his master vice, his dominant weakness? Every man has one. Not a single one of the answers we give to these questions can be irrelevant to forming an opinion about the author of a book and about the book itself – that is, if we suppose we are dealing with something other than a treatise in pure geometry.[2]

Sainte-Beuve's method became one of the strong guiding forces in nineteenth-century Spanish American literary criticism. The method, combined with the popular tendency to tell the story of the lives of writers, gave great emphasis to the biographical approach which entered the twentieth century with considerable momentum. The approach has been widely adopted in this century and has been used with various modifications in the case of Rubén Darío.

Powerful impetus was also given to the biographical approach in Rubén Darío's criticism by Darío's own writings on his life and works. Conscious of the importance of his career, Darío in two important books, *La vida de Rubén Darío escrita por él mismo* (published originally in several instalments in *Caras y Caretas*, Buenos Aires, 1912), and *Historia de mis libros* (appearing first in three issues of *La Nación* in 1913), produced material that would serve as the point of departure for subsequent biographers. Besides the principal books mentioned, shorter items dispersed throughout his work, such as his 'Diario,'[3] 'Los colores del estandarte,'[4] 'Yo soy aquél,'[5] 'Prólogo que es página de mi vida'[6] and some of his other prologues, 'Canción de otoño en primavera,'[7] *El oro de Mallorca*,[8] and 'Epístola a la señora de Lugones,'[9] also prompted, for various reasons, other writers to contribute to the same subject.

Darío's *Vida* is an account of his experiences from his earliest childhood to the time of writing. He describes his unstructured education, his tormenting dreams, his search for literary opportunities, his precarious economic situation, his amours, his travels, his contacts with literary and political figures, and his health. He makes reference to and quotes some of his childhood poetry, recalls some of the notable figures he wrote about in *Los raros*; and of his major poetic works he discusses only *Prosas profanas*. He mentions only eight poems from this book, describing the circumstances in which seven of them were written and repeating José Enrique Rodó's comments about the musicality of the eighth, 'Sonatina.' *Azul* is mentioned only twice, in contexts that deal primarily with Juan Valera; and there is no reference whatsoever to either *Cantos de vida y esperanza* or *El canto errante*.

Using as the epigraph to his *Vida* Benvenuto Cellini's statement that all distinguished men should write their autobiography, and not before the age of forty, Darío begins his account by mentioning his eligibility for the task with regard to age. But he immediately indicates the tentative nature of his effort by continuing: 'Así doy comienzo a estos apuntamientos, que más tarde han de desenvolverse mayor y más detalladamente.'[10] Similarly, he closes his discussion of the few poems dealt with in his *Vida* by stating: 'Tanto éstas como otras poesías exigirían bastantes exégesis y largas explicaciones, que a su tiempo se harán.'[11] His treatment of the books *Azul*, *Prosas profanas*, and *Cantos de vida y esperanza* which constitutes *Historia de mis libros* is also brief and enticing. These works, then, and others in which he touches on aspects of his life and works provided a basic design on which later writers, who found the biographical approach attractive, could elaborate. Sometimes, too, Darío provokes further investigation of his life by making allusions to situations that promise to be sensational. He mentions in the *Vida*, for instance, that shortly after the death of his first wife he had a terrible experience in Managua, that Federico Gamboa had written about this experience, but that in deference to Darío's wishes he had left his account unpublished. Darío closes his discussion of the incident with the remark, stimulating for later biographers: 'Es precisa, pues, aquí esta laguna en la narración de mi vida.'[12] Also, in the course of narrating the *Vida*, Darío noticed errors committed in earlier sections which he allowed to stand in his text. He pointed out, for instance, that the episode concerning Captain Andrews occurred during his second voyage to Spain and not during his first, in 1892, as he had stated earlier in the text. Because of the possibility of further errors he kept reminding his readers: 'advierto que bien puedo equivocarme, de cuando en cuando, en asuntos de fecha, y anteponer o posponer la prosecución de sucesos ... no me valgo para estos recuerdos sino de mi memoria.'[13] Darío's death came less than four years after he wrote his *Vida*. And his failing health during those years, prevented him from returning, in any sustained way, to his autobiography. It was left to others to augment, verify, correct, and interpret the information he had offered. His manifest importance as a poet, his tentative autobiographical work, the interest evoked by his life as he portrayed it, all combined with the growth in popularity of the biographical approach to literary criticism to produce serious and voluminous biographical studies of Darío's life and works.

Different emphases are encountered in these works not only concerning the aspect of Darío's life to which their authors pay particular attention but also to the extent to which they relate biographical facts to his literary works. Of the studies that deal comprehensively with his life the earliest are most dependent on his autobiographical works. Even his contemporary, Enrique Gómez Carrillo, whom Darío regarded as a friend, but who often used a gentle sarcasm in his treatment of Darío, and who was better acquainted with him personally than any of his subsequent biographers, made use of the autobiographical writings, particularly the *Vida*, and part IV of the 'Dilucidaciones,' in his essay 'Una visita a Rubén Darío.'[14] Gómez Carrillo portrays Darío in Mallorca in 1907 as a pathetic figure defending himself from detractors. He also reports, erroneously,[15] that Darío wrote nothing in Mallorca that indicated any sensitivity to his surroundings. Elsewhere, in a tone that conveys some resentment, he tells of his encounter with Darío in 1890 when he arrived in Guatemala to become publisher and editor of *El Correo de la Tarde*. He introduces him quite agreeably: 'llegó a Guatemala, ya coronado de rosas, el gran Rubén Darío,'[16] but proceeds to picture him mockingly as running from one president to the next – from José Manuel Balmaceda of Chile to Francisco Menéndez of El Salvador to Manuel Lisandro Barrillas of Guatemala – and as squandering the funds of *El Correo de la Tarde*, leaving Gómez Carrillo unpaid for his contributions to the newspaper. He also declares, unfairly, that 'para Rubén, mientras menos español era algo, más valía.'[17] For him, Darío in his later years was 'envenenado por el alcohol y la vanidad.'[18]

Máximo Soto-Hall, with emphatic benevolence, recounts aspects of the story of Darío's life in Central America, reporting conversations with the poet and referring to his autobiography. These were the methods that Eduardo de Ory[19] and José María Vargas Vila[20] had used a year after Darío's death to give more extensive but wholly laudatory portraits of his career.

Francisco Contreras,[21] who had a longstanding friendship with Darío, followed the poet's own procedure of attempting to discuss life and work separately and used the substance of Darío's *Vida* and *Historia* unstintingly. This procedure resulted in extensive commentary on Darío's works. Arturo Torres-Ríoseco continued this trend in his *Vida y poesía de Rubén Darío*,[22] but added much new material on Darío's life, giving a fuller account of this aspect than he had done in his earlier book *Rubén Darío: casticismo y americanismo. Estudio precedido de la biografiá del poeta.*[23] He also undertook a substantial discussion of Darío's books of poetry. In the intervening years valuable new information for Darío's biography had been contributed by Alberto Ghiraldo whose *El archivo de Rubén Darío* was first published in 1940[24] and in its fuller and definitive form in 1943.[25] Ghiraldo himself, however, had done scarcely any meaningful interpretation of Darío's correspondence, carried out between 1896 and 1911 with and about literary figures, which constitutes the major part of the *Archivo*. Juan Antonio Cabezas does not seem to have taken advantage of the *Archivo*; and, although his book is entitled *Rubén Darío: un poeta y una vida*,[26] he concentrates on Darío's life, taking the poetry to represent the poet's states of mind during the various historical circumstances in which the different collections were written. Of the aesthetic aspect of the poetry he says very little, offering instead a selection of poems with the following stated purpose: 'Y ahora una breve antología de Rubén cerrará la segunda parte de este libro biográfico. Un intermedio para que el lector tenga su personal y espiritual coloquio con el poeta, sin la intervención del biógrafo.'[27]

In the introduction to his *La dramática vida de Rubén Darío* of 1952, Edelberto Torres wrote of Darío:

> Quedan muchas zonas de su existencia no exploradas y algunas lo han sido parcialmente. Ni siquiera poseemos el itinerario preciso de sus pasos por el mundo, mucho menos la localización de los hitos de su evolución mental. De uno y otro aspecto, sólo han sido señalados los sitios que él mismo marcó como lugares de residencia o de visita, y aquellos grandes momentos en que dio al mundo sus libros y poemas más conspicuos. La cronología de su producción ofrece un extenso campo de investigación, porque gran número de artículos y poemas, aun los ya recopilados, carecen de identificación temporal que permita seguir el hilo evolutivo en el dédalo de su proficua labor.[28]

This statement by the author of the most extensive biography of Darío so far written indicates the difficulty of arriving at a completely satisfactory account of the career even of a writer who was famous throughout his lifetime and who died in this century. Beyond the aim of telling as complete a story as he can of Darío's life, Torres attempts to tell it, as his title indicates, as entertainingly as possible. He therefore foregoes the scholarly responsibility of documenting his work and defends himself on those grounds in the preface to the second edition (reproduced in the third edition)[29] from criticism of this lack of documentation by E.K. Mapes.[30] Torres does achieve his aims. His narration of some of the episodes is exciting, if not sensational.[31] All the topics touched on in Darío's *Vida* are explored energetically in *La dramática vida*, as Torres used all the sources of information that were available to him. The *Archivo* compiled by Francisca Sánchez, Darío's Spanish companion, was an additional source employed in the fourth edition of Torres's book.[32]

In his book *Este otro Rubén Darío*, Antonio Oliver Belmás celebrates the acquisition by the University of Madrid (or by Spain, as he asserts) of the *Archivo* of Francisca Sánchez on 25 October 1956. 'Por haber sido yo el primer catalogador de los documentos cedidos a España por doña Francisca Sánchez,' he writes, 'debía moralmente al mundo un libro que se apoyara en esos amarillentos papeles.'[33] For the purposes of a biographer, this *Archivo* is helpful above all for clarifying some of Darío's literary and personal relationships and for tracing his itinerary with new precision. Oliver Belmás devotes extensive sections of his book to these aspects, paying particular attention to Darío's relations with Juan Valera, Marcelino Menéndez y Pelayo, and especially Miguel de Unamuno, as well as mentioning Darío's contacts with a large number of other Spanish and Spanish American writers. His travels within Spain and in the neighbouring Spanish territories are carefully dealt with. And there is an initial emphasis on Darío's association with Navalsáuz, Francisca Sánchez's native village, which Darío visited for the first time in October 1899 and where the materials that were to form the *Archivo* were kept before being moved to Madrid. For the rest, the author deals with various topics, some of them concerned with intrinsic aspects of Darío's poetry, others with aspects of his early life that had been dealt with more thoroughly by other biographers. There is no apparent intention on Oliver Belmás's part to treat exhaustively in this book all the important topics offered by Darío's work. He has dealt subsequently with other important areas in other publications, which will be mentioned in later chapters. *Este otro Rubén Darío*, by having recourse to the *Archivo* of Francisca Sánchez, contributes significantly to knowledge of Darío's relations with Spain.

The first comprehensive biography of Darío to appear in English was that of Charles D. Watland.[34] Unlike Oliver Belmás, he presents a precise chronological story of Darío's life in a work that is not as expansive as that of Torres but which has essential documentation and is the product of careful research, with works from Darío's *Vida* to the *Archivo* of Francisca Sánchez being included among his sources. Like Torres's work, however, *Poet Errant* does not attempt to make any detailed assessment of Darío's poetry.

Intimate and vast knowledge of Darío's life is also shown by Jaime Torres Bodet who set himself many goals in his biography.[35] He views

Darío's career in the light of his social, political, and economic circumstances, at the personal, national, and continental levels. Like almost all the biographers mentioned so far in this chapter, he surveys Darío's life, covering the topics Darío himself had considered in presenting his *Vida*. He provides apt comments on Darío's works and relates them to his life in a sober, deeply reflective way. As a consequence of attempting all this in a relatively short work, some aspects receive cursory treatment and his documentation is somewhat capricious; but his achievement in the field of biographical criticism, of relating meaningfully the life and the works of the poet, is great. So also is Enrique Anderson Imbert's in his book, *La originalidad de Rubén Darío*.[36] He gives a detailed account of Darío's life and career and analyses of his principal works. The relationship of life to work is the indispensable foundation on which the book rests; for Anderson Imbert's definition of originality is satisfied here by his view of Darío's literary work as the authentic expression of a unique existence and development.[37]

There are many useful works dealing with Darío's biography which do not aim at being comprehensive. They deal with stages of Darío's life, with his experiences in specific countries, and with his relations with certain figures. Several of these works have contributed greatly to the work of the comprehensive biographers. Useful information on Darío's earliest days is provided by Juan de Dios Vanegas and Alfonso Valle.[38] Biographers have acknowledged their debt to those who have written about Darío's formative years, such as Diego Manuel Sequeira,[39] who has provided indispensable documents concerning Darío's early work in Central America, Gustavo Alemán Bolaños,[40] whose work on Darío in Guatemala has been refined by Thomas Irving[41] and Evelyn Uhrhan Irving,[42] Ernesto Mejía Sánchez,[43] who has provided richly documented studies of Darío in Central America, and Raúl Silva Castro,[44] who has contributed a valuable study of Darío in Chile. Other studies such as that of Ventura García Calderón,[45] for example, contribute to this aspect of Darío's biography. Apart from the records of Darío's life in Central America and Chile mentioned above, important studies have been devoted to his relations with citizens of or his stay in Argentina,[46] Costa Rica,[47] Cuba,[48] the Dominican Republic,[49] Ecuador,[50] Mexico,[51] Panama,[52] Uruguay,[53] Venezuela,[54] Brazil,[55] Portugal,[56] the United States,[57] Spain,[58] Cataluña,[59] Asturias,[60] Andalucía,[61] Mallorca,[62] and Italy.[63] In addition to the treatment given in these works to the part of Darío's biography that dealt with his relations with his intimate acquaintances[64] and with personalities of his epoch, many specific investigations of these topics have been made.[65]

The biographers' reliable findings may be summarized as follows. Félix Rubén García Sarmiento was born in Metapa (now Ciudad Darío), Nicaragua, on 18 January 1867. His parents, second cousins, were descendants of Darío Mayorca, and Darío came to be a patronymic attached to his descendants. Rubén was taken to León in his infancy to live with his great aunt and her husband, Félix Ramírez, who was his godfather and adoptive father, his parents having separated a month before he was born. 'El matrimonio de Manuel García – diré mejor de Manuel Darío – y Rosa Sarmiento,' writes Darío, 'fue un matrimonio de conveniencia, hecho por la familia. Así no es de extrañar que a los ocho meses, más o menos, de esa unión forzada y sin afecto, viniese la separación.'[66] He signed his first school-books with the name Félix Rubén Ramírez in the kindergarten run by Jacoba Tellería which he started to attend in 1870. In 1874 he entered public school and his writing of verses was stimulated by one of his teachers, Felipe Ibarra. He attended a private school for a brief time in 1887, for which his fees were paid by an uncle. He had to withdraw when he fought with that uncle's son. From 1878 to 1880 he attended a Jesuit school and began to read Latin and Greek. A member of the staff, a Colombian known as Padre Valenzuela, was a poet. He encouraged Darío who at this time was already much in demand as a village poet, writing epitaphs on behalf of the bereaved and songs for festive occasions. His first published poem 'Una lágrima,' an elegy, appeared on 26 June, 1880 in the Nicaraguan newspaper El Termómetro ; and he continued to publish from then on with some frequency in the Nicaraguan periodical El Ensayo. He signed all these publications with the name Rubén Darío.

In March 1881, the Instituto de Occidente was founded in León. Darío studied there and was impressed by its first director, José Leonard y Bertholet, a Polish exile, a liberal and a freemason. Darío soon began to be critical of the Jesuits and left the Instituto shortly after Leonard, under pressure from the Jesuits, resigned a post he had held for only two months. Apart from the rebellious religious and political ideas which Darío had acquired from Leonard and which were strengthened by his reading of Juan Montalvo, he received a good introduction to French literature which was to have decisive importance in his literary career. Only the fact that Darío taught Spanish grammar on a part-time basis at a private school run by his friend Francisco Castro saved him from being apprehended by the state as a vagrant after he left the Instituto. One of his projects at this time was to collect his early work in a manuscript entitled 'Poesías y artículos en prosa.' The collection remained unpublished. In an attempt to attract his government's attention and to get support for studies which he hoped to undertake in Europe he left León for Managua in

FIGURE 1
Rubén Darío in 1898

FIGURE 2
Minister for Nicaragua in Madrid, 1908

1882. The government agreed to finance his education, on condition that he attend a Nicaraguan institution, but Darío regarded his quest as a failure. In August he left for El Salvador where he was well received by the president Rafael Zaldívar and where he continued his literary activities. He read his ode 'Al libertador Bolívar' on 24 July 1883, in the Teatro Nacional de San Salvador – an effort which pleased Zaldívar. Further-more, a valuable literary relation with the Salvadoran poet Francisco Gavidia sprang up.

Darío returned to Nicaragua in late 1883 and in the following year joined the staff of the president Adán Cárdenas, giving particular atten-tion to matters affecting the plan for a Central American Union. On 16 and 22 October 1884 the first published criticism of Darío's work appeared in *El Diario Nicaragüense* (Granada), a two-part article entitled 'La ley escrita de Rubén Darío' by Ricardo Contreras. Darío worked in the Biblioteca Nacional in Managua in 1885 and came to know the volumes of the *Biblioteca de autores españoles* in the Colección Rivadeneyra. In that year too his book *Epístolas y poemas* was printed. It was bound and distributed in 1888 with the title changed to *Primeras notas*. On 8 January 1886 the newspaper *El Imparcial*, with Darío as one of its founders, published its first number in Managua. He was persuaded by General Juan José Cañas to take advantage of the literary climate of Chile, and he received modest financial support from President Cárdenas for the ven-ture. In making his plans to leave for Chile, he agreed to represent his paper as well as *El Mercado* and *El Diario Nicaragüense*.

He arrived in Valparaíso, Chile on 24 June 1886, and in Santiago de Chile at the beginning of August. He entered fully into the flourishing literary activity that had enticed him, as it had enticed several leading Spanish American writers before him, to that country. He contributed an article to *El Mercurio* of Valparaíso on the eruption of Momotombo, which had occurred shortly before he left Nicaragua. Soon he left for Santiago where he worked for the newspaper *La Epoca* and established good relations with Pedro Balmaceda Toro, the son of the president of Chile. With the help of this friendship Darío gained access to several influential people as well as to important publications. In collaboration with Eduardo Poirier he wrote the novel *Emelina* which was entered unsuccessfully in a competition sponsored by the newspaper *La Unión*. His *Rimas*, in imitation of Bécquer's, also failed to win a prize in a competition sponsored by Federico Valera. However, his *Canto épico a las glorias de Chile* did share first prize in another division of the competition with a poem by Pedro Nolasco Préndez on the same subject. When the prizes were announced in Santiago in September 1887, Darío was there, having returned from Valparaíso where he had gone in March of the same year to take up a job as a customs inspector. Five months later he forfeited the job through poor attendance. His *Canto épico* and *Rimas*, or *Otoñales*, were published in a volume containing the distinguished entries in the Valera competition.[67] His collection *Abrojos* was published in the same year. In the meantime he prepared *Azul* for publication. José Victoriano Lastarria, whom he had asked to write the prologue, died in June 1888, but Darío's friend Eduardo de la Barra undertook the task. This prologue, before appearing in the first edition of *Azul*, was printed in the newspaper *La Tribuna* on 20 and 21 August. In December Darío received news of his father's death. He left Chile for Nicaragua in February 1889, submitting his first article to *La Nación* on departure.

En route to Nicaragua he visited Ricardo Palma in Lima. After spending three months in Nicaragua he went to El Salvador in June where he was cordially received by the president, Francisco Menéndez. There, he founded and directed *La Unión*. On 21 June of the following year he and Rafaela Contreras contracted a civil marriage. During Darío's wedding celebration, Menéndez died in a *coup d'etat* led by Carlos Ezeta. Darío then fled to Guatemala where, again welcomed by a president, this time Lisandro Barrillas, who gave him the necessary funds, he launched the newspaper *El Correo de la Tarde*. His biography of Pedro Balmaceda, who had died in 1889, was published in Guatemala in 1890 with the title *A. de Gilbert*, a pseudonym used by Balmaceda. The second, enlarged edition of *Azul*, now with an additional prologue by Juan Valera, was also published in Guatemala in 1890. Valera's prologue was composed of his two 'Cartas americanas' concerning Darío, which had appeared in *El Imparcial* of Madrid on 22 and 29 October 1888.

Rafaela arrived in Guatemala early in 1891; and the religious celebration of their wedding took place on 11 February of that year. In August they left for Costa Rica where, on 11 November, his son Rubén Darío Contreras was born. After contributing articles to *La Prensa Libre*, directed by Francisco Gavidia, he joined the staff of *El Heraldo* in March 1892, serving there for two months before returning to Guatemala. There he received news that he had been named secretary of the Nicaraguan delegation to the celebrations in Spain of the Fourth Centenary of the discovery of America. He returned to Nicaragua in late June to prepare for his journey to Spain, which began in the following month. Stopping briefly in Cuba, from 27 to 30 July, 1892, on the way to Spain, he met Julián del Casal. On arrival in Spain, he was warmly received by Juan Valera, Gaspar Núñez de Arce, Ramón de Campoamor, and Menéndez y Pelayo among others. His return journey provided another visit to Cuba, where he spent 5 and 6 December.[68] He also visited Colombia and met the writer and statesman Rafael Núñez, who promised to arrange a diplomatic post for him in Argentina. Rafaela died in El Salvador on 26 January 1893 and on 8 March Darío married Rosario Emelina Murillo who was fantasized in his novel *Emelina*. A son was born to Rosario some six weeks after their marriage. In April he received news that he had been named Consul of Colombia to Argentina.

The generous stipend attached to the post enabled him to go to New York, where he met José Martí, and then to Paris and a meeting with Paul Verlaine and Jean Moréas. He spent two months in Paris and reached Buenos Aires on 13 August, beginning almost immediately to write for *La Nación* and other Argentinian dailies. His consular duties were negligible. In 1894 he founded, with Ricardo Jaimes Freyre, the short-lived *Revista de América*. Rafael Núñez died in September 1894, and the Colombian government soon suppressed Darío's diplomatic post. His mother Rosa Sarmiento died in El Salvador on 3 May 1895, and in the Argentinian autumn of that year Darío spent some time on the island of Martín García recuperating from a fit of alcoholic depression. But 1896 was to be a better year for him. He was named secretary to Carlos Carlés, the director of postal services for Buenos Aires; and *Los raros* and then *Prosas profanas* were published in that city.

In December 1898, he was sent to Spain by *La Nación* to report on the state of that country after the war between Spain and the United States. He reached Barcelona on 1 January 1899 and went to Madrid on 4 January. There he met Francisca Sánchez and went to discover her native village Navalsáuz in October of that year. After covering the Paris Exposition for *La Nación* in 1900 he travelled through Italy and was granted an audience by Pope Leo XIII. A daughter, Carmen, was born to him and Francisca in April 1900. In the following year he returned to Madrid where his daughter died. He spent August of that year with Francisca in Dieppe, France. *Peregrinaciones*, *España contemporánea* and the second edition of *Prosas profanas*, enlarged with twenty-one new poems and with the study of the first edition by Rodó appearing as an unsigned prologue, were all published in 1901. In the following year his translation of Gorki, *Tomás Gordeieff*, appeared in Barcelona and was published subsequently in Paris, where Darío became acquainted with Antonio Machado. During the previous three years he had met Unamuno and had established friendships with Juan Ramón Jiménez and Valle Inclán.

In 1902 Darío was named Consul of Nicaragua to Paris. His first son with Francisca, Rubén Darío Sánchez, nicknamed 'Phocás, el campesino' by his father, was born, only to die two years later in 1905. Darío travelled extensively through southern Spain and to Gibraltar and Morocco in 1904. In the same year, on the invitation of the Mexican Felipe López, he travelled through Germany, Austria, Hungary, and Italy; and his *Tierras solares* was published in Madrid. He moved to Madrid with his family in February 1905 and on 28 March read 'Salutación del optimista' at the Ateneo de Madrid. The month of August was spent in Asturias and, with his good friend Juan Ramón Jiménez helping him with the final arrangements, he published *Cantos de vida y esperanza* in Madrid. The second, enlarged edition of *Los raros* came out in Barcelona in that year; and the third and definitive edition of *Azul*, with some of the material of the second edition omitted, was published in Buenos Aires.

In May 1906, Darío travelled to England and Belgium; and in July he left for Rio de Janeiro to serve as secretary of the Nicaraguan delegation at the Pan American Conference. He wrote 'Salutación al águila' at the conference. After a brief visit to Buenos Aires he left for Paris and went to Mallorca in November with his family to spend the winter, suffering again from the ill effects of alcohol. In Mallorca he worked on his book *El canto errante*, and on other poems as well as on a novel *La isla de oro*, which he did not finish. Meanwhile his *Oda a Mitre* was published in Paris and his *Opiniones*, in Madrid. Rosario Murillo had gone to Paris while he was in Mallorca; and Darío, in order to avoid seeing her, went to Brittany shortly after his return from Mallorca, leaving his friend Luis Bonafoux to negotiate with her. She demanded to see Darío and did see him in August 1907 in Quenat, Brittany, where he gave her two thousand francs. The publication of his *Canto errante* at this time provided Darío with much needed funds. On 2 October the second Rubén Darío Sánchez, nicknamed 'Güicho' by his father, was born, Darío left for Nicaragua at the end of the month and on arrival received a tumultuous welcome. He remained there until April 1908.

His purpose in going to Nicaragua was twofold: first, to obtain a divorce from Rosario so that he could marry Francisca – the *Archivo* of Francisca Sánchez in Madrid contains a code that was designed to inform Francisca promptly of the result of his quest – and, second, to secure the kind of diplomatic post that would make him financially comfortable. He did not achieve the first purpose but had some success with the second. He was sent to Spain by President José Santos Zelaya to represent Nicaragua as Minister to Spain. He was also put in charge of the consulate in Paris. In 1909 he made visits to Paris and travelled to Italy; and his book *El viaje a Nicaragua e intermezzo tropical* was published. The successor of President Zelaya, José Madriz, named Darío the delegate to the celebrations of the centenary of Mexico's independence in 1910. On the way to Veracruz from Saint-Nazaire he stopped in Havana to attempt to clarify his mission since he had received news that Madriz had been overthrown. He proceeded to Veracruz despite not hearing from Nicaragua. Porfirio Díaz noted that Darío was received with popular acclaim in Veracruz, and, recognizing an anti-United States motive in the acclaim, prohibited Darío from proceeding to Mexico City. Darío returned to Europe after a financially difficult fourth stay in Cuba. His diplomatic career was at an end, but his literary career continued with the publication of *Poema del otoño y otros poemas* in Madrid.

In March 1911, two wealthy Uruguayan brothers, Armando and Alfredo Guido, offered Darío a small salary to edit in Paris a monthly magazine called *Mundial*, to be published in Spanish. In desperate financial straits, he accepted, knowing he was being exploited. He wrote several of the articles in the series he called 'Cabezas' for *Mundial*. He also published a collection of articles entitled *Letras* in Paris. *Mundial* was a success; and the Guidos launched *Elegancias* aimed at female readers. In addition, in 1912, they organized a world tour to publicize the magazines. Darío was the featured member of the tour which visited Barcelona, Madrid, Lisbon, Rio de Janeiro, São Paulo, Montevideo, and Buenos Aires. He was welcomed triumphantly in Buenos Aires where he dictated *La vida de Rubén Darío escrita por él mismo* for the journal *Caras y Caretas*. Another collection of articles, *Todo al vuelo*, appeared in Madrid. In poor health, he returned to France, arriving in November. In May of the following year he was joined in Paris by Francisca, their son 'Güicho,' who like Rubén Darío Contreras survived to adulthood, and Francisca's sister María. He lived in Mallorca from October to December and then returned to Madrid after a stay in Barcelona. His *Historia de mis libros* appeared on 1, 6, and 18 July 1913 in *La Nación*.

In 1914, Darío went with his family to live in Barcelona and from there a fellow Nicaraguan Alejandro Bermúdez persuaded him to undertake a trans-Atlantic speaking tour on behalf of world peace. Before leaving Barcelona he assembled the last of his books of poetry to be published during his lifetime, *Canto a la Argentina y otros poemas*. In November he wrote 'La gran cosmópolis' in New York; and on 4 February 1915, he read his poem 'iPax!' before the Hispanic Society at Columbia University. Invited to Guatemala by Estrada Cabrera to participate in the *Fiesta de Minerva* and to recuperate from illnesses that were plaguing him at this time, he arrived there on 29 April and was joined by Rosario Murillo and Rubén Darío Contreras. His health deteriorated seriously and he was moved to León, Nicaragua at the beginning of 1916, accompanied by his friend Dr Luis Manuel Debayle. *La Nación*, always his dependable and appreciative employer, offered to pay all his expenses. Darío's illness was diagnosed as atrophic cirrhosis of the liver. Two operations, one on 8 January, another on 2 February, did not help him. He died on 6 February 1916 and a passionate struggle involving Rosario's family and Debayle over claims to parts of his body followed. A local judge intervened and decided that his brain, heart, and kidneys should go respectively to Rosario, Debayle, and the University of León. The Nicaraguan church and state paid him the highest honours at his funeral; and his death was genuinely mourned by the people.

Critics have supplemented these biographical facts with comments on Darío's character and personality. Much has been written about the instability of his private life: about his inability to proceed in a disciplined and consistent manner in affairs of the heart and of the flesh, and about a lack of a sense of responsibility in his domestic life. His relations with Rosario Murillo especially, his readiness to travel alone, his lapses into bouts of heavy drinking and into visits to houses of ill repute have been cited to substantiate the finding that he was of weak and unstable character. Oliver Belmás's contributions in particular have given some balance to this picture of disorderliness. He, like some others, has noticed the sporadic nature of Darío's bohemian activities and, after a careful accounting of the various diplomatic and journalistic assignments and creative tasks performed by Darío, has pointed out that such voluminous and carefully composed production demanded hard work.[69] It is often the fate of those who are regarded as geniuses that little credit accrues to them for the time and effort required to produce their work and that their eccentricities become exaggerated out of all proportion. It seems too that the economic and professional necessity for Darío to travel without his wife during his first marriage, except in Central America, should be pointed out. He was living in precarious economic circumstances in Argentina, occupying a diplomatic post that had no real reason for existence at that time. While it is clear that he fled from Rosario Murillo, the biographers of the last fifteen years have been nearly unanimous in considering Darío's relationship with Francisca Sánchez a serious one – showing that he attempted to give their liaison the status of matrimony and that he wanted her to be with him in America during his last days.

Darío's timidity has also been widely commented on by his biographers. In one of his self-portraits, in the initial poem of *Cantos de vida y esperanza*, 'Yo soy aquel,' he described himself as 'tímido ante el mundo,' tending thus to present timidity as one of his permanent characteristics. From its various manifestations, however, it would seem that Darío's timidity, like so much else concerning him, is made complex and

FIGURE 3

FIGURE 4

interesting by contradictions and by change. On the one hand, as a precocious young writer he actively demanded attention. Even in the early stages of his career he asserted his right to live as a writer, to make a living from and win social recognition and prestige through his writing. It hardly seemed to occur to him that this expectation was unusual in Spanish America; and so, apparently unabashed, he addressed his requests to the most illustrious citizens of the countries in which he lived. The contrast between the daring required to make requests of important figures and the timidity which he felt in the presence of these figures is well portrayed by Darío in his account of his first visit to El Salvador and his encounter with the president, Rafael Zaldívar.[70] This contrast between daring conception and timid execution is evident on several occasions in the poet's life. It is shown later, for instance, in his arrival as a nineteen-year-old in Santiago. Darío's description in his *Vida* of a scene in which he is met at the railway station aptly conveys his apprehension by representing the humbleness that must have been apparent to the distinguished gentleman who met him.[71] In his triumphant return to Nicaragua in 1907 this characteristic is again evident.[72] Suggesting that the older Darío was more withdrawn and reserved, Enrique Gómez Carrillo writes, with the ambivalent admiration that characterizes his comments on Darío:

> Los que no han conocido al pobre gran poeta sino más tarde ... no pueden imaginarse lo que aquel hombre era en el año 1890. Ligero, vivo, curioso, enamorado de la vida, lejos de encerrarse en torres de marfil, acercábase al pueblo para ver palpitar sus pasiones. Trabajando en cualquier parte, a cualquier hora, ocupábase lo mismo de la crónica de tribunales, o de las revistas de modas, que de los chismes sociales o de las intrigas políticas.[73]

This progressive withdrawal seems to be accompanied by a corresponding growth of the component in his work that is the result of deep reflection.

Since Darío's life was dedicated chiefly to his art, it is unwise to judge any aspect of his life without taking into account his achievement, his attitude to his art, and his thoughts about the reception of his effort. It is necessary too to contemplate the possibility that his art might determine certain of his views on life. Darío was fully confident in his ability as a poet at all stages of his career. He seemed to know that he was the best poet of his time writing in Spanish, and he valued poetry as a manifestation of the highest human activity. His generosity in material things seemed to reflect a belief that with his art he was rich indeed, just as his generosity in his judgment of the work of others showed that he did not expect them to reach his standards. But he was also aware of the propensity of others to misunderstand his achievement, to neither appreciate his talent nor allow the rewards he deserved. Much of this is displayed in what is perhaps the most important autobiographical summation of his career: the conclusion of *Historia de mis libros*, written in a valedictory tone which reveals that Darío, at age forty-six, considered his career to be almost at an end. He writes:

> Y el mérito principal de mi obra, si alguno tiene, es el de una gran sinceridad, el de haber puesto 'mi corazón al desnudo,' el de haber abierto de par en par las puertas y ventanas de mi castillo interior para enseñar a mis hermanos el habitáculo de mis más íntimas ideas y de mis más caros ensueños.

> He sabido lo que son las crueldades y locuras de los hombres. He sido traicionado, pagado con ingratitudes, calumniado, desconocido en mis mejores intenciones por prójimos mal inspirados; atacado, vilipendiado. Y he sonreido con tristeza. Después de todo, todo es nada, la gloria comprendida. Si es cierto que 'el busto sobrevive a la ciudad,' no es menos cierto que lo infinito del tiempo y del espacio, el busto como la ciudad, y ¡ay!, el planeta mismo, habrán de desaparecer ante la mirada de la única Eternidad.[74]

Darío's statement leans heavily on the negative aspects of his reception and not a little on pathos. By being an autobiographical representation of the subject of the unappreciated artist, featured in much of his work, particularly in *Azul*, the statement might seem to corroborate his claim for sincerity in his work. On the other hand, the statement may be taken as reflecting a one-sided view that does not reveal a sincere picture of the poet's situation. Such are the complexities of the question of sincerity in literature.

Certain theoretical implications and specific practical problems which derive from the application of the biographical method to Darío need to be considered at this point. The method, as has been said, proceeds from the assumption that the life of a writer has an explicable bearing on his literary creations and that the facts of this life provide crucial elucidation for the work. One of the liveliest and most comprehensive claims for the importance of the biographical approach in contemporary criticism was made by Leon Edel in his series of lectures subsequently published as his book, *Literary Biography*. Measuring the biographical against other approaches, he writes:

I am inclined to think that the 'modern' critics are trying to narrow down the critical act far more than is necessary, and to achieve a kind of 'pure' criticism possible only through a species of self-delusion, in the process of which the critic equates himself with the common reader. Even as no historian could write the history of France without looking into Germany, so no critic, I hold, can explicate – the very word implies this – anything without alluding to something else ... The votaries of opinion and fancy would do well to hearken to the biographer who can materially assist them. For faced with modern art – the surrealist poem, the abstract painting, the intricate composite symbolism of works such as *Finnegans Wake* – criticism finds itself admittedly forced, sometimes in a rage of bafflement, into speculation or inarticulateness. When art becomes abstract to this degree the author is speaking wholly from his private language; and any critic who tries to read his meaning by any other process than the biographical indulges in guesswork and creates his own work of art upon the edifice of the other; he projects his own feelings and can discuss only his relationship to the work. Where abundant material is available, the biographer can offer a reasonably clear understanding of the creator, and our understanding of that personage should make his work more intelligible.[75]

While there is a paucity of explicit rationale for the biographical approach by those who have employed it with regard to Darío, there can be little doubt, from the rationale implicit in their practice, that Edel's statement would be approved in great part by them. The belief that biography provides facts that can be applied to the criticism of an author's work to yield more valid results than can be achieved by criticism that is 'speculative,' or 'poetic,' or 'creative,' or 'pure' would appear to be the main justification of their practice. In the last three decades, however, there have been strong theoretical pronouncements concerning the limitations of the biographical approach. Thus René Wellek and Austin Warren write:

The biographical approach forgets that a work of art is not simply the embodiment of experience but always the latest work of art in a series of such works; it is drama, a novel, a poem 'determined,' so far as it is determined at all, by literary tradition and convention. The biographical approach actually obscures a proper comprehension of the literary process, since it breaks up the order of literary tradition to substitute the life cycle of an individual. The biographical approach ignores also quite simple psychological facts. A work of art may rather embody the 'dream' of an

> author than his actual life, or it may be the 'mark,' the 'anti-self' behind which his real person is hiding, or it may be a picture of the life from which the author wants to escape. Furthermore, ... the artist may 'experience' life differently in terms of his art: actual experiences are seen with a view to their use in literature and come to him already partially shaped by artistic traditions and preconceptions ... The poem exists; the tears shed or unshed, the personal emotions, are gone and cannot be reconstructed, nor need they be.[76]

This statement reflects ideas put forward by Alfonso Reyes in his essay 'La vida y la obra.'[77] Such theoretical statements have been followed by the increasing practice of criticism which has applied itself primarily to the works themselves; and the achievements of some of this criticism would lead one to judge as too sweepingly negative Edel's characterization of the 'pure' critics. In fact, his characterization seems to apply only to the kind of criticism which attempts a re-creation of the original work and which has come to be known as creative criticism, the kind that José Enrique Rodó used in commenting on 'Era un aire suave' and other poems from *Prosas profanas*. But already at the time of Edel's lectures other kinds of intrinsic analysis which he might have taken into account were being practised.[78]

On the other hand, the speculative quality denounced by Edel in criticism that is concerned with the work itself is to be found in the two principal processes of literary biography: that of using the works themselves as material evidence for conclusions about the life and that of relating the findings about the life to the works. It would seem that basic assumptions concerning the concept of sincerity form the premise for the biographical approach; for, without a belief that poetry is the authentic representation of one's self, the two principal processes of literary biography mentioned above would not become preoccupations for students of literature. This concept of sincerity is one that held sway during the Romantic period, existing in close relationship with the ideal of spontaneity in expression. It is one of the Romantic tendencies that survived among several of the Modernist poets in Spanish America, so that Darío and Martí in particular frequently professed their sincerity.[79] It is necessary, however, to put Darío's claim of sincerity into proper perspective. Darío's essential self-identification was as an artist, a poet. This is clear from all his autobiographical writings and from his 'Palabras liminares,'[80] his 'Prefacio'[81] to *Cantos de vida y esperanza*, and his 'Dilucidaciones.'[82] There are echoes in all these writings of declarations he made in 'Los colores del estandarte': 'En verdad, vivo de poesía ... No soy más que un hombre de arte. No sirvo para otra cosa.'[83] Sincerity for him meant, to a degree that is singular among the Spanish American poets of his time,[84] fulfilment of his poetic capability; and the means of this fulfilment was an unfettered, eclectic, and ubiquitous search for the highest level of harmonious expression. This is a mode of sincerity then that would be difficult to apprehend, except in a superficial way, through biographical study. It has been said since the Romantic period that there are two kinds of poets, the 'objective' and the 'subjective,' or better, those who write with greater and those who write with lesser distance from their apparent selves. But this greater and lesser distancing may be discerned in different poems by a single poet. Darío's 'Marcha triunfal' and 'Caupolicán,' for instance, would belong to the former category, and others like 'Yo soy aquel ...' and 'Canción de otoño en primavera' to the latter. It is to this latter category of poems that the biographical approach would seem most readily applicable. And, indeed, the poems mentioned as examples of this kind of poetry in Darío's work show correspondences with Darío's biographical reality. In this regard they are, especially 'Yo soy aquel ...,' useful for a determination of Darío's self-identification and of his view of his own development. Many interesting comments may be derived from comparing Darío's views with those of others concerning his life and literary career. On the other hand, certain contradictory views in the examples chosen indicate that the poems are not reliable biographical documents. The principal contradiction between the poems concerns the view of youth presented. In 'Yo soy aquel ...' youth is portrayed bitterly in the well-known stanza:

> Yo supe de dolor desde mi infancia;
> mi juventud ...,¿fue juventud la mía?
> sus rosas aún me dejan su fragancia,
> una fragancia de melancolía ...[85]

The also well-known opening verses of 'Canción de otoño en primavera' carry a contrasting picture:

> Juventud, divino tesoro,
> ¡ya te vas para no volver!
> Cuando quiero llorar, no lloro ...
> y a veces lloro sin querer.[86]

Such a contradiction suggests that the poems, rather than subscribing to a reliable biography, represent certain possible and different emotional attitudes. Each poem develops its representation in a distinct way, and the success with which it does this would seem to be the central issue on which its value as a poem rests. The question of sincerity of representation, when sincerity means biographical authenticity, thus becomes quite insignificant.

Finally, in order to illustrate further some of the merits and limitations of the biographical method, comments are necessary on some of the specific practices carried out with regard to Darío. The first practice deals with the deduction of his life from his works, and concerns the interpretation of parts of *El oro de Mallorca*. Darío declared the novel to be autobiographical and suggested that its protagonist Benjamín Itaspes represented Darío himself. The Itaspes-Darío identification has been accepted almost unanimously by Darío's biographers and details from the novel have been used to clarify vexing problems in Darío's biography. Alberto Ghiraldo, for example, quotes Itaspes discussing his amatory life and uses Itaspes's words as an explanation of Darío's broken relations with Rosario Murillo. Ghiraldo's stated purpose is to 'desvelar un misterio a través de cuyos cendales aparece Darío con los colores de la verdad.'[87] It would appear to be risky indeed to use material that comes in the context of an artistic whole as decisive and factual biographical evidence. An artistic whole demands that all the details of its composition be fashioned to contribute to its coherence; and *El oro de Mallorca*, like the poems discussed above, must be regarded warily as a biographical source.

Darío's own *Vida* too has created more problems than have been discussed so far in this chapter. It has been pointed out that it contains errors and important omissions. Unlike the original autobiography, St Augustine's *Confessions*, the *Vida* was not addressed to its author's Maker who knew all and from whom there was nothing to hide. Writing for his contemporaries and for posterity Darío suppressed some materials, embellished others, and distorted still others by making fiction of certain aspects of his reporting.[88] Such, for instance, is his reporting of his early sexual fantasies,[89] which has given impetus to the sometimes inexpert application of psychology.[90] Juan Antonio Cabezas's discussion of Darío's racial-psychological formation, for instance, displays wild and untidy speculation. He writes:

> Pocas almas como la de este poeta habrán reflejado en sí las influencias de la tierra y habrán vivido profundamente el drama biológico de su mestizaje espiritual y carnal ... Desde la infancia es agitada su alma por un íntimo frenesí sexual. Vendaval interior, semejante al trágico 'amok' que posee a los indígenas malayos.[91]

Related to Cabezas's comments are others made by Cecil Maurice Bowra and Arturo Torres-Ríoseco which reflect a theory of the racial determinism of poetic expression. To Bowra certain shortcomings in Darío's poetry derive from the fact that 'he had Indian blood in his veins' and that 'his simple, natural character was better suited to a less elaborate, less sophisticated, and less ambitious art.'[92] Torres-Ríoseco refutes the specific conclusions at which Bowra arrived. However, he uses Bowra's method although he adds a concept of climatic and cultural determinism. He writes:

> Yo creo todo lo contrario: que el temperamento tropical del poeta y la ardentía de su sangre negra le acercaban al concepto de poesía decorativa del parnasiano y, por otro lado, su herencia indígena, su sensibilidad hiperestésica, la indecisa cultura de su juventud, su creencia en mitos y supersticiones le colocaban en un plano simbolista.[93]

Neither Indian blood nor Black blood nor tropical climate explains adequately any characteristic of Darío's poetry. The human range of attitudes towards literature and talents for creating literature is not circumscribed by race or by climate. Torres-Ríoseco's references to cultural factors ring more true. Emphasis is placed on Darío's indigenous cultural heritage by Angel Lázaro[94] and Jorge Campos.[95] This aspect is elaborated on in the article entitled 'El oro, la pluma y la piedra preciosa: Indagaciones sobre el trasfondo indígena de la poesía de Darío'[96] by José Juan Arrom. In this study, not only is the presence of the indigenous element in Darío's work explained, but an account is also offered of how the diverse components of the Spanish American cultural background dispose some of its people to the attractions of foreign cultures. He writes:

> esa cultura del Nuevo Mundo, que nos caracteriza, conforma y motiva, no es exclusivamente europea, ni exclusivamente africana, ni exclusivamente indígena: la nuestra es una cultura de síntesis en que participan, en mayor o menor grado, según la región, las culturas que en ella se suman. De ahí que a todo americano de espíritu alerta le sea fácil adentrarse, por sendas que le son íntimamente familiares, en la cultura de otros pueblos. Y eso es, en realidad, lo que hizo Darío: captó, sin que en el proceso de captación intervinieran para nada el ángulo facial o el color de la piel, las mejores esencias de España, y de Francia, y del resto de Europa, para unirlas, con sabia alquimia personal, a las arcanas esencias que había acumulado en los años formativos de su niñez centroamericana.[97]

The trend in Darío criticism developed by Lázaro, Campos, Arrom, and to some extent by Torres-Ríoseco reveals a Jungian rather than a Freudian orientation. Its findings are generally more verifiable than those that relate traits of personality to precise situations in the literary works.

The biographical approach, then, as it has been applied to Darío, has achieved several successes and shown certain limitations. When it has been concerned with pure biography, with telling accurately the facts and events in Darío's life – the circumstances of his birth and upbringing, his education, his decisive experiences, the order of his publications, his travels, his acquaintances and friendships, his health, his social and political milieu, etc. – it has provided indispensable material for literary history. And, as has been shown, great effort and skill have been put into the research that has yielded this material. From the point of view of literary criticism, however, the biographical approach has been used without striking benefit. This has been so and indeed seems necessarily so largely because the attempt to identify the details of an integral work of literary art, that is, a work that is imaginatively coherent, with details of the life of its author entails speculation. Even when correspondences between the two seem convincing, biographical authenticity has literary value only when it is made to function as an integral part of the fiction.[98] The biographical approach, then, has limited usefulness in establishing the value of works of art.

CHAPTER TWO

Socio-Political
Considerations

Criticism that tends to examine poetry primarily from the point of view of its relation to society has, like biographical criticism, formed a long-standing and much practised part of the criticism of Darío's work. Such criticism is, of course, related to the biographical in the sense that to be born into and to live in certain social and political circumstances is a part of a writer's biography. But the sociological critics, giving primacy to the writer's social responsibility, take the view that it is desirable for him to represent in his writings the basic social and political problems facing the community to which he belongs. This attitude has deep roots in the Spanish American tradition and is a natural complement of much of Spanish American literature.

From the late eighteenth century, the years preceding Independence, and throughout the period of social upheaval and readjustment during the first two-thirds of the nineteenth century, Spanish American literature and literary criticism tended to be identified closely with the social reality of the area. This tendency was challenged during the last third of the century by the attitude, promoted chiefly by Darío, of detachment from social questions. While Darío could write literature that demonstrated this detachment and while his own pronouncements and criticism suggested a new status for literature and put emphasis on the craft of literature, he could not decisively affect critical practice among his contemporaries. The pull towards literary Americanism continued to assert itself and from the field of criticism strong voices were heard attempting to redirect literature to its traditional course of identification with Spanish American reality.

The tradition began in modern Spanish American literature when writers, in the spirit of the Enlightenment, took the view that literature ought not to be an isolated exercise and that the man of letters ought to interest himself in all aspects of American life. Writers came to find the movement towards independence and the determination of a direction for Spanish America after independence to be absorbing subjects. Andrés Bello, José Joaquín Fernández de Lizardi, José Joaquín de Olmedo, José María Heredia, Domingo Faustino Sarmiento, José Hernández, and others contributed through debates or through the subjects treated in their literary production to defining the new Americanism. And even though there was some disagreement among them – Bello's and Sarmiento's over language usage and Bello's and Echeverría's over the role of the Hispanic tradition, for instance – they were all committed to the task of representing Spanish American reality in their writings.

The Argentinian, Esteban Echeverría, gave emphatic expression to the doctrines of literary Americanism and liberalism in his *Dogma socialista* (1846); and his years of exile in Uruguay contributed to stimulating keen interest in these concepts among intellectuals in Montevideo. This interest was sustained by another Argentinian, Juan María Gutiérrez (1804–78), who was perhaps the outstanding Spanish American literary critic of his time. As a member of the Asociación de Mayo[1] formed by Echeverría in 1838 he subscribed to the concepts of Americanism, Romanticism, and liberalism in literature. But beyond that he placed high value on the aesthetic element in literature, regarded the classical writers with favour, recognized the Hispanic heritage and, as a creative writer, was not bound by the burning social and political issues of his time. Unlike Echeverría, Mármol, and Sarmiento, who confronted the Rosas régime in their writings, Gutiérrez, in his novel *El capitán de Patricios*, preferred to write in the manner of sentimental romanticism.[2] Gutiérrez, then, although continuing the demand for literary Americanism, was disposed to eclecticism in his approach to literature and gave a broad interpretation to Americanism.

His epoch was followed by the rise of the Modernists, whose literary interests took them beyond Americanism. But in the last fifth of the century, when they were active, the work of Hippolyte Taine, along with other French models of the period, won widespread attention in Spanish America. His emphasis on 'la race,' 'le milieu' and 'le moment,' and his interest in determinism and historical causation in the assessment of literature were to give further stimulus to the concept of literary Americanism. And at the end of the century in his work entitled *Rubén*

Darío: Su personalidad literaria: Su última obra (1899), José Enrique Rodó uttered what must be regarded as one of the most famous statements of nineteenth-century literary criticism when he declared that 'Rubén Darío no es el poeta de América.'[3]

There were important critics, however, who, in the period immediately preceding the appearance of Rodó's essay, were expressing views to which the Uruguayan critic's are superficially similar. Two critics in particular, Paul Groussac and Manuel Gondra, promptly evaluated, in terms of the nineteenth-century attitudes of literary Americanism, the kind of literature which Darío was practising and the theories he had formulated about this literature. Paul Groussac in two articles, '*Los raros*' and '*Prosas profanas*,' in November 1896 and January 1897 respectively, expressed his disapproval of what he understood to be Darío's too faithful following of French examples. In the first article he writes: 'Lo peor del caso presente es que el autor de *Los raros* celebra la grandeza de sus mirmidones con una sinceridad afligente, y ha llegado a imitarlos en castellano con desesperante perfección.'[4]

Groussac concludes his study by asking doubtingly whether Darío's orientation

> puede entrañar promesa alguna para el arte nuevo americano, cuya poesía tiene que ser, como la de Whitman, la expresión viva y potente de un mundo virgen, y arrancar de las entrañas populares, para no tornarse la remedada cavatina de un histrión. El arte americano será original – o no será. ¿Piensa el señor Darío que su literatura alcanzara dicha virtud con ser el eco servil de rapsodias parisienses, y tomar por divisa la pregunta ingenua de un personaje de Coppée?
>
> Qui pourrais-je imiter pour être original?[5]

Groussac returns to the question of Spanish American intellectual originality in his article '*Prosas profanas*' of 1897. And, viewing Darío's situation now against the historical background of Spanish America, and somewhat patronizingly, Groussac tends to be more sympathetic to Darío than he was in the earlier article. He writes: 'Siendo, pues, un hecho de evidencia que la América colonizada no debe pretender por ahora a la originalidad intelectual, se comete un abuso de doctrina al formular en absoluto el reproche de imitación europea, contra cualquier escritor o artista nacido en este continente.'[6] Groussac, nevertheless, remained dissatisfied with certain aspects of Darío's work, especially with what he considered the poet's complacency in proposing (in the 'Palabras liminares') directions that lead away from Spanish American reality. But in his assessment of Darío's poetic techniques he sees elements that possess high value:

> Para ser completo y justo, hay que saborear la pieza misma con sus mil detalles del estilo: la cincelada orfebrería de las palabras, nombres, verbos, y adjetivos de elección, que se engastan en la trama del verso como gemas en filigrana; el perpetuo hallazgo – tan nuevo en castellano – de las imágenes y ritmos evocadores de la sensación, en que se funden ciertamente elementos extraños, pero con armonía tan sabia y feliz que constituye al cabo una inspiración.[7]

The recognition of such merit in Darío's writing led Groussac to predict that when the early phase of the poet's production had passed he would sing 'libremente la verdad y la vida, con una eficacia y maestría de que dan bella muestra algunas piezas de su presente colección.'[8] Groussac, then, admired Darío's talent, but he desired to see in his poetry an originality based on reality that was recognizably American. In this he was true to the predominant current of nineteenth-century Spanish American literary criticism.[9]

A year after Groussac's study of *Prosas profanas* was published in *La Biblioteca* there appeared in *La Democracia* (Asunción) an essay entitled 'En torno a Rubén Darío'[10] by the Paraguayan writer and statesman Manuel Gondra. Gondra knew Groussac's studies of Darío's works and in his own essay has recourse to some of the Argentinian's negative arguments; nevertheless, in his effort to totally condemn Darío's writing he attacks Groussac as well as Eduardo de la Barra and Leopoldo Alas for whatever favourable opinions they might have held of Darío's work. The burden of Gondra's attack is against what he considers to be the lack of regard for the intellectual quality of Spanish America exhibited by Darío in his 'Palabras liminares' to *Prosas profanas*. Gondra relates Darío's proclamations in the 'Palabras liminares' to his poetic practice in *Prosas profanas* in the following terms:

> Insinuándose en ellos como depositario de una doctrina artística, cuya revelación hará el día en que la intelectualidad americana haya subido de nivel, Darío ha venido a colocarse en una posición bien difícil ...
> Admirabilísimo artífice de versos él, no hallo en toda su obra lo que pueda autorizarle a presentarse como tal Mesías de un arte nuevo, siendo sí, y esto no se podrá negar, un prodigioso talento de imitación el suyo, talento

que necesita dar una nota personal, propia, para que se le distinga de los
diversos grupos poéticos en que fragmentariamente puede ser colocado.[11]

For Darío to write in the 'Palabras liminares' of 'la absoluta falta de
elevación mental de la mayoría pensante de nuestro continente'[12] is for
him to show not only gross disrespect for his contemporaries but also to be
ungrateful, according to Gondra. Other essays, collected in Gondras's
Hombres y letrados de América, reflect their author's interest and pride in
the writers and political philosophers who were contributing to the intellectual life of Spanish America. He seems dismayed, then, that Darío
should so sweepingly belittle them, especially since his success was
largely due to the recognition and praise they gave to his poetry. Gondra
asks further why Darío refuses to give a clearly elaborated statement of
his aesthetic views in order to help his fellow Spanish American writers
out of the inferior state he considers them to be in, if he in fact believes, as
he states in the 'Palabras liminares' that 'la obra colectiva de los nuevos de
América es aún vana, estando muchos de los mejores talentos en el limbo
de un completo desconocimiento del mismo Arte a que se consagran.[13]
Gondra's irritation at Darío's self-proclaimed superiority and apparent
disdain for Spanish America motivated, at least in part, his unwillingness
to see significant value in Darío's poetry and to declare that 'el *modernismo* pasará sin haber enriquecido la Filosofía del Arte con un solo
principio, ni la técnica con una sola fórmula.'[14] He considers that Darío's
statement, 'Si hay poesía en nuestra América, ella está en las cosas viejas,
en Palenque y Utatlán,'[15] implies an attempt to impose a severe limitation
on the 'copiosas fuentes de inspiración poética de la lira americana: la
naturaleza y la historia de nuestro continente,'[16] and he wonders whether
Darío would be capable of representing such remote American reality.

In a speech that Gondra gave at the unveiling of a statue of Alberdi in
Buenos Aires, he made clear his admiration for the nineteenth-century
Americanist tendency of integrating literature and politics.[17] He was
strongly predisposed to admire Spanish American literature that followed
the prescription of Bello, of Gutiérrez, and of Echeverría. He therefore
judges Darío negatively and foreshadows some of Rodó's reactions when
he observes that the poet

> no ha demostrado ... tener el *sentimiento de América*. Y creo que se
> entenderá bien esta expresión. Sus versos pueden leerse en toda su
> extensión, sin que se diga una sola vez: ésas son las llanuras, ése es el cielo,
> ésas las hembras o ésos los varones de América. Si por casualidad se

tropieza con un rasgo de americanismo en sus poesías, es americanismo de pacotilla europea.[18]

Gondra was doubtless irritated too by the casualness with which Darío took aim at cherished traditional views: that the poet confronted long-standing literary concepts with what could be viewed as a series of unelaborated points no doubt seemed provocative to him. His response was to aim his own intemperate attack at the 'Palabras liminares,' to reject them, to find fault with the arguments of whoever found originality in any aspect of Darío's work, to criticize adversely the poet's versification and to require him to adhere to traditional concepts by presenting Spanish American reality in his work.

Rodó's famous statement, 'Rubén Darío no es el poeta de América,' is made with such emphasis in the first paragraph of his essay that it would be easy to understand it to be the summary of a negative opinion of Darío's books, Azul and Prosas profanas. But, in fact, it represents only one part of his reactions: the other, more substantial, part concerns his admiration for Darío's artistic skill, for his bold, irrepressible poetic imagination, for the confidence with which he introduces a new mode of poetry. And it may be said that Rodó's total reaction indicates dramatically the conflict and indeed the crisis faced by a critic who subscribed to the concept of literary Americanism for some time during the Modernist period.

The evolution of Rodó's opinion of Modernism may be noticed in his articles published between 1895 and 1897 in the Revista Nacional de Literatura y Ciencias.[19] In the article entitled 'El sentimiento de la naturaleza' which appeared on 10 August 1895 and which forms a part of his study 'El americanismo literario' he quotes with enthusiasm Juan Bautista Alberdi's approving comments on Esteban Echeverría's poetry: 'Leyda, Regreso, Flor del aire – afirma Alberdi, que en su juicio de la obra de Echeverría supo acertadamente apreciar la nota de originalidad que aquel sentimiento comunicaba al espíritu y la forma de la nueva poesía – dejaban entrever, ya en el fondo, ya en los accesorios, la fisonomía peculiar de nuestra naturaleza.'[20]

This positive seconding of an appraisal that gives value to poetry which represents American reality is followed by other laudatory words: 'El poeta de la regeneración social y política vivirá, más que por la excelencia de su arte, por la grandeza del propósito y la originalidad del pensamiento que propagó y en el que germinaba la solución futura del problema fundamental de la nacionalidad, la idea que determinó su forma orgánica.'[21] With such views on the value of Americanism it is not surprising that Rodó's early reactions to Modernism should be negative and that he should have continued to show this negative reaction for some time. The year 1897, however, proved to be critical and decisive in his thinking about the movement. A letter to Leopoldo Alas dated 30 June 1897 shows that at that time he viewed Modernism with disfavour. He informs Alas that

> Otro de los puntos sobre los que yo quisiera hablar detenidamente a Vd. es el de mi modo de pensar en presencia de las corrientes que dominan nuestra *nueva* literatura americana. Me parece haberlo afirmado alguna vez: nuestra reacción antinaturalista es hoy muy cierta, pero muy candorosa; nuestro modernismo apenas ha pasado de la superficialidad. En América, con los nombres de *decadentismo* y *modernismo*, se disfraza a menudo una abominable escuela de trivialidad y frivolidad literarias: una tendencia que debe repugnar a todo espíritu que busque ante todo, en literatura, motivos para sentir y pensar.[22]

Modernism is for him a new kind of decadence and he observes that to the 'decadentismo *gongórico*'[23] which has burdened Hispanic literature has been added a 'decadentismo *azul*.'[24] In an article entitled 'Un poeta de Caracas' which appeared in the *Revista Nacional* in August of the same year, he treats the question more fully:

> Muy avenido a que la poesía americana abra su espíritu a las modernísimas corrientes del pensamiento y la emoción, se inicie en los nuevos ritos del arte, acepte los procedimientos con que una plástica sutil ha profundizado en los secretos de la forma, no me avengo igualmente a que, extremado y sacando de su cauce el dogma, bueno en sí, de la independencia y el desinterés artísticos, rompa toda solidaridad y relación con las palpitantes oportunidades de la vida y los altos intereses de la realidad. – Veo en esta ausencia de contenido *humano*, duradero y profundo, el peligro inminente con que se ha de luchar en el rumbo marcado por nuestra actual orientación literaria. Al modernismo americano le matará la falta de vida psíquica. Se piensa poco en él, se siente poco. Le domina con demasiado imperio un vivo afán por la novedad de lo aparente, que tiene a la frivolidad muy cercana.[25]

He then concedes great stature to Darío and makes him an exception to his charges, even though he expresses all this in terms that do not quite show approval of Darío's literary preoccupations:

> A Rubén Darío le está permitido emanciparse de la obligación humana de

la lucha, refugiarse en el Oriente o en Grecia, *madrigalizar* con los abates galantes, hacer la corte a las marquesas de Watteau naturalizándose en el 'país' donoso de los abanicos. – Una individualidad literaria poderosa tiene, como el verdadero poeta según Heine, el atributo regio de la irresponsabilidad.[26]

A month later, in another letter to Leopoldo Alas, he makes a distinction between modernism and decadentism. It is probable that towards the end of the same year he began his famous study of Darío in which he declares: 'Yo soy un *modernista* también.'[27]

Rodó's study reflects his own history as a literary critic and is a composite of all the critical directions he had taken in the past and was being made to take at the time of writing by the power of Darío's work. It is fitting, then, that he begins by assessing Darío in terms of the tradition of literary Americanism in its most basic sense. He states that there is nothing in Darío's poetry by which one could recognize 'al americano de las cálidas latitudes, y al sucesor de los misteriosos artistas de Utatlán y Palenke,'[28] and describes him as an anomaly that historians of national civilizations such as Hippolyte Taine and Henry Buckle would not be happy to discover. When Rodó declares that there is room in the most elevated and human poetry for 'cierta impresión de americanismo en los accesorios' and adds that 'aun en los accesorios, dudo que nos pertenezca colectivamente el artista de que hablo,'[29] his concept of 'americanismo en los accesorios' vividly recalls that above quoted statement of Alberdi (see p. 30) and reveals how prominent in Rodó's consciousness are the theoretical premises concerning Americanism that were formulated earlier in the century. But apart from pointing out Darío's 'antiamericanismo involuntario,'[30] Rodó pays him high compliments in the first section of his essay, calling him 'sutil y delicado artista'[31] and 'gran poeta exquisito.'[32]

The rest of the study is devoted to an elaboration of these compliments, which takes place in two stages. First, the positive value of words such as 'sutil,' 'delicado,' 'exquisito' is established by his justification of Darío's departure from the traditional Americanism, and, secondly, by means of fairly detailed comments on some of the poems, he explains his favourable impression of *Prosas profanas*.

Rodó sees certain limitations in Americanism. He states that nature and country life are the only two truly American literary sources and allows that: 'los poetas que quieren expresar, en forma universalmente inteligible para las almas superiores, modos de pensar y sentir enteramente cultos y *humanos*, deben renunciar a un verdadero sello de americanismo original.'[33] When he examines previous Spanish American poetry he finds that, precisely because of its close relationship to social and political reality, it has been undistinguished. He explains that 'toda manifestación de poesía ha sido más o menos subyugada en América por la suprema necesidad de la propaganda y de la acción. El arte no ha sido, por lo general, sino la forma más remontada de la propaganda; y poesía que lucha no puede ser poesía que cincela.'[34] Such a background of poetry in the nineteenth century, with its principal feature being an *'utilitarismo batallador,'*[35] is enough, as Rodó sees it, to cause the free and non-committed work of Darío to stand out clearly for its originality.

Rodó was intimately familiar with the currents in literary criticism of his age. In his two studies of Juan María Gutiérrez and his essay, 'La crítica de Clarín,' he not only gives incidental appraisals of the Spanish American critics but also comments on the sociological attitudes of Mariano José de Larra, Emilia Pardo Bazán, Hippolyte Taine, Théophile Gautier, and Jean-Marie Guyau, on the erudite approach of Menéndez y Pelayo, on the aestheticism of Juan Valera, and on Gustave Flaubert's ability to discuss 'la obra en sí, por su composición y su estilo.'[36] Whenever he mentions Sainte-Beuve he tends to cite the French critic's 'sustitución del estudio de la obra por el del escritor.'[37] But there is another aspect of Sainte-Beuve's work that Rodó treasures in himself and which he might have adopted partly as a result of his wide reading. It is his breadth of view, his ability to deal sympathetically with a wide range of works. He had declared in 'Notas sobre crítica,' published in the *Revista Nacional* on 10 January 1896, that: 'Sin cierta flexibilidad del gusto no hay buen gusto. Sin cierta amplitud tolerante del criterio, no hay crítica literaria que pueda aspirar a ser algo superior al eco transitorio de una escuela y merezca la atención de la más cercana posteridad.'[38] Having found Darío's work to be only negatively susceptible to a sociological critical approach, Rodó readily recognized the originality of the poetry and allowed himself to be carried along by its spirit. He was thus obliged to discuss the literary rather than the biographical personality; and he dealt with the poetry itself by means of elaborate, imaginative re-narration, in well wrought prose, of such poems as 'Era un aire suave,' 'Blasón,' 'Palimpsesto,' and 'Sinfonía en gris mayor.' He praised the inventiveness and musicality of Darío's versification, the fitting sophistication of the title 'Prosas profanas,' and in writing of the imagery of the book he approximates Darío's language: 'Está lleno de imágenes, pero todas ellas son tomadas a un mundo donde genios celosos niegan la entrada a toda realidad que no se haya bañado en veinte aguas purificadoras.'[39] Rodó concludes here, as he does in his obituary entitled 'En la muerte de Rubén

Darío' published in *Nosotros* (February 1916), that there is no doubt about Darío's greatness, even though poetic art in Spanish America could not accommodate many Daríos, if indeed there could be others capable of his particular excellence. But the spirit of renewal, which Darío as the dominant Modernist championed, opened the way to other literary efforts that were also within the Modernist range. Rodó indicates that his own writing is a token of this conviction, and, in this sense, he states:

> Yo soy un modernista también; yo pertenezco con toda mi alma a la gran reacción que da carácter y sentido a la evolución del pensamiento en las postrimerías de este siglo; a la reacción que, partiendo del naturalismo literario y del positivismo filosófico, los conduce, sin desvirtuarlos en lo que tienen de fecundos, a disolverse en concepciones más altas.[40]

Rodó's study occupies a special place among the critical studies that have been devoted to Darío's work. The study itself reflects the process of development of Spanish American literary criticism in response to a new mode of writing. Its author noticed excellence in this poetry which was different from the poetry that had gone before it and responsibly starts his appraisal by evaluating the work from the perspective of the predominant critical trend of his time. By beginning in this way, he seems convincingly to yield, in the later part of his study, to Darío's poetry, to grant it the kind of imposing stature, the autonomy which he considered it to deserve.[41]

In his essay entitled 'Rodó y Rubén Darío,' Edoardo Crema[42] has suggested that, on the basis of Rodó's failure to write again about Darío's work,[43] it would seem that Rodó reverted to concerning himself with writers who recognized their moral responsibility to represent what Rodó called 'las palpitantes oportunidades de la vida y los altos intereses de la realidad.'[44] Crema attempts to substantiate his opinion by referring to Rodó's conversations, held after 1899, as they are reported by Pérez Petit and Osvaldo Crispo Acosta (Lauxar), in which Rodó is represented as repudiating Darío's poetry.[45] Whether Crema's suggestion is valid or not, it is a fact that there are later critics who have tended to see Rodó as being adversely critical of Darío in his study of the poet's work,[46] and who have regarded him as one of the initiators of a critical approach to Darío that would have preferred to see Darío representing literary Americanism: critics, in short, whose efforts are essentially a response to the statement 'Rubén Darío no es el poeta de América.' For this reason and because in his major essay, as well as in his overall criticism of Modernism, he does begin from the position of a literary Americanist, he is considered here among the critics whose major tendency is social or political, even though his work on Darío goes beyond his deep social interest.

In his prologue to Darío's *Peregrinaciones*, Justo Sierra disputed the statement that Darío was not the poet of America, a statement which, as we have seen, was prefatory to Rodó's positive evaluation of *Prosas profanas*. Sierra has the impression of resonances that are distinctly Spanish American when he listens to Darío's poetry. Darío's open-spiritedness is also to Sierra evidence of Darío's Americanism. He writes:

> ¿Por qué dicen que no sois un poeta de América … ? Si, sois americano, pan americano, porque en vuestros versos cuando se les escucha aten-tamente suenan rumores oceánicos, murmurios de selvas y bramidos de cataratas andinas; y si el cisne, que es vuestro pájaro heráldico, boga sin cesar en vuestros lagos helénicos en busca de Leda, el cóndor suele bajar a grandes saltos alados de cima en cima en vuestras estrofas épicas; sois americano por la exuberancia tropical al través del cual sentís lo bello; y sois de todas partes, como solemos serlo los americanos, por la facilidad con que repercute en vuestra lira policorde la música de toda la lira humana y la convertís en música vuestra.[47]

The first known defender of Darío's Americanism, then, gives an en-thusiastic but impressionistic and undocumented response to Rodó's statement.

Without going into the background of Rodó's statement, without considering the critical tradition to which Rodó largely adhered, Federico de Onís makes the following judgment:

> Cuando Rodó escribió su magnífico ensayo sobre *Prosas profanas* cometió el error de decir que Rubén Darío no era el poeta de América, sólo porque en aquel libro faltaban los temas americanos. No es una obra más americana porque trate de asuntos americanos; de hecho la más de las obras que tratan de ellos son europeas, aunque se hayan escrito en América, como ocurre con tantas imitaciones de Chateaubriand o Bernar-dino de Saint-Pierre. El valor y la originalidad de Rubén Darío, lo que constituye la esencia de su poesía, es algo genuinamente americano, aunque proceda, como América misma, de orígenes europeos. El americanismo original hay que buscarlo en una sensibilidad nueva, y *Prosas profanas*, con su delectación en los temas helénicos o versallescos o de la España antigua, con su gusto por el lujo, el refinamiento y la sensualidad, con su desarraigado cosmopolitismo y su capacidad asimala-

dora e imitativa, muestra uno de los lados más significativos de la sensibilidad americana.[48]

The cogency of Federico de Onís's statement from a contemporary view of literary history can hardly be denied. Yet it may be wondered whether the concepts contained in it are fundamentally different from those of Rodó. Rodó seems to have meant that in the traditional sense Darío was not the poet of America, that he did not treat the accustomed American subjects, but beyond that he seems to recognize that room must be made in America for Darío when he says: 'Habíamos tenido en América poetas buenos, y poetas inspirados, y poetas vigorosos; pero no habíamos tenido en América un gran poeta exquisito.'[49] In fact, all the elements that Onís enumerates as comprising 'el americanismo original' are observed by Rodó as being factors in the 'renovación literaria' that Darío's work meant for America and for the Hispanic world in general and which Rodó came to welcome in his essay. In a kind of *envoi* to his essay Rodó expressed the wish that Darío during his imminent visit to Spain would be able to inspire the youth of Spain to new expression too: 'Llegue allí el poeta llevando buenos anuncios para el florecer del espíritu en el habla común, que es el arca santa de la raza.'[50] Rodó went to the extent, then, of encouraging the spread of interest throughout the Hispanic world in the kind of poetry Darío was writing.

Rodó's compatriot, the novelist Mario Benedetti, has related the language of Rodó's essay to incidents in the relationship between Rodó and Darío and found that Rodó had a deep conviction that the Spanish American writer ought to 'incorporarse a la milicia hispano-americana.'[51] He believes that this conviction kept Rodó from ever having fully approved of Darío's work. Benedetti's own view of Darío has usually coincided with the view he believes Rodó to have had. In a paper read in Varadero, Cuba, and published in a special number of *Casa de las Américas* which commemorated the centenary of Darío's birth, he repeated his thesis that Darío kept his authentic, American self apart from his writing and wrote instead a literature of complete evasion and alienation. He concluded his address by declaring: 'que ya sabemos que cumple cien años, claro, pero que no los representa.'[52] The Venezuelan poet and critic Rafael Pineda,[53] who contrasts Darío with Neruda, and the Chilean poet Enrique Lihn[54] have expressed views similar to those of Benedetti.

Another Cuban journal which published a number dedicated to Darío during 1967, *L/L* (*Boletín del Instituto de Literatura y Lingüística*), contains articles that go beyond a vaguely Americanist tendency to a scientific, Marxist position. In his article entitled 'Cronología del modernismo,' José Antonio Portuondo,[55] who has always seemed to respond to the appeal of his Cuban compatriot Enrique José Varona for a scientific, disciplined approach to literary criticism, situates the literary activity of the Modernist movement within the main political and social events of the period 1880–1909. This period began with Martí's arrival in New York and ended just before the outbreak of the Mexican revolution. He follows other Caribbean writers, Pedro Henríquez Ureña and José Arrom, in their generational emphasis and adopts Julius Petersen's view that 'las experiencias literarias más amplias son aquellas que no se refieren a las formas literarias sino que conmueven la estructura fundamental del hombre entero de una época'[56] and identifies the moving force of the generation to be 'la penetración imperialista.'[57] Portuondo goes on to specify the ways in which imperialism decisively affected Spanish American life:

> El imperialismo es, por una parte, torrente de capitales foráneos que impulsa el nacimiento y desarrollo de una burguesía de nuevos ricos semejantes al 'rey burgués' descrito por Darío en *Azul*, y por otra, con la industrialización de nuestras tierras, surgimiento de un proletariado urbano con conciencia de clase e incipiente organización sindical.[58]

His 'Esquema cronológico de la generación modernista' is conceived with the idea that 'la cronología permite ver el proceso de decomposición económica y política de Nuestra América alimentando la evasión modernista y la denuncia naturalista.'[59] For Portuondo, however, unlike other writers of Marxist orientation, 'evasión' does not determine that the writing of the period should be valued negatively. His high regard for Darío is ultimately clear from his study: 'Esta rica y tensa atmósfera preñada de contradicciones, alienta la vida y la obra del más grande poeta del siglo, Rubén Darío. El movimiento impulsado por él da nombre a toda la generación.'[60]

He does not discuss here the factors that constitute this greatness. The study, however, implies that Darío's greatness rests on the manner in which he represents evasion and anguish: that is, on the writing itself, on the composition of his works, works which relate, negatively, to a precise socio-political condition. The same conclusions concerning Darío are arrived at in his essay 'Martí y Darío: polos del modernismo.'[61] The approach followed by Portuondo in these articles is similar to that followed in his essay 'Angustia y evasión de Julián del Casal'[62] in which the work of the Cuban poet is seen as a reflection of his political circumstances.

Portuondo is also the author of the foreword, entitled 'Centenario de Rubén Darío,'[63] which introduces the special number of *L/L* dedicated to the poet. In an introduction to the studies included in the 'Homenaje,' one can perceive varying levels of enthusiasm shown by him for the approaches employed by the different authors. He describes, for instance, the contribution of Roberto Friol ('Rubén Darío en su página,' pp. 50–75), an article that deals with the ontological justification for certain important symbols – particularly 'el cisne' – in Darío's poetry, as being 'de raíces idealistas.' This description, coming from a point of view that gives primary importance in criticism to the work as a reflection of the dominant political and economic conditions operative in the society of which the literary work ought to be a symbol, can hardly be taken as laudatory. Portuondo is flexible, however. That he values Darío's works and the approach to their criticism for more than their political significance is shown in his highly complimentary comments on Juan Marinello's contribution, of which he says: 'Juan Marinello, maestro en estas disciplinas, nos da una imagen total, sintetizadora, en su brillante 'meditación de centenario.'[64] In his article, Marinello proposes a unity in Darío's poetry which, he suggests, may be considered as representing 'el aliento inmortal que nace de su preocupación desvelada, de su grito desesperado y del dolor de su esperanza.'[65] Like Portuondo, he believes that this 'grito desesperado' and 'dolor' have their roots in the historical reality of Latin America; and he too speaks with some censure of 'un sentido idealista de la creación.'[66] But Marinello also places great emphasis on Darío's poetic expression and on his role in renovating poetic language. Paraphrasing the judgment of the Spanish critic Enrique Díez-Canedo, he states that 'Rubén Darío abrió las ventanas a la poesía hispánica en su día.'[67] He cites as distinctive, too, Darío's belief in creative liberty and lauds his ability to be resolute, clear, and decisive in his expression, an ability which he finds common to the great poets.

It is noteworthy, then, that these two outstanding Cuban critics, Portuondo and Marinello, demand much more than an explanation of the relation of the work to its social and political background. Their appreciation of Darío seems to be based to a great extent on the poet's skilful, imaginative, and pioneering expression. That Portuondo, one of the leading Marxist critics in Spanish America,[68] regards Darío as 'el más grande poeta del siglo' (presumably of the last one hundred years) is a tribute both to these qualities in Darío and to Portuondo's thorough understanding of the complex relation between art and society.[69]

The Russian writer Fiodor Kelin takes yet another position and that, emphatically, regarding Darío's relation to society. In his article entitled

'Rubén Darío'[70] he offers the view that the poet has been subjected to 'Incomprensión y burla por parte de la sociedad burguesa.'[71] He declares further that Darío 'no fue nunca "sacerdote del arte puro," como preten-den presentarlo algunos críticos del campo reaccionario. El mismo, en sus opiniones sobre el arte, se manifestó siempre en "contra del culto a la palabra" y exigía en la poesía no sólo 'música del verbo" sino también "música de las ideas."'[72] These opinions, the tenacity with which they are held being emphasized by the use of adverbs like 'siempre' and 'nunca,' are given without any compunction to demonstrate the errors of the many critics who have disagreed with his views, especially concerning the poetry Darío wrote between 1888 and 1905.

Kelin states that Darío in his later work abandoned Modernism which had become decadent; but then adds that

> Darío es amado del lector de hoy afín a él no por sus puntos de vista estéticos, aunque ellos sean muy interesantes, sino porque *toda su obra* está imbuida de gran contenido humano, de ardiente amor al hombre, de inquietud por su destino ... La poesía de Darío, *en cualquier etapa de su vida*, fue un ardiente y sincero canto a la libertad.[73]

Although Kelin's statements apply to the whole of Darío's work, when he comes to use specific poems to illustrate his points he selects them all from Darío's later books; and here he finds Darío fruitful with ideas and prophecies. When Darío writes in 'Salutación del optimista' that 'algo se inicia como vasto social cataclismo/ sobre la faz del orbe,' Kelin interprets him to have perceived 'vivamente la proximidad de gigantescos cambios sociales.'[74] Bourgeois society is characterized as hostile in 'Los motivos del lobo.' But, continues Kelin, Darío refused to escape from this society; he did not take refuge in the ivory tower. Instead he prepared Spanish American youth for liberty by promoting 'la revolución intelectual.' He sees Darío as believing, like Pushkin, that there would come a time when all nations would unite – a belief that led him to campaign firmly for peace and to condemn German militarism, English aggression in Spanish America, and North American imperialism. In this regard Kelin considers it significant that Darío's last poem is '¡Pax!.' Thus as far as the degree of positive socio-political relevance he sees in Darío is concerned, Kelin is not outdone by any critic who has examined Darío's work.[75]

Other writers have been more selective in their evaluation of Darío's social and political commitment. In several of his books and articles published in the nineteen thirties and forties Arturo Torres-Ríoseco advanced the view that 'a pesar de la huida de la realidad, las obras de Darío contienen otra nota más por la cual no sólo es "el poeta de los cisnes," sino también "el poeta de América." Desde *Cantos de vida y esperanza*, en particular, se manifiestan vigorosamente en sus obras temas pan-hispánicos y americanos.'[76] Enrique Anderson Imbert sees a hiatus in Darío's social interest lasting from the period preceding *Azul* to 1904. In his essay 'Rubén Darío, poeta,' first published in 1952 as the prologue to an anthology of Darío's poetry prepared for the Fondo de Cultura Económica of Mexico, he noticed several manifestations of political liberalism in Darío's poetry before 1888 – his support for Central American unity, his attack on political tyranny, etc. He recognizes in the *Cantos de vida y esperanza* 'la vuelta a la preocupación social. Reaparecen – pero con las virtudes de un estilo soberbio – las actitudes de Darío anteriores a *Azul*: la política, el amor a España, la conciencia de la América española, el recelo a los Estados Unidos, normas morales, etc. ... '[77]

In his book *La poesía de Rubén Darío* (Buenos Aires: Losada, 1948), a book that will be discussed in some detail later in this study, Pedro Salinas devotes a chapter to 'La poesía social.' He considers Darío to be 'un americano completo'[78] and explicates several poems that demonstrate the range of his political and social positions. 'A Colón,' 'Raza,' and 'Los cisnes' reflect Darío's anxiety over the desperate straits faced by Spanish America and Spain; 'Salutación del optimista' carries his vision of hope for the Hispanic peoples; 'A Roosevelt' gives his sense of the conflict feared by the Spanish American people; 'Salutación al águila' and 'iPax!' demonstrate his deep desire for peace, and 'Canto a la Argentina,' his hope for human solidarity. But Salinas ultimately forges a link between this social poetry, which he treats as a sub-theme in Darío's poetry, and what he regards as the main theme, Darío's 'afán erótico.'[79] He does this, not altogether convincingly, by claiming that Darío's yearning for peace was derived from his desire to preserve his erotic spirit.

Nine years after Salinas's book appeared, Edelberto Torres, with his article entitled 'Introducción a la poesía social de Rubén Darío,'[80] contributed another focus to the discussion of Darío's social and political commitment. He suggests that Rodó's denial of American sentiment in Darío should now be clearly refuted and, after admitting that some of Darío's own statements are damaging to a refutation of Rodó's claim, refers to Justo Sierra's and Pedro Salinas's views to support the case he will make. (He does not, however, take into account Salinas's ultimate argument concerning Darío's eroticism.) Torres goes on to establish his case, chiefly by examining some of Darío's post-1896 poetry and by relating this poetry to historical facts. He also quotes in full a work by Darío entitled 'iPor qué?'[81] (1892), a vitriolic attack on social injustice.

The proposition that concern for social and political questions coexisted with other concerns throughout Darío's career is advanced by Antonio Oliver Belmás and also by José Ferrer-Canales in articles that were published as contributions to volumes in honour of Darío's centenary. Oliver Belmás observed in his article 'Lo social en Rubén Darío' that

> en Rubén hay muchos poetas: el medieval, el romántico, el parnasiano, el simbolista, el modernista, amén del religioso, del esteta, del filosófico, del folklórico, del humorista, del cívico y del social ... El poeta social en Darío no se contradice con el aristo. Nace en su juventud y perdura ya toda la vida, en alternancia con las demás cuerdas de su lira.[82]

Oliver Belmás begins tracing the social aspect of Darío's works with the period 1881–3. He continues to see social emphasis in *Azul* (1888) and in poems written throughout Darío's stay in Chile (1886–8). In his article 'La vendimia cívica,' José Ferrer-Canales remarks like Oliver Belmás that Darío's 'lira tenía cuerdas múltiples.'[83] Ferrer-Canales begins his examples of the social aspect of the poet's writings where Oliver Belmás and Anderson Imbert begin; and, like Oliver Belmás, he sees poetry with this tendency in works written in Chile, such as 'El salmo de la pluma,' the sonnets 'La revolución francesa,' and the stories 'El rey burgués,' 'El fardo,' and 'La canción del oro' from *Azul*. He gives a more comprehensive list of examples of social emphasis than Oliver Belmás – encompassing those of Torres Ríoseco, Salinas, Edelberto Torres, and Anderson Imbert – from Darío's later poetry.

Two other writers show that Darío's social concern extended both to the Americas and to Spain. Focusing his attention on Darío's prose writings, Pedro Agramonte[84] has seen Darío not only as continuing the Americanism of Juan Montalvo and of José Martí but also as defending threatened Hispanic traditions. Perhaps the most thorough treatment of the subject of Darío's Americanism and Hispanism so far is Jaime Delgado's 'Rubén Darío, poeta transatlántico.'[85] Delgado examines in detail works and attitudes that go beyond the range covered by Ferrer-Canales; and in his enthusiasm, ignoring writers like Gondra, he writes 'Que Rubén Darío es un poeta esencialmente hispanoamericano, es decir, radical y propiamente americano, creo no ha habido nunca nadie que haya osado ponerlo en duda.'[86] He goes on to demonstrate Darío's concern for Spain in several poems.

Criticism of Darío's work with an Americanist, a sociological, or a political focus has been widespread and has yielded varying results. Sometimes, as in the cases of Paul Groussac, Manuel Gondra, and, to a certain degree, Mario Benedetti, the discovery of an absence of Americanist sentiment on Darío's part brings negative evaluation from the critics. But positive evaluation may be granted, as was done by Rodó and Portuondo, despite the finding of a tendency by Darío to avoid American reality. And sometimes, as with Fiodor Kelin, a critic may identify in Darío's work complete attachment to great social and political causes and make a positive evaluation. Finally, positive evaluation is also made of Darío's work when it is observed, as José Ferrer-Canales, Antonio Oliver Belmás, and Jaime Delgado did, that social concern was one of the enduring facets of that work.

Several problems arise from the attempt to assess Darío as a writer from the perspective discussed in this chapter. First of all, critics have often made their observations on the basis of different parts and quantities of Darío's work. For instance, Groussac commented only on *Azul* and *Prosas profanas*, while Delgado examined selections from the complete works. Of course, the stage Darío had reached in his career when they wrote had a bearing on these critics' findings. The time at which the critics made their assessments is significant for other reasons. Darío's contemporaries expected him to use his talent to make a direct contribution to Spanish American life, to promote the grandeur of American landscape, to portray decisive moments in the history of the area, to convey the collective fears and aspirations of its people. The demand for a close relationship between the writer and social reality has become widespread in Spanish America and will no doubt continue to grow. In his essay entitled 'La realidad americana y la literatura,' in which he attacks those writers whom he considers to be practitioners of 'magical realism,' Portuondo writes:

> El pecado mayor de estos escritores es haber perdido de vista la relación existente entre el poeta y la realidad, entre la literatura y la sociedad en que se produce, en haber querido hacer de la historia privada la matriz del desorden público, haber elevado a la categoría de héroes al impotente y al sicópata, haber sustituido la auténtica rebelión con una estéril ansiedad y una angustia sin salida y sin enemigos visibles.[87]

Although Portuondo's comments are not aimed at Darío, they reflect an attitude that has considerable impact on Darío's readers.[88]

But while it remains doubtful that Darío sustained a literary position that contributed to any doctrine for radical social and political change in Spanish America, it also is doubtful what influence literature, as an instrument for radical change, has on society. Jean-Paul Sartre, the advocate of engaged literature in his *Qu'est-ce que la littérature* (1948), in

1961 manifested discouragement concerning the role of literature. He voiced this discouragement in an interview with Oreste Pucciani shortly after returning from Cuba with the conviction that the Cuban people had changed and that literature had very little to do with that change. Sartre says:

> Up to the age of forty! I believed ... that people could be changed through literature. I no longer believe that. People can certainly be changed, but not through literature, it would seem. I don't know just why. People read and they seem to change. But the effect is not lasting. Literature does not really seem to incite people to action.[89]

The element of doubt concerning the social effectiveness of literature and the difficulty, in any case, of assessing this effectiveness are problems facing those critics who share the premise that a writer can influence society. Problems may arise too, however, in defining a writer's socio-political position. The various pronouncements of Darío's critics on the subject of what constitutes Americanism is indicative of the perils to be encountered in attempting to determine a writer's social adequacy. With increasing political and sociological sophistication this difficulty is compounded; and differences, sometimes fine differences, in political and social perception may result in drastically opposing evaluations of literature. One striking example of this is apparent in the evaluation of Kafka's works by two Marxist critics, Roger Garaudy and the late Georg Lukács. Garaudy extols Kafka's greatness, sees him as representing the struggle against alienation and declares besides that it is 'les interprétations pseudo-marxistes' which see Kafka as 'un petit bourgeois décadent au pessimisme corrosif.'[90] Lukács's interpretation is that, despite Kafka's aesthetic appeal, he is one of the chief exponents of 'decadent modernism' and is therefore not to be admired, unlike Thomas Mann, whom he considers as furthering 'critical realism.'[91] Such, then, may be the difficulties of assessing the precise social or political posture of a writer.

Finally, there is the problem of evaluating the relative importance of the aesthetic and the social aspects of the works studied. Even those literary theorists who are most insistent on political content also recognize that aesthetic quality is crucial. Mao Tse-tung, for example, in one of his 'Talks at the Yenan Forum on Art and Literature' said: 'What we demand is unity of politics and art, of content and form, and of the revolutionary political content and the highest possible degree of perfection in artistic form. Works of art, however politically progressive, are powerless if they lack artistic quality.'[92]

It has also been recognized, however, that harmony between the two aspects is difficult for the writer to achieve and, even when it is achieved, for the reader or audience to perceive. Among those who have commented insistently on this problem is the playwright Bertolt Brecht who in his essay on the 'Epic Theatre' entitled 'Theatre for Learning'[93] remarked on the disadvantage to the instructive elements in art because of the ability of the naturally more appreciated artistic elements to distract the public. On the other hand, the public's opinion of the aesthetic elements may be fashioned by their judgment of the social or political attitudes reflected by the work. Gondra's reaction to *Prosas profanas* may be seen as an example of this. And it often happens that preoccupation with the socio-political orientation leaves no room for any analysis of the aesthetic elements of the work.

Rubén Darío's explicit and implicit views on socio-political questions have varied. His expression of contempt for one side of an issue could easily be followed by his praise for another aspect of that same side; and his interventions in issues were sometimes as surprising as were his withdrawals at other times. Apart from the often cited examples of this – his attitude to US hegemony in Spanish America, for example[94] – it is interesting to note that his article '¿Por qué?,' cited above, in which he delivered a strong attack against social inequality in a style unusual for Darío in its bluntness, was written in 1892 when some of the poems of *Prosas profanas* had already begun to appear. Yet it is still possible to discern a constant factor in his socio-political positions. This is his liberalism – an attitude that from time to time is open to condemnation from both conservatives and revolutionaries. Darío steadfastly showed his belief in the right to liberty, self-determination, and independence of different countries and different peoples, but he was far from advocating any methods by which these should be achieved or any specific social or political system. This is reflected, to take some scarcely studied examples of these attitudes, in his view of China and Japan.[95] With regard to China, Darío's initial references in *Azul* showed the frivolousness of his acknowledged early guide to that country, Pierre Loti. In time, however, referring to the ancient excellence of Chinese culture and to the eighth-century poet Li Po (701–62), he became seriously concerned about the situation of the Chinese people at the turn of the twentieth century, about the indignities they suffered at the hands of foreign exploiters who were goaded on by racist motivations.[96] With regard to Japan, too, Darío later showed concern that the ancient cultural patterns be preserved. In a prologue to Enrique Gómez Carrillo's *De Marsella a Tokio* he expresses his satisfaction that Japan is seeming to achieve this when he writes:

Yo sería de los que juzgan odiosa la influencia europea en la tierra de los
vencedores de Rusia (el Japón), si no estuviese convencido de que esa raza
no cambia en su fondo, y de que a pesar de la importación de las levitas, del
socialismo, del parlamentarismo y del sombrero de copa, existe en el
japonés la intangibilidad de su espíritu y de sus antiguas tradiciones.[97]

In his essay 'Congreso social y económico iberoamericano,'[98] dealing with
the socio-economic conditions in Spain in 1900, Darío, as an economic
historian, sees strengths in Spain's past that seem to be waning in
contemporary time. In some of his best known poetry and prefaces to his
books of poetry the same inclination to see in the past the true excellence
of Spanish American civilization is also evident. All these instances of
historicizing are undertaken by Darío in an attempt to encounter the
spiritual and social values and ancient traditions which, if they can be
maintained in their respective modern societies, will indicate that these
societies are free, self-determined, and independent. The perception and
appreciation of these values and traditions require the flexible liberalism
which marked Darío's attitude towards socio-political questions. And,
indeed, this attitude parallels Darío's attitude towards literature, which
was his real commitment.

CHAPTER THREE

Literary History

To the aspects of literary history that have been dealt with in the preceding chapters may be added considerations on precise topics that have been of focal interest to literary scholarship dealing with Rubén Darío. These topics are Darío's place in Hispanic literary history, particularly his place in Modernism, and his influences and sources.

As with the examination of works dealing with his biography, so also in discussing his place in Modernism, it is useful to start with Darío's own opinions. He was the first to use the term *modernismo*; and he was, of all the Spanish American writers who are thought to be associated with the movement, the one who most conscientiously involved himself with its theory. His initial use of the term in the essay 'La literatura en Centro-América' (1888) was in the context of praise for the creative work of his first important critic, the Mexican Ricardo Contreras. It was used as a synonym for *modernidad*, to explain the fact that Contreras was nicely in keeping with the times, that he was a developed writer who reflected a knowledge of the historical processes by which the contemporary state of literary expression was reached. Darío wrote of Contreras:

> Es preciso haber leído algo de este literato, conocer los chisporroteos de ingenio que riega a cada paso en sus períodos, su erudición maciza, llena, fundamental, su facilidad de producir, sus principios literarios razonados, el brillante encadenamiento de su prosa, su pureza en el decir al par que el absoluto modernismo en la expresión, de manera que es un clásico elegante, su estilo compuesto de joyas nuevas de plata vieja, pura, sin liga, para apreciarle.[1]

Two years later in an article entitled 'Fotograbado,' an account of his visit to and impressions of Ricardo Palma, he wrote precisely on Modernism as a movement, giving it for the first time the definition with which all later historians of the movement would have to contend. The definition also comes in a context of praise, this time for the broad knowledge, keen perception, and flexibility shown by Palma in literary matters:

> El es decidido afiliado a la corrección clásica, y respeta a la Academia. Pero comprende y admira el espíritu nuevo que hoy anima a un pequeño pero triunfante y soberbio grupo de escritores y poetas de la América española: el modernismo. Conviene saber: la elevación y la demonstración en la crítica, con la prohibición de que el maestro de escuela anodino y el pedagogo chascarrillero penetren en el templo del arte; la libertad y el vuelo, y el triunfo de lo bello sobre lo preceptivo, en la prosa, y la novedad en la poesía; dar color y vida y aire y flexibilidad al antiguo verso que sufría anquilosis, apretado entre tomados moldes de hierro. Por eso él, el impecable, el orfebre buscador de joyas viejas, el delicioso anticuario de frases y refranes, aplaude a Díaz Mirón, el poderoso, y a Gutiérrez Nájera, cuya pluma aristocrática no escribe para la burguesía literaria, y a Rafael Obligado, y a Puga Acal, y al chileno Tondreau, y al salvadoreño Gavidia, y al guatemalteco Domingo Estrada.[2]

In a prologue to Jesús Hernández Somoza's *Historia de tres años del Gobierno Sacasa* (1893) Darío refers to Ricardo Contreras and to Modesto Barrios as pioneers in introducing to America what Darío seems to consider at this time to be the primary element in Modernism: the contemporary French example.[3] He would appear to be moving away at this time from the broadly inclusive examples of Modernists that he had given in 1890 when writers like Rafael Obligado, Manuel Puga y Acal, and Domingo Estrada were included. He was later to be more severe in his characterization of nineteenth-century writing while maintaining his eclectic view of Modernism. Thus, on the one hand he regarded the Romantic spirit as a continuing and indispensable factor in Modernist writing: 'Románticos somos ... ¿Quién, que Es, no es romántico?'[4] On the other hand, his view of early nineteenth-century poetry as represented by Bello and Olmedo is not positive. Elaborating in *Historia de mis libros* on his statement made in the 'Palabras liminares' to *Prosas profanas* that 'Si hay poesía en nuestra América, ella está en las cosas viejas,'[5] he writes:

> no se tenía en toda la América española como fin y objeto poéticos más que la celebración de las glorias criollas, los hechos de la Independencia y la

> naturaleza americana: un eterno canto a Junín, una inacabable oda a la
> agricultura de la zona tórrida, y décimas patrióticas.[6]

In his essay 'Los colores del estandarte' (1896) he refers to *Azul* (1888)
and to his own role as the initiator of Modernism when he states:
'publiqué el pequeño libro que iniciara el actual movimiento literario
americano.'[7] Three years later in the essay 'El modernismo' he writes of
the distinctive quality that Modernism had given to Spanish American as
compared with Peninsular literature.[8] And in the preface to *Cantos de
vida y esperanza* of 1905 he declares that 'El movimiento de libertad que
me tocó iniciar en América se propagó hasta España, y tanto aquí como allá
el triunfo está logrado.'[9] The opinion – it is too vague to be called a precept
– which he held steadfastly regarding Modernist writers was that they
should be exceptionally aware of the possibilities of literary expression
and strive to use these possibilities with a freedom limited only by concern
for lofty authenticity.[10]

The discussion of Modernism by other critics has often been undertaken with the simultaneous intention of assessing Darío's role in the
movement. This was so during his lifetime and it has continued to be so.
The works of Rodó, Gondra, and Groussac, discussed in Chapter 2, are
examples of those who examined the question during Darío's lifetime,
and Pedro Henríquez Ureña's view, expressed in an essay of 1905, ought
to be added here. In his famous essay entitled 'Rubén Darío,' he considers
the Nicaraguan poet to be the outstanding modernist. He writes:

> Sabido es ... lo que Rubén Darío ha significado en las letras hispano-
> americanas: la más atrevida iniciación de nuestro *modernismo*. Fue él
> mucho más revolucionario que Casal, Martí y Gutiérrez Nájera, y en
> 1895, quedó con la muerte de estos tres, como corifeo único. Su influencia
> ha sido la más poderosa en América durante algunos años, y su reputación
> una de esas que en la misma actualidad se tornan legendarias.[11]

The controversy concerning the movement and Darío's role in it has
continued since his death with different perspectives being lent by time.
These varying perspectives may come from different critics or they may
show themselves in the course of one critic's career.[12]

Federico de Onís, for instance, has made declarations that have been
quoted selectively to support one position or another. In 1934 he characterized Modernism in very comprehensive terms, calling it

> la forma hispánica de la crisis universal de las letras y del espíritu que inicia
> hacia 1885 la disolución del siglo XIX y que se había de manifestar en el

arte, la ciencia, la religión, la política y gradualmente en los demás
aspectos de la vida entera, con todos los caracteres, por lo tanto, de un
hondo cambio histórico cuyo proceso continúa hoy.[13]

In 1952 he gave the movement a definition that lends itself to quotation by
those who see Martí as the central figure of Modernism. He wrote:

> Si miramos el modernismo, como debe mirarse, no como una escuela
> literaria, sino como una época, que fue el principio de ésta en que vivimos
> todavía, Martí se nos impone como el creador y sembrador máximo de las
> ideas, formas y tendencias que han tenido la virtud de perdurar en ella
> como dominantes y que están cada vez más llenas de posibilidades para el
> futuro.[14]

It should be added, however, that this sentence is part of a passage in
which Onís was agreeing partially with Darío's view of Martí as a precursor of Modernism. In the following year Onís implied that the movement
had dispersed leadership in a prosperous Spanish America when he wrote:

> el Modernismo surgió, no en España, sino en América, como obra de
> individualidades aisladas y pequeños grupos selectos en el momento
> mismo en que las naciones hispanoamericanas habían llegado, cada una a
> su modo, a su organización interna, y habían entrado en un largo período
> de relativa paz, estabilidad y prosperidad.[15]

Later in the same year in his essay 'Martí y el modernismo' Onís attempted to erase any distinctions he might have made between 'modernismo'
and 'modernidad.' He declared:

> Nuestro error está en la implicación de que haya diferencia entre 'moder-
> nismo' y 'modernidad,' porque modernismo es esencialmente, como
> adivinaron los que le pusieron ese nombre, la busca de modernidad.[16]

In his latest comments on the subject, in his essay entitled 'La poesía
iberoamericana,' he refers to Darío's key role in the movement. He
mentions the harmonizing in Spanish America of Symbolism and Parnassianism and states:

> Este fenómeno extraordinario de armonía y síntesis de escuelas sucesivas
> en Europa es el que define el Modernismo hispanoamericano de 1882 a
> 1905, con Rubén Darío como figura central, movimiento capital en las
> letras de lengua española.[17]

Onís thus comes ultimately to speak of a Spanish American Modernism and to underline Darío's central importance in the movement.

In 1944 Enrique Díez-Canedo gave explicit recognition to Darío's place in Modernism when, succinctly manifesting much of the range of Federico de Onís's views, he wrote:

> la escuela que en literatura se conoce con la denominación de 'modernismo' tiene ... por figura principal, a un gran poeta de América, a Rubén Darío. Quizá la palabra escuela no sea la más propia para calificar a las tendencias literarias que bajo aquella denominación se agruparon. El modernismo es más que una escuela: es una época; y su influjo sale del campo literario para ejercerse en todos los aspectos de la vida. Como escuela literaria, no ha encontrado su denominación; pero ha ido a dar con ese nombre, y de tal suerte se la ha pegado, que ya no es posible sustituirlo por otro.[18]

By mentioning the inadequacy of the term 'escuela,' and by proposing the word 'época' as a substitute, Díez-Canedo offers a term that applies well to Onís's characterization of Modernism of 1934 and that was to have further acceptance. The use of the term 'movimiento,' however, as it was initially employed by Darío himself and then by Pedro Henríquez Ureña,[19] became the consensus word among writers on Modernism.[20]

Pedro Henríquez Ureña, Díez-Canedo, and, on occasion, Onís indicate that, although the Modernist movement is wide in its embrace, its focal point is literary, with Darío playing the central role. Other critics have upheld this view. Arturo Torres-Ríoseco, for example, writing about those poets who, in his opinion, were the precursors of Modernism, declares:

> Estos cuatro poetas [Julián del Casal, Manuel Gutiérrez Nájera, José Asunción Silva and José Martí] son los antecesores de Rubén Darío; en cierto modo son también modernistas, ya que en sus temas y en su estilo presentan las características esenciales del modernismo. Sin embargo, la evolución hacia la nueva escuela no se ha efectuado en forma completa en ellos, y por eso a menudo hay en su poesía una regresión hacia la forma y el espíritu románticos.[21]

Enrique Anderson Imbert certainly considers Darío to be the central figure in the movement.[22] And Fernando Alegría is much more positive than any critic mentioned so far in his evaluation of Darío's historical importance. In fact, he questions the convention of talking about Modern-

ism as a movement embracing many poets, and declares instead that
Modernism was the poet Rubén Darío. He writes:

> the critics say a new poetic movement was born in Spanish America and
> they name it 'modernism.' They exaggerate, or, rather, they mistake the
> facts. What happened is that a new poet, a great poet, was born in Central
> America, and this poet absolutely dominated Spanish and Spanish Ameri-
> can poetry for about twenty years. *He* was modernism, he and a few
> talented disciples, and when he died modernism died with him ... His
> magic touch sent his disciples away with the dangerous notion that they
> too were demi-gods. After his disappearance modernism faded in the
> winds of our materialistic age like a cloud of golden dust. [23]

Fernando Alegría's view as well as those that give Darío clear primacy
in the Modernist movement have not gone unchallenged. In fact, such
views have been strenuously refuted, particularly by Ivan A. Schulman
and Manuel Pedro González. Both in their *Martí, Darío y el modernismo* [24] and in Schulman's *Génesis del modernismo* [25] the case is put for a
fuller view of Modernism than is usually presented. [26] Schulman proposes
in the former book that, instead of considering Modernism to have lasted
from 1888 to 1916 (the period spanning Darío's career), [27] the movement
might be considered to last from 1882 to 1932 and indeed to continue up to
the present time, particularly as evidenced in certain quests for style
manifested in the contemporary Spanish American novel. He sees the
movement as syncretic, embracing several contradictory and paradoxical
positions. Further, those writers regarded as precursors of Modernism by
Torres-Ríoseco, for instance – Casal, Silva, Gutiérrez Nájera and Martí –
are judged by Schulman and González to be full-fledged Modernists. All
this leads to their main point as far as Darío is concerned: that in relation
to the Modernist movement in general not only is Martí as important as
the Nicaraguan poet as an innovator but Martí's innovations antedate and
are the source of many of those attributed to Darío. They accordingly
dispute the claim made by Darío himself and by many of his critics that he
is the initiator of Modernism in Spanish America. Neither Schulman nor
González shows that Martí as a writer is clearly superior to Darío. Their
opinions of Martí are not markedly different from those given in more
summary form by Darío himself who again and again expressed deep
admiration for the Cuban whom he regarded as 'Maestro,' [28] 'un gran
poeta en prosa' [29] and also as 'buen poeta, en verso.' [30] Schulman classifies
as exaggerated Osvaldo Bazil's statement that 'sin Martí no habría
Darío.' [31] On the other hand, Schulman, in the chapter 'Darío y Martí'

from his later book, presents examples of the influence of Martí on Darío which may not be real cases of influence at all.[32] It is necessary, though, to make a distinction between Schulman's and González's writings on their subject. The former attempts to make his case through a patient study of the literary history of the period, founded on a stylistic basis. His remarks are generally circumspect. González is wide ranging in his methodology and rhetorical in his style of reporting. In his aim to reduce Darío's stature so that Martí's may be correspondingly enhanced, he does not refrain from the occasional recourse to speculative statements intended to cast doubt on the authorship of some of Darío's writings, nor to some rumoured aspersions that have been cast on Darío's masculinity.[33] Both Schulman and González wish to establish an evaluation of the Modernist writers that would minimize the generally conceded present difference in literary stature between Darío and such writers as Martí, Guillermo Valencia, José Asunción Silva, and González Martínez.

In concluding an article that summarized efficiently his numerous writings touching on the subject of Darío's place in Modernism,[34] Manuel Pedro González writes:

> Por último, hay que hacer una revaloración de Rubén Darío con criterio sereno, objetivo y competente. La crítica rubeniana – con muy raras excepciones – adolece de proclividad ditirámbica, de tono apologético. Más que exégesis rigurosa, el noventa y nueve por ciento de los que sobre él han escrito han adaptado una actitud apoteótica. Es hora ya de que se abandone esta postura alucinada y trivial que ha conducido a una apoteosis hiperbólica y absurda. Negar el don poético de Darío sería una necedad tan ilógica y arbitraria como la glorificación que de él han hecho sus apasionados devotos. Lo que necesitamos es la revaloración docta y justa que nos dé la medida exacta de su genio. Hasta ahora se ha hecho de Darío la piedra angular del modernismo y se le ha exaltado a un rango que es a todas luces falso por lo exagerado y subjetivo. Antes y después de él se dieron en aquel magnífico florecimiento literario varias figuras de igual o superior estatura que la crítica subjetiva y mal informada ha desdeñado o preterido.[35] ,

These are strongly contentious statements, made by a researcher whose presented evidence is based chiefly on questions concerning the original-ity and precedence of elements found in the works of Darío and his contemporaries. It must also be said that the assessment given of Darío here comes from a point of view that readily, perhaps too readily, sees an inadequate representation of Modernism in Darío's work of the period before *Cantos de vida y esperanza*. It is this pre-1905 period which Juan Marinello[36] judges to be the modernist period. In doing this he proposes, in his book of 1959, the other pole of extreme views regarding the scope of Modernism by considering the movement to be strictly aestheticist. Largely because he sees the movement as not representing the real interests of the Spanish American people, as evading a search for the causes of their anguish, his opinion of it is negative, though he shows high regard for Darío's artistic skill. In fact, as we shall see later, when he comes to assess Modernism in terms of poetic art, he holds Darío in unrivalled esteem.

The impact on Darío of developments in the socio-economic life of Latin America, mentioned by Portuondo (as discussed in Chapter 2), is intriguingly explored and carried to different conclusions by Angel Rama in his book *Rubén Darío y el modernismo*.[37] While Portuondo and Marinello see the modernist reaction as one of evasion of the issues raised by these socio-economic developments, Rama discovers an intimate relationship between Modernism and the intensified functioning of capitalism in Latin America in the late nineteenth and early twentieth centuries. He concludes that Modernism is not in any way a reaction against capitalism, but a reflection in the field of art of some of its characteristics. According to Rama, the individualism, subjectivism, independence, and quest for novelty which are manifestations of Modernism are also manifestations of the liberal philosophy that underlies capitalism. The concept of the marketability of the literary product is one that comes to the fore in the modernist period and there is an awareness of the public, an international public, as consumers. The artist develops a corresponding self-awareness of his position as a professional. Rubén Darío, of whom Rama says 'Si él no es todo el modernismo, es sin duda su más llamativa bandera,'[38] led Spanish American writers in adapting the new attitudes to literary endeavour, and became in so doing one of the two or three greatest and most influential poets in the history of Hispanic literature. Rama's view of Darío's career and the enthusiastic assessment he makes of his poetry demonstrate once more the many-faceted importance of Darío's work as seen from a historical perspective.

As Manuel Pedro González's work itself suggests, a study of Darío's writing primarily from the perspective of literary history does not promise to provide 'la revaloración docta y justa que nos dé la medida exacta de su genio.'[39] Even when Darío's poetry is found to have clearly derivative elements, his work, both historically and aesthetically, has seemed, to the overwhelming majority of his critics, to represent the outstanding writing of his epoch. Writers whose careers partially overlap the period of Modernism as defined by Schulman have had their positive say in this regard. Vicente Huidobro, César Vallejo, Octavio Paz, and Pablo Neruda are among them,[40] as is Jorge Luis Borges who in 1967 wrote:

> Todo lo renovó Darío: la materia, el vocabulario, la métrica, la magia peculiar de ciertas palabras, la sensibilidad del poeta y de sus lectores. Su labor no ha cesado y no cesará; quienes alguna vez lo combatimos, comprendemos hoy que lo continuamos. Lo podemos llamar el Libertador.[41]

And the following passage from the sober version of Mario Benedetti's article 'Rubén Darío, Señor de los tristes' is further and more precise testimony to Darío's contribution to later practitioners of the literary art:

> Buena parte de la mejor poesía en español, escrita y publicada en los últimos veinte años, tiene en él un antecedente, no forzado sino natural. Puede mencionarse el *Canto a la Argentina* como un borrador del *Canto general*. Pero hay otros anuncios. Casi todos los estudios sobre Darío comienzan afirmando que el Modernismo está muerto, y de esa afirmación deducen urgentemente que la poesía de Darío está igualmente muerta. Por eso me parece oportuno señalar que en la producción de Darío hay muchos poemas (y no siempre escritos en los últimos años) que se evaden hasta de las más amplias definiciones del Modernismo. Singular-mente, son esas fugas las que me parecen de una más palmaria actualidad. Poemas como 'Allá lejos' o los que integran la serie 'A Francisca,' están augurando toda una corriente de actualísima poesía intimista, franca, tierna y a la vez despojada. La 'Epístola a la señora de Leopoldo Lugones' es tan inobjetablemente actual que puede leerse como si hubiera sido escrita la semana pasada, es decir sin que sea necesaria una previa acomodación histórica de nuestro ánimo. Octavio Paz califica este poema de 'indudable antecedente de lo que sería una de las conquistas de la poesía contemporánea: la fusión entre el lenguaje literario y el habla de la ciudad.' Habría que agregar que toda una concepción del prosaísmo poético, tan importante en la poesía que actualmente se escribe en América Latina y en España, se halla prefigurada en ese poema escrito en 1907.[42]

An examination of the writings of the critics who have attempted to place Darío's work within a historical perspective and especially to see it in terms of the Modernist movement reveals a wide variety of views. This variety, which is as evident during Darío's lifetime as after it, indicates, nevertheless, that one of the often adduced aims in studying literary history – that of discovering the tastes of different ages[43] – is to some extent achievable. After struggling with the terms 'Decadence' and 'Symbolism,'[44] Darío's earliest critics were guided by the poet himself to the term 'Modernism' and to the principal example of what it meant. It was Rodó, whose work on Darío I have dealt with in Chapter 2, who in his magnificent essay 'Rubén Darío, su personalidad literaria, su última obra'[45] displayed dramatically the struggle that Spanish American criticism, with its nineteenth-century tradition of literary Americanism, faced before it could come to partial acceptance of Darío and of Modernism. The legacy of literary Americanism has continued into the twentieth century. And for this and other reasons – such as the tendency to broaden the definition of Modernism, the desire to promote the value of other writers, and the attractiveness of vanguardist literary movements – the view that Darío is superior to his contemporaries has not by any means been unanimous. It would seem, nevertheless, that the arguments to the contrary are not sufficient to refute the position that Darío is the dominant figure in a movement that consciously strove to renovate, broaden, and uplift Hispanic literary expression; that some of the tools at his service could have been acquired from such contemporaries as Martí, Gutiérrez Nájera, Casal, and Silva, but that he went beyond them in his ubiquitous and eclectic search for tools; that the movement ended with Darío and ought to be distinguished from 'modernidad';[46] and that because it was successful many of its elements have served and continue to serve other practitioners of the art, as is evident, for example, in Pablo Neruda's poetry and prose and in the work of others who, as Borges has said, have tried futilely to combat Darío.

And, in fact, to speak only of Darío's primacy over his contemporaries in the Modernist movement may be to give insufficient emphasis to the uniqueness claimed for him in a recent trend in commentary on Modernism. This trend is important because it has brought into clear focus a view that was presented earlier with less precision. The trend was initiated by Fernando Alegría in 1965 with the statement quoted above to the effect that Darío was Modernism. Juan Marinello, one of the leading writers on Modernism and on José Martí, continued this trend in a statement that represents a substantial revision of his opinion. In his essay, 'Rubén Darío: Meditación de centenario,'[47] Marinello declares that, although he still believes that Martí's work is 'de un hecho de distinta naturaleza y mayor alcance, en que el Modernismo queda inserto,'[48] his earlier view of the relationship between Martí and Darío[49] as Modernists was misplaced. He examines Spanish American literature from 1880 to 1920 and finds that, in that great period,·poetry is the most distinguished genre while Martí's strength was prose. Marinello names all the important poets of the period and adds:

> No está bien llamarles modernistas porque, integrando la hermosa etapa superadora, no responden a los ademanes del jefe de la escuela ... Nadie discutirá que dentro de esa Edad de Oro de la literatura continental aparece Rubén Darío, 'el de las piedras preciosas,' como el poeta de más estatura ... El Modernismo, que es como decir Rubén Darío, es un tramo fragante de la modernidad, o de la universalización de la literatura latino-americana si se prefiere, que cuaja en lo lírico su voz más duradera.[50]

Marinello's view of Darío's place in Modernism, then, has come to correspond to Alegría's. So, too, has Anderson Imbert's who in 1967 wrote:

> Darío ha llenado el período del Modernismo. Es el Modernismo. Todos los temas, tonos, tendencias, técnicas se dan en él. Su compleja personalidad ha escrito páginas suficientes para ilustrar cualquier aspecto del Modernismo, en verso y en prosa, sobre superficies tranquilas o bajo tormentosas profundidades, con difíciles elegancias y con confesiones en el estilo de la plática, con exotismos y con americanismos, para un Arte por el Arte y para una literatura comprometida ...[51]

And the earlier writers discussed above, Arturo Torres-Ríoseco, for instance, who hold that Modernism coincides with Darío's career and that such poets as Martí, Silva, Gutiérrez Nájera, and Casal were precursors of Modernism, may also be seen as considering too that Darío was Modernism – was the figure whose literary practice and theory gave form and substance to a Spanish American literary movement that preceded similar literary and other movements, also called Modernist, which appeared with varying characteristics in different centres of Western literature.

INFLUENCES AND SOURCES

Darío's work has also been examined extensively from the point of view of its sources and of the literary influences that have been exerted upon it. Some of his earliest critics investigated these aspects and their work has given rise to further studies.

In the prologue to the first edition of *Azul* (1888) the Chilean Eduardo de la Barra remarks on the variety of influences detectable in Darío's work. He mentions Victor Hugo, Paul de St Victor, Alphonse Daudet, Bernardin de Saint-Pierre, Jorge Isaacs, and Catulle Mendès in this regard, but adds:

> Son en verdad estilos y temperamentos muy diversos, mas nuestro autor de todos ellos tiene rasgos, y no es ninguno de ellos. Ahí precisamente está su originalidad. Aquellos ingenios, aquellos estilos, todos aquellos colores y harmonías, se aúnan y funden en la paleta del escritor centro-americano y producen una nota nueva, una tinta suya, un rayo genial y distinctivo que es el sello del poeta ... Su originalidad incontestable está en que todo lo amalgama, lo funde y lo armoniza en un estilo suyo, nervioso, delicado, pintoresco, lleno de resplandores súbitos y de graciosas sorpresas, de giros inesperados, de imágenes seductoras, de metáforas atrevidas, de epítetos relevantes y oportunísimos y de palabras bizarras, exóticas aun, mas siempre bien sonantes.[52]

Later in the same year, in the first of his 'Cartas americanas' dealing with *Azul* ..., the Spanish writer Juan Valera dwelt on the French element in Darío's writing, declaring:

> Veo, pues, que no hay autor en castellano más francés que Vd. Yo lo digo para afirmar un hecho, sin elogio y sin censura. En todo caso, más bien lo digo como elogio ... lo primero que se nota es que está Vd. saturado de toda la más flamante literatura francesa. Hugo, Lamartine, Musset, Leconte de Lisle, Gauthier, Bourget, Sully-Proudhomme, Daudet, Zola, Barbey d'Aurevilly, Catulle Mendès, Rollinat, Goncourt, Flaubert y todos los demás poetas y novelistas han sido por Vd. bien estudiados y mejor comprendidos. Y Vd. no imita a ninguno: ni es Vd. romántico, ni naturalista, ni *neurótico*, ni decadente, ni simbólico, ni parnasiano. Usted lo ha revuelto todo: lo ha puesto a cocer en el alambique de su celebro, y ha sacado de ello una rara quintaesencia.[53]

Like Eduardo de la Barra, then, Valera sees originality in the way in which Darío used his sources; but, of the two, Valera tends more to isolate the French presence in Darío's first important book. That Valera, despite his above claim that he points to this French influence rather as a form of 'elogio,' is really quite uneasy about its presence can be seen in his letter of the following week, 29 October 1888. Admitting his difficulty in establishing his preference between Darío's prose and poetry, he writes: 'En la prosa hay más riqueza de ideas; pero es más afrancesada la forma. En los versos la forma es más castiza.[54] There is no doubt that Valera's words here betray a negative evaluation of 'afrancesada' and a positive evaluation of 'castiza.' That he was motivated in his comments by concern for the weakening impact of Spanish literature and a corresponding strengthening of the impact of French literature on Spanish American writing can be seen from his conclusion to this second letter where he writes:

> Con todo, yo aplaudiría muchísimo más, si con esa ilustración francesa que en Vd. hay se combinasen la inglesa, la alemana, la italiana, y ¿por qué no la española también? Al cabo, el árbol de nuestra ciencia no ha envejecido tanto que aún no pueda prestar jugo, ni sus ramas son tan cortas ni están tan secas que no puedan retoñar como mugrones del otro lado del Atlántico.[55]

Valera's attitude represents the first important reaction in terms of established traditions to the departure signalled by the first stage of the Modernist movement. The second important reaction is that shown at its best in the way Rodó tackled and resolved the problem of the break with the tradition of literary Americanism posed by the first 'gran poeta exquisito'[56] of Spanish America. Darío having rejected the options of *casticismo* and of *americanismo literario*, and Nicaragua being without an established literary tradition, his contemporaries found in the French resonances of his early important poetry a trait useful for discussing his work in terms of influence and source.

Darío himself contributed to this trend in the criticism of his work. He wrote of French influence regarding *Azul* ... in his essay 'Los colores del estandarte' in the following terms:

> El *Azul* ... es un libro parnasiano y, por tanto, francés. En él aparecen por primera vez en nuestra lengua el 'cuento' parisiense, la adjetivación francesa, el giro galo injertado en el párrafo clásico castellano; la chuchería Goncourt, la *câlinerie* erótica de Mendès, el encogimiento verbal de Heredia, y hasta su poquito de Coppée.
>
>   Qui pourrais-je imiter pour être original? me decía yo. Pues a todos. A cada cual le aprendía lo que me agradaba, lo que cuadraba a mi sed de novedad y a mi delirio de arte; los elementos que constituirían después un medio de manifestación individual.[57]

He was later to write, in his autobiography,[58] that at this time Santiago Estrada, José Martí, and, above all, Paul Groussac were his guides in prose writing. And his revelations in the same work[59] about his early readings have provided useful data for those critics who have emphasized his Hispanic influences.

This emphasis became particularly prominent in commentary on Darío's poetry published in 1905 and after; and the two areas of influence – the French and the Hispanic – came to be dealt with respectively in two important books. In 1925 Erwin K. Mapes contributed through his *L'influence française dans l'œuvre de Rubén Darío*[60] the most extensive study of the subject that has been done; and, combined with his 'Innovation and French influence in the Metrics of Rubén Darío,'[61] it established Mapes as the most important contributor to this aspect of Darío studies. The place of the Hispanic tradition was first described comprehensively by Arturo Torres-Ríoseco in his book *Rubén Darío. Casticismo y americanismo.*[62] He elaborated on an aspect of this book a year later in his article 'Casticismo en la obra de Darío: Resurrecciones e innovaciones métricas.'[63] At the same time it was becoming conventional to associate *Azul* and *Prosas profanas* with the period of French influence and the later poetry with Hispanic influence. Max Henríquez Ureña demonstrates this position in two separate studies, the first being 'El intercambio de influencias literarias entre España y América durante los últimos cincuenta años (1895–1925)'[64] and the other, 'Las influencias francesas en la literatura hispanoamericana.'[65]

Other influences on Darío's writing were suggested as critics turned their attention more and more to the search for sources of specific poems. Arturo Marasso has produced the most extensive and erudite work of this kind.[66] He recognizes the French writers already named, in addition to others, as providing sources for Darío's works but he also gives great importance to other sources such as the Bible, classical mythology – either directly through Ovid and Homer or through such French works as the *Dictionnaire des Antiquités grecques et romaines* by Daremberg and Saglio and René Ménard's *Mythologie dans l'art ancien et moderne* – Plato, Dante, Shakespeare, and the Hispanic literary tradition. Marasso makes a painstaking attempt to specify from all these sources the precise materials used by Darío in his individual works, a difficult task indeed, given Darío's complexity and eclecticism. Alejandro Hurtado Chamorro in his book *La mitología griega en Rubén Darío*[67] suggests that Darío used the world of Greek mythology to exteriorize symbolically his natural Hellenism, his personal sentiments. Hurtado accordingly explores the symbolic substance of figures of Greek mythology often used by Darío – Venus, Leda, Psyche, Apollo, Pan, and Orpheus. Serious studies of Darío's literary preparation have been made by Ernesto Mejía Sánchez in his already mentioned book *Los primeros cuentos de Rubén Darío*[68] and in his essay 'Las humanidades de Rubén Darío.'[69] These studies as well as Marasso's have been useful indeed to Dolores Ackel Fiore whose book *Rubén Darío in Search of Inspiration*[70] demands some fairly detailed comments.

The book contains most of the valuable insights provided by those scholars who had previously investigated Darío's sources; and it contributes new ones. The author shows that Darío's main access to the classics was by way of translations such as Federico Baráibar's *Poetas líricos griegos* and José Ignacio Montes de Oca y Obregón's *Poetas bucólicos griegos* and *Odas de Pindaro*, as well as other translations by Francisco Javier de Burgos and Marcelino Menéndez y Pelayo. Moreover, the classics came to Darío through all those already mentioned by other critics and by Darío himself and through others such as Paul-Armand Silvestre, Leconte de Lisle, Henri de Régnier, Paul Adam, Jules Laforgue, Pierre Loti, Jean Moréas, Paul Verlaine, and Stéphane Mallarmé. She also points to 'castizo' influences by writers such as Santa Teresa, Góngora, Gracián, Quintana, Valera, and Menéndez y Pelayo. She sees Darío, then, as cultured, well read, but not possessing scholarly knowledge of the classics. Thus, she points out that John Brand Trend in his article '*Res metricae* de Rubén Darío'[71] credits Darío with a technical knowledge of the placing of accents in Latin that the poet could not have had; and she agrees with Pedro Salinas that "'lo griego" was for Darío not "un objeto de conocimiento" but rather "un norte para deseos sueltos en busca de rumbo.'"[72] Biblical and liturgical references have great weight in Darío's work, she adds; and the combination of all these elements makes for a highly individual style. She finds that the myths in Darío's work were not impersonal as they were for the Parnassians, that he could use Greco-Roman personalities to express his Christian beliefs. She concludes that

> Darío ... stands out for the way he makes ... Greco-Roman vocabulary distinctively his own ... he employs it with flexibility and originality. He even ventures to create his own Greco-Roman words such as *pandórico*, *fáunico* and *kalofónico*, in seriousness and in jest, in prose and in verse, with the admirable agility with which he has always known how to harmonize models, sources and materials of the most varied origin.[73]

A concluding paragraph such as this reveals the sensitive understanding of Darío's work and of literature shown by Fiore throughout her study. She always shows that each poem is different and that the meaning and aptness of each word must be determined within the structural context of each poem. She understands, too, that the attribution of precise sources to the works of a real poet is a precarious undertaking and wisely prefers to suggest a combination of sources in dealing with Darío's poems.

The medieval period has also been proposed as containing sources for Darío. Francisco López Estrada[74] has presented the most comprehensive study done so far of this aspect of Darío's sources. Other studies of narrower scope have been made of the subject by Francisco Sánchez-Castañer,[75] María Pilar Pueyo Casáus,[76] Giuseppe Bellini,[77] Bernardo Gicovate,[78] Eduardo Neale-Silva,[79] Pedro Henríquez Ureña,[80] and José María de Cossío.[81] Referring to some of these studies and to appropriate works of Darío – the early poem 'La poesía castellana,' for instance – López Estrada suggests, as does Concha Zardoya, that Darío's lyrical roots are in the *Poema de Mío Cid*, in Berceo, Juan de Mena, and other medieval Spanish poets. Beyond this he finds that medieval influences often come indirectly to Darío through the Pre-Raphaelites; but he notices, as does Pueyo Casáus, the direct influence of Dante.

The search for sources has also focused on North America with the efforts of scholars such as Fernando Alegría,[82] John Englekirk,[83] José Agustín Balseiro,[84] and Humberto de Castro[85] pointing to the influence of Walt Whitman and Edgar Allan Poe. Nor have German writers such as Goethe, Wagner, Nietzsche, and Heine been ignored as influences on Darío.[86]

Having referred to the difficulty faced by those who would establish precise sources and influences for Darío's writings, I should like now to illustrate this difficulty by examining attempts to establish the source of one of Darío's famous poems, 'Lo fatal.' In 1932 Amado Alonso expressed the view that 'La fuente de "Lo fatal" es una cuarteta de Miguel Angel.'[87] The precise quatrain is a reply to one by Giovanni Strozzi which was inspired by the statue *La Notte* sculpted by Michelangelo for the Medici monument. Michelangelo's quatrain reads:

> Caro m'è'l sonno e più l'esser di sasso,
> Mentre che'l danno e la vergogna dura.
> Non verder, non sentir m'è gran ventura;
> Però non mi destar, deh! parla basso.[88]

Alonso contends that 'Lo fatal' 'es un poemita de fisonomía muy singular dentro de la producción de Rubén,'[89] and that this is so because its condition as a response to Michelangelo's verses determines its stylistic features, especially the directness of its expression. He predicted, besides, that in the then imminent appearance of Arturo Marasso's book, which he thought would be entitled *Las fuentes de Rubén Darío*, further evidence would be given to justify his own claim that Michelangelo's verses were indeed the source for 'Lo fatal.' Marasso's book appeared two years later; but apart from a statement that 'Amado Alonso estableció una sabia correspondencia estilística entre esta poesía y la célebre estrofa de Miguel Angel,'[90] it gives no reinforcement to Alonso's claim. Instead in that and in later editions of his book as well as in his article on 'Lo fatal'[91] Marasso mentions other possible sources – Boscán, Homer, Cicero, Sophocles, *The Book of Job*, Fernán Pérez de Oliva, Mallarmé, and others. He declares, however, that the chief source of Darío's poem is Claude Bernard's *Introduction á l'étude de la médecine expérimentale*, adding for intended emphasis:

> ¿Cómo no leer, por ejemplo, la *Ciencia experimental* de Claudio Bernard? Un poeta de la sensibilidad de Darío no ha leído nunca *todos los libros*. Pero los ha presentado en la atomósfera intelectual donde se vive. Y especialmente los libros que por su prestigio persuaden con eficacia irresistible.[92]

Thus Darío, in Marasso's view, by direct or indirect means, found in Bernard's book the chief source for his poem.

Six years after Marasso's book appeared, Carlos Oscar Cupo, in his article 'Fuentes inéditas de *Cantos de vida y esperanza*,'[93] offered the view that Bécquer's influence is decisive in 'Lo fatal.' Cupo first cites thematic resemblances between the last two verses of Darío's poem and the last stanza of Bécquer's second *rima*:

> Ese soy yo, que al acaso
> Cruzo el mundo, sin pensar
> De donde vengo ni a donde
> Mis pasos me llevarán,[94]

as well as this stanza from his fourth *rima*:

> Mientras la humanidad siempre avanzando
> No sepa a dó camina:
> Mientras haya un misterio para el hombre
> Habrá poesía.[95]

Cupo then alleges that Bécquer's influence is also noticeable in the versification of Darío's poem. He writes:

'Lo fatal' lleva la distribución de un soneto en alejandrino que resulta
incompleto porque Rubén sustituye el terceto final por dos versos libres;
eneasílabo uno y heptasílabo el otro. ¿No es esto una clara consecuencia de
que Bécquer haya escrito su rima II en versos octosílabos? ¿Puede no haber
una influencia musical?[96]

In 1964 Jesús Castañón Díaz published the same finding about the source
of the metre of the last two lines of 'Lo fatal.'[97] It would be difficult to
agree wholeheartedly with Cupo and with Castañón Díaz. Indeed, the
most remarkable feature about the break with the alexandrine in the last
two verses of the poem and the disruption of the sonnet form in what
might have been the final tercet is the aptness of this formal disruption
when it is seen in the essential light of its correspondence to the state of
despair expressed climactically in the words of the verses. As a result,
original, inventive, and subtle coherence is achieved in the poem. This
kind of observation has not been made by these critics about the
versification of 'Lo fatal,' while the preoccupation with sources has con-
sumed much energy.

Then, in 1967, Julieta Gómez Paz in an article entitled 'Rubén Darío y
Rosalía de Castro'[98] refers only to Amado Alonso's finding that
Michelangelo's verses are the source of 'Lo fatal.' She disputes the finding
and suggests instead that Darío wrote his poem after reading Rosalía de
Castro's *Follas novas* and that the poem 'Amigos vellos' gave Darío his
initial creative impulse for his poem. She quotes from 'Lo fatal' several
lines or parts of lines that bear resemblance to works by the Galician
poet, and on this basis suggests that the source of the poem lies in Rosalía
de Castro's work.

Three years before Gómez Paz's article appeared, Emilio Carilla examined the claims of Alonso and of Marasso and found them both wanting
in persuasiveness. Carilla proposed simply that the poem could have come
from Darío himself without any prompting by a precise literary source,
that the directness of the language could have been the result of the kind of
strong feeling that Darío had been showing at about the time of the
writing of the poem – in other poems such as 'A Phocás el campesino.' He
suggests further that certain biographical experiences, such as the death of
Darío's son, the first Rubén Darío Sánchez, nicknamed Phocás, turned his
thoughts towards death. It is possible to raise certain objections to
Carilla's findings, to argue, for instance, that we cannot be certain of the
date of composition of the poem or of the real mood or moods of Darío as
he composed it. Nevertheless, Carilla's approach, in so far as it attempts to

turn attention from outside sources and back to Darío himself, aids in bringing the poem within a more ascertainable critical perspective.[99] And his conclusions can be strengthened by other observations. The language of the poem is not as unique in its directness among Darío's poems as Alonso claims it to be. Several other poems of this and later periods of his poetry reveal similar expression – the 'Nocturnos,' 'A Phocás,' and in another vein, the 'Epístola a la señora de Lugones,' for example. Further, the concepts developed in 'Lo fatal' are, as students like to point out, not far removed from the commonplace. Darío might have reflected on them at a tender age and several times thereafter or he might have heard them expressed by a villager in Metapa or Navalsáuz. It would seem unlikely that a precise literary source was necessary for the poem's composition; and the plethora of precise sources suggested tends to confirm doubts that any one claim is valid.

The preceding discussion of 'Lo fatal' and its suggested sources was not intended to negate the view that, as T. S. Eliot expressed it: 'No poet, no artist of any art, has his complete meaning alone. His significance, his appreciation is the appreciation of his relation to the dead poets and artists.'[100] Far less was it intended to suggest that profitable studies involving Darío's sources do not exist.[101] Its purpose was rather to demonstrate certain perils that waylay the quest to discover influences and sources, the elusiveness of precision that is inherent in this exercise and the self-perpetuating speculation that may result. Above all, emphasis on this other extrinsic critical activity seems inordinate when it is compared with the relatively few intrinsic examinations of Darío's writing that have been undertaken to this point.

Undoubtedly the investigation of Darío's place in literary history and of his sources has yielded numerous studies that have been useful and will continue to be useful to Darío students. These studies have helped to establish Darío's place among writers and to discover the links between him and other writers. One point that is applicable to both types of study needs, however, to be made. It is that the nature of literature, its dependence on a proliferation of words and images to reveal human experiences that may be similar, gives rise to resemblances between works or parts of works of different authors even when no contact of any kind exists between them. Claims of influence and source made on the basis of resemblances are thus unreliable.[102] Similarly, when a writer's work has achieved the distinction and versatility that Darío's has, it illuminates certain aspects of the writing of his contemporaries and predecessors, so that, to a certain degree Darío 'crea a sus precursores,' as Borges has

termed the phenomenon.[103] In such cases a certain paradoxical anach-
ronism is involved when we speak of influences and sources. And it is a
fact that several of Darío's Spanish American contemporaries and of his
French predecessors, for instance, have figured in literary history thanks
mainly to Darío's career.

CHAPTER FOUR

Towards the Intrinsic:
Philosophy, Themes, Motifs, Metrics and Language

The study of Rubén Darío's thought, of the ideas that may be gleaned from his writings, has not been undertaken with great fruitfulness or persistence. The lack of fruitfulness has been shown by those who attempt earnestly to demonstrate the presence of rigorous and profound thought in his works, while the lack of persistence is shown by those who abandon quickly the search for rigorous thought in his writings and deal instead with the author's *Weltanschauung*, with his *intuición del mundo*, or with his 'themes.'

In the first of these falls C. Rangel Baez's study, 'The Poetry of Ideas in Darío and Nervo,'[1] which is an unsuccessfully developed attempt to link Darío to certain French thinkers, such as Jean-Marie Guyau, René Descartes, Henri Bergson, and Ernest Renan. In the second category are the many critics who are apt to use the word 'pensamiento' in titles of their studies of Darío's work but who usually define the word in terms that indicate that the authors do not aim to elucidate any rigorous thought structure therein. Thus Abelardo Bonilla in his book *América y el pensamiento de Rubén Darío* wrote that

> Darío, gran poeta y brillante cronista, no pensó honda ni rigurosamente en los campos conceptuales y dialécticos ... Al hablar de pensamiento poético nos referimos entonces a la concepción del mundo y a la voluntad de forma del vate, y nuestro propósito es analizar en los poemas de Darío el contenido ideológico, y si se quiere filosófico, de la intuición poética. Este contenido ... nos interesa en cuanto tiene de genuinamente americano.[2]

In a similar vein, Roberto Armijo in his book *Rubén Darío y su intuición del mundo* declares that 'Rubén Darío careció del sólido andamiaje filosófico que sirviera de soporte mental a su obra. El sedimiento de su mundo ideológico, es pobre, limitado ... No estaba dentro de las corrientes de la moderna filosofía, sino que esgrimía ideas completamente extemporáneas.'[3] Nor does Pablo Antonio Cuadra in his 'Introducción al pensamiento vivo de Rubén Darío' understand 'pensamiento' to involve rigour or consistent method. Rather he posits the view, which is a radical departure from his youthful opinions, that Darío's thought is American and declares: 'Equivocábamos a Rubén porque nos colocábamos demasiado cerca de su propia multiplicidad. Cuando nos alejamos, aunque desconcertados, adquirimos la perspectiva y descubrimos su unidad. Su unidad era América, Hispanoamérica.'[4] The writers mentioned above who have found that Darío was not in any profound sense a philosopher have not used their discovery as a form of censure. This has not been true of some other writers, of Cecil Maurice Bowra, for example. He uses what he considers to be Darío's lack of philosophical grounding, his lack of an ability to deal with real mysteries, to substantiate a negative attitude towards certain aspects of the poet's work.[5]

The question of how ideas in poetry should be valued has a long history and it harbours many complexities. When, for example, Plato indicated in Books II and III of the *Republic* the undesirability of the presence of poets in his ideal republic because he considered them to be liars, he failed to make the distinction between delusion and illusion, between the poet's capacity to deceive and his creative exercise of imagination. Centuries later Samuel Johnson[6] and then Samuel Taylor Coleridge,[7] infinitely more accommodating than Plato if not to the ideas themselves within literary works at least to their aesthetic effect, recommended – as Coleridge expressed it in his *Biographia Literaria*, Chapter XIV[8] – a 'willing suspension of disbelief' with regard to the statements made in the course of a literary work. Following up on the implication in Coleridge's position that poetry states only provisionally in order to produce an emotional effect and that, in the light of this, statements made in a poem should be dissociated from literal truth, I.A. Richards proposed the term 'pseudo statement,'[9] a term that allows validity for a statement only within the context of the poem or other literary work to whose structure it contributes. This view conforms to Richards's position that poetry is emotive rather than referential. For Alfonso Reyes, statements within literary works have their validity within those works, and their truthfulness in any referential sense must be regarded as suspect. He writes: 'La literatura, mentira práctica, es una verdad psicológica. Hemos definido la literatura: *La verdad sospechosa.*'[10] The tendency to discount the philosophical importance of statements that form part of literary works is shown too by T.S. Eliot. For him the achievement of a poet lies not in creating ideas but in demonstrating how it feels to hold certain adopted views. Thus the poet's concern is not so much with the beliefs themselves – though these should show a certain maturity – as with finding the objective correlatives appropriate for conveying their emotional charge. For Eliot and for most of the writers discussed here, then, the aesthetic aspect of a poem overshadows in importance the ideological statement; and the excellence of a writer hardly depends on his strength in the field of philosophy. Thus Eliot could declare that neither 'Shakespeare nor Dante did any real thinking.'[11]

There are writers, Miguel de Unamuno, for example, whose fictional work represents another dimension of their consistent philosophical probings into the mysteries of life. Such fictional works may usefully be considered from the point of view of their affinity with the ideas that form the core of the philosophical work,[12] particularly after the primary task of assessing the features that contribute to the distinctiveness of each fictional work has been undertaken. There are also concepts expressed in works which, considered in isolation, outside the frame of their literary setting might seem valuable in themselves. Yet, as far as the assessment of a literary work is concerned, the study of the philosophical idea contextually, as contributing to the structure of the work, rather than referentially, would seem to be the preferable procedure. And the idea conveyed by the work need not be complex, sophisticated, or form an important contribution to the history of thought.[13] This position, or at least the aspect of it that attaches little importance to the quality of thought beyond the requirement that it should be sufficient to sustain the sense and emotion of a poem, seems to be implicitly accepted by most of the critics who have studied the verse and prose of Rubén Darío.

One of the consequences of this is the attention that has been paid to themes rather than to substantial philosophical ideas in his work. The work that has won greatest acclaim as a study of the thematic aspect of Darío's work is Pedro Salinas's *La poesía de Rubén Darío*, subtitled *Ensayo sobre el tema y los temas del poeta.*[14] Salinas presents the basis of his study in the following terms:

> 'Cada loco con su tema,' dice el refrán. Así igualmente, cada gran poeta
> con el suyo, el tema vital que desde los adentros preside misteriosamente
> sobre los otros temas, los literarios. Se presenta en la vida espiritual del
> autor con más persistencia que los demás. Y con mayor frecuencia que los
> demás se representa en su obra a la que sirve de recóndito centro de

irradiación, de principio constantemente activo, para sus varias creaciones. Tema humano, genérico, preocupación del alma, nacido con ella, es anterior a cualquier intento de su expresión particular en un arte determinado ... Se sobreentiende que ese tema vital es algo muy distinto y mucho más general que los temas peculiares que en cada arte se han venido formando a compás de los siglos. El tema del poeta para proyectarse en poesía se va buscando los asuntos que, en cada caso, le parecen más afines a su querencia. Por lo general no se acaba ni agota en una obra, en un asunto.[15]

Salinas goes on to state that the poet's theme is sometimes easily discernible, while at other times it is so difficult to apprehend that the insufficient critic gives only a partial or, at worst, a completely erroneous interpretation of the work. Salinas states, too, that the theme supersedes the author's purpose: 'Es lo puesto – por inexplicable agencia – sobre lo propuesto.'[16] He allows, however, for sub-themes which are departures from the main theme and insists that the 'tema vital' should not be expected to conform to the writer's biography. Salinas declares that the detection and study of the poet's central theme is the critic's highest task. He writes:

Se me figura la función más deseable del estudio de un poeta la delicada discriminación de su tema, su cuidadosa separación de los temas segundos, o subtemas; el precisar el curso que sigue, através de la obra, resolver las contradicciones aparentes que velan su presencia, llegando por fin a la visión del creador entero y verdadero, salvada de mutilaciones y limpia de desenfoques.[17]

Having thus established the theoretical basis for his study, Salinas embarks on an examination of Darío's poetry which for the detail of intrinsic interpretation and the volume of poetry studied has not been surpassed in Darío criticism. His concept of the variety of forms and tones in which the poet's theme may occur allows him to consider a wide variety of types of Darío's poems. These poems are related explicitly to the principal theme, eroticism in its hedonistic, tragic and agonizing forms, to which Darío's life was implicitly related in the introductory biographical chapters. The book thus gives an overwhelming impression of elegant completeness. Nevertheless, it becomes apparent that eroticism, the 'tema vital' that Salinas recognizes in Darío's work, does not convincingly emerge from all of Darío's poetry with the degree of dominance and exclusivity that Salinas claims for it, that by yoking his sub-themes –

social preoccupation and the idea of art and the poet – to the principal theme he exceeds extravagantly his earlier theoretical formulation concerning the place of sub-themes. Moreover, it can be perceived that in some cases, had the poems been viewed more openly, the discoveries that support the claims made by Salinas for their connection to the 'tema vital' might not have proved to be substantive[18] and that a fuller explication of certain poems would lead to the discovery of a wide diversity of primary themes in Darío's work.[19] Implicit in Salinas's theory of the 'tema vital' is the presence of a *Geist* that presides over all the artist's expression. Even though there are other distinguished writers who have shared this view, Francisco Ayala,[20] for instance, it may still be wondered whether the quest for unity in an artist's work is not usually carried out at the expense of comprehensiveness in the viewing of his production. This may be wondered especially in the case of an artist like Rubén Darío who was not so much bound by subjects as by his quest for excellence of expression.

Salinas has not been unique in attempting to identify one precise theme as the 'tema vital' in Rubén Darío's work. Citing Salinas's very words, quoted above, concerning the involuntary nature of the functioning of a principal theme, Catalina Tomás McNamee identifies a different principal theme in Darío's work from that identified by Salinas. For her the ubiquitous theme in Darío's work is Catholicism. In the conclusion to the abstract of her doctoral thesis, 'El pensamiento católico de Rubén Darío,' she repeats the usually made qualification concerning the use of 'pensamiento' as applied to Darío and writes of the Catholic theme as follows:

> Como hemos insistido desde el principio, este gran nicaragüense fue siempre más poeta que filósofo. Por consiguiente, su 'pensamiento' religioso no consistió en una serie de abstractas especulaciones teológicas; más bien, tal pensamiento fue, en él, un acto de todo su ser ... Y el corazón de Rubén fue un órgano católico; en los cantos que de él fluyeron – sean himnos sagrados o prosas profanas – se oye siempre el eco de la gran armonía cristiana que resuena por toda la creación. A veces, el poeta, con plena conciencia e intención explícita, se puso a cantar la hermosura de la Esposa o la bondad del Divino Señor; otras veces, en medio de una melodía profana brotaría espontáneamente – se diría, casi a pesar suyo – el tema católico. No importa. Allí está el motivo que se percibe – ya fuerte, y sutil – en toda la obra rubeniana.[21]

Salinas's theory, then, is used by Tomás McNamee to arrive at conclusions different from his about Darío's principal theme, and thus the problem of identifying a 'tema vital' in Darío's work is underlined.

Other claims for the prominence of religion as a theme in Darío's work have been made by writers like Jaime Concha,[22] Hernán Díaz Arrieta,[23] Julio Ycaza Tigerino,[24] Pedro Barreda-Tomás,[25] Mary Avila,[26] Lola E. Boyd,[27] and Enrique Anderson Imbert,[28] although, with the exception of Concha, religion is not identified by these writers as the 'tema vital' in the sense that Salinas defines this term. These studies have reflected for the most part the view that there are other themes in Darío's work that claim primary attention, themes that arise from and are common to different groups of poems and which are not necessarily to be subsumed under any one dominant theme. Anderson Imbert, although granting the predominance of the erotic 'en Darío – como en casi todos los hombres,'[29] recognizes a variety of other important themes in Darío's work. In *Cantos de vida y esperanza*, for instance, aristocratic evasion and social preoccupation (see Chapter II) are viewed by him as important themes. And he identifies in different poems themes which contribute to a demonstration of Darío's preoccupation with the enigmatic meaning of life. The place of art in life, for instance, is shown in such poems as 'Yo soy aquel,' 'Pegaso,' and 'Melancolía.'[30] Pleasure as a problematic phenomenon is seen by him to be the theme of 'Programa matinal' and of other poems, and time is seen as a metaphysical preoccupation, particularly in his later poetry with the many references to 'otoño.' Life as a bitter mystery is the theme identified by him in the 'Nocturnos' and other poems of the same period such as 'No obstante,' 'Filosofía,' '¡Oh miseria de toda lucha por lo finito!' 'Phocás el campesino,' '¡Ay, triste del que un día ... !' and 'Lo fatal';[31] and death as revealing the secret of life is the theme understood in such poems as 'Augurios' and 'Thánatos.' The multiplicity of themes in Darío's work is given noteworthy attention also by Julio Ycaza Tigerino.[32] Apart from his already mentioned study of the religious theme, he makes, on the basis of detailed examination of many of Darío's poems, observations concerning temporal, magical, ethnic, Americanist, and other themes. Ramón de Garciasol had studied most of these themes, though less effectively, a few years earlier.[33]

Darío's concern for justice and freedom has been examined as a theme in his work especially with regard to the treatment of black people. Richard L. Jackson has studied the topic with careful attention to Darío's essays, fiction, and poetry and has found Darío to be 'reivindicador de los oprimidos, exponente de la poesía negra, conocedor de la raza negra.'[34] In another important study of the theme, René L.F. Durand[35] cites evidence from Darío himself and from Luis Alberto Sánchez, Leopoldo Lugones, Amado Nervo, Francisco Contreras, and Ricardo Rojas to make the case that Darío had African forebears. Durand then proceeds to examine 'la négritude' in Darío's poetry and finds that this element occurs throughout. He also suggests that, more than being one of the decorative elements characteristic of Modernism, Darío's celebration of blackness constitutes authentic lyricism and that in this he anticipates poets like Léopold Senghor of Senegal and other poets of 'négritude.' A view diametrically opposed to those of Jackson and Durand is presented by Gastón Baquero, who, among his many disparaging comments in his study of Darío, states that 'Rubén Darío ... tenía por los negros el desprecio habitual de la sociedad hispanoamericana de su tiempo.'[36] While it can hardly be denied that Baquero's view is sustainable by an essay like Darío's 'La raza de Cham'[37] and that consequently there is some inconsistency in Darío's position, it would seem that the burden of his preoccupation with the subject shows a sensitive concern for the well-being of black people.

It will have been noticed that the term 'theme' has been used with some variety of meaning by Darío's critics. I have already commented on Salinas's use of the word in terms of his concept of the 'tema vital'; and in the last case studied, that of the concern for fairness and justice towards black people, the word 'theme' is used by the critics to denote the thesis or doctrine of Darío's works that deal with this subject. That is to say, the distinction may be made here between 'subject' – the treatment of blacks – and 'theme' – that blacks should be treated fairly and with justice. When the word is used in this way there is no uncertainty as to its meaning and it conforms well to the concepts of 'guiding idea,' 'moral,' 'lesson,' and 'pronouncement,' as distinguished from 'subject,' 'situation,' or 'plot.'[38] No such clarity exists when the word is applied to Darío's non-didactic and purely imaginative works. In such cases it is usually employed to represent the abstract concepts embodied in the structure of those works. Wolfgang Kayser, giving an example from Spanish Golden Age literature, states that 'El tema de *La estrella de Sevilla* es "la palabra dada."'[39] This use of the term is widespread, not only with regard to Darío but in modern criticism as a whole. But 'theme' used in this non-didactic sense would seem to be of only peripheral value; it tends to signify a vague component of a literary work. Kayser, for instance, says hardly more about its usefulness in literary analysis than what is quoted above; and Meyer Abrams[40] has pointed out that the specified theme of a given poem is usually only one of several abstract statements that can fit the poem, that the specified theme is usually so general that it can apply to an indefinite number of other poems, and that the theme of a purely imaginative work does not function, as it does in a didactic work, as the doctrine which the whole poem may be seen to represent.

The practice of studying themes in Darío's purely imaginative works reveals many of the limitations mentioned by Abrams. Above all, when several of Darío's poems are studied to demonstrate the presence of a given theme, there is an inevitable fragmentation and unbalancing of those works. The fact that the same poems have been used by different critics to illustrate different themes reveals the vague and general nature of theme as a basis of analysis. Also, the varying degrees of intensity with which a theme is developed is the kind of illuminating consideration that is not always offered by those who identify themes. Other poets of less skill than Darío have written poems in which may be identified themes that have been observed in Darío's poetry. What distinguishes Darío from these other poets depends not so much on the themes evoked in his poetry as on the effective structuring and coherence he achieves.

The study of motifs to show how they help to determine ultimate aesthetic effects in Darío's works has been carried out admirably by Erika Lorenz[41] with regard to musical elements. She carries out a detailed study of the structure and function of sonorous elements in Darío's writing. Her patient exploration of the linguistic and metrical bases of the often-mentioned musicality of his poetry is carried out within the frame of whole poems and she concludes that in Darío's poetry there is development from the verbal harmony of *Azul* and *Prosas profanas* to the ideal harmony of *Cantos de vida y esperanza* and *El canto errante*.[42]

Another related kind of study, the tracing of the development of a symbol in Darío's writing is carried out by Concha Zardoya in her article 'Rubén Darío y la fuente.'[43] She shows the evolution of the meaning of 'la fuente' from its first mention in one of his poems of 1880 as something purely decorative to its use as a symbol of love and death in the poems of 1914 dedicated to Francisca Sánchez. It is necessary to note here too Alan S. Trueblood's thorough article 'Rubén Darío: The Sea and the Jungle.'[44] He examines 'Sinfonía en gris mayor,' 'Tarde del trópico,' 'Sinfonía,' 'Marina,' 'Caracol,' and 'Revelación,' and concludes that in Darío's work there is 'an interconnected symbolism of sea and jungle, expressive at once of elemental vitality and of cosmic harmony.'[45] Trueblood sees this symbolism as reaching transcendental proportions and as conforming with Pythagorean principles in Darío's later poetry. And Raymond Skyrme's 'The Meaning and Function of Music in Rubén Darío: A Comparative Approach'[46] goes beyond a mere examination of melodic effects to deal penetratingly with symbolic meaning in Darío's work. In addition to its examination of music, Skyrme's study should be considered akin to those of Darío's transcendental sensuality done by Gullón and Trueblood. Another extensive and profound study of symbolism in Darío's poetry has been contributed by Jaime Giordano in his book *La edad del ensueño.*[47] He views Darío's poetry as distinctly symbolist, containing many echoes of Poe and Mallarmé; and he explains that 'una poética simbolista habrá de quedar ligada y atada sin remedio a una poética del ensueño.'[48] His procedure is to deal with leitmotifs or, as he calls them, 'motivos conductores' such as 'Fuente,' 'Forma,' 'Luz,' 'Mar,' 'Jungla,' 'Cruz,' 'Ascención,' and 'Anunciación'; to show how they function and lead to a sense of unity in all of Darío's work, from his early romantic period to his later work where he participates in the cult of mystery. The complex symbolic patterns detected by Giordano provide eloquent rebuttal to opinions such as those presented by Bowra about the absence of sophisticated symbolism in Darío's work.

Comment on Darío's enterprising use of metre and versification formed a small part of the studies done on his work by most of his earliest critics. His achievement in this regard soon became so generally recognized that, since the early twentieth century, studies devoted to Hispanic versification have abounded in examples from his works. And several studies have dealt exclusively with metre and versification in Darío's poetry.

Pedro Henríquez Ureña has made studies of Darío's versification in all the contexts mentioned above. He paid adequate attention to the formal aspects of Darío's writing in his early study (1905) of *Cantos de vida y esperanza*; and his essays of 1918, 1919, and 1920 on aspects of Spanish versification give due emphasis to Darío's work.[49] He has also studied in detail the origins of the verse form of specific works of Darío,[50] as mentioned in Chapter 3. Among other studies that have been devoted entirely to Darío's metrics are, in the chronological order of their appearance, those by Tomás Navarro Tomás,[51] Erwin K. Mapes,[52] Julio Saavedra Molina,[53] Francisco Maldonado de Guevara,[54] Juan Francisco Sánchez,[55] Mercedes Pinilla Ecijo,[56] and Antonio Oliver Belmás.[57] All these studies tend to demonstrate Darío's willingness to be innovative, the ubiquitousness of his search for metrical models, and the mastery with which he adapted these models to his own expressive system. These studies have usually been carried out in the belief that, as Pedro Henríquez Ureña has stated it, 'La principal innovación realizada por Darío y los *modernistas* americanos ha consistido en la modificación definitiva de los acentos: han sustituido con la acentuación *ad libitum* la tiránica y monótona del eneasílabo, del dodecasílabo hijo de las viejas coplas de arte mayor, y del alejandrino.'[58] Henríquez Ureña goes on to discuss other verse forms that he considers to be used innovatively by Darío, but he sums up the part of his study dealing with form by commenting soberly on the limitations inherent in discussing form in isolation. He writes:

Todo lo dicho y aun todo lo citado quizás no bastarían a justificar el alto puesto que el futuro asignará a Rubén Darío en la historia del verso castellano, si en ello no fueran implícitos el alto ingenio y la general inspiración del poeta. Axioma es ya: cada gran manifestación artística crea su propia forma. La forma sólo debe interesar cuando está hecha para decir alguna belleza: armonía del pensamiento, música del sentir, creación de la fantasía. 'Todo lo demás es *literatura*.'[59]

Investigations of Darío's language have yielded valuable results. Edmundo García Girón, for instance, has contributed an edifying study of 'La adjetivación modernista en Rubén Darío.'[60] Raimundo Lida[61] and Daniel Devoto[62] have shown that language usage developed by Darío facilitated the poetic expression of later poets. Devoto mentions García Lorca particularly as one of the beneficiaries of Darío's work. Eduardo Carreño[63] and John Turner[64] have examined different aspects of his use of grammar, and Oliver Belmás[65] has written a brief account of the poet's use of Americanisms. Ricardo Molina[66] has contributed a lucid, integral, and concise study of Darío's use of language. The methods employed in these studies have tended to be philological and grammatical rather than structurally linguistic and the studies have been carried out with the purpose of displaying certain characteristics of modernist expression, of assessing Darío's achievement in this area of his activity, and of fixing his place among the writers of his time.[67]

One book that treats all of the topics dealt with in this chapter is Salvador Aguado-Andreut's *Por el mundo poético de Rubén Darío*.[68] He studies 'themes' such as time, life, love, and death, assesses the use of sensation and evocation to give symbolic associations to such motifs as light, and comments on several aspects of Darío's language and metrics. All this is done after an extensive comparison of Darío with Victor Hugo.

These studies, then, of philosophy, themes, motifs, and language use detailed evidence from Darío's works to come to general conclusions about aspects of his art. Only seldom do they entail any attempt at evaluating the works from which the evidence is taken.

CHAPTER FIVE

Structural Analysis

The first known piece of literary criticism that attempts to evaluate a specific Darío work by means of detailed analysis of the intrinsic features is Ricardo Contreras's essay entitled 'Crítica literaria: "La ley escrita," oda por Rubén Darío.' This article was published in two instalments in *El Diario Nicaragüense*, No. 85, 16 October 1884 and No. 90, 22 October of the same year.[1] In fact, Contreras's article may be regarded as the first serious study ever done of Darío as a writer. There is nothing haphazard about the approach and his study shows his adherence to a definite critical method. He consciously undertakes an analytical stance and indicates that it is on the basis of intrinsic merit, as differentiated from historical considerations, that the real value of poets can be assessed. He thus advises the reader 'No pierda miserablemente su tiempo leyendo a nuestros poetas que no tienen sino mérito extrínseco en cuanto representan un *momento* histórico de nuestra naciente literatura nacional.'[2]

Contreras declares at the beginning of his essay that Darío is 'el único escritor en verso que a mi juicio merece en la República';[3] and having said that and classified himself as 'muy parco en alabanzas,'[4] he goes on to scrutinize the diction of 'La ley escrita,' pointing out the flaws in wording and the effect of these flaws on the imagery and, ultimately, on the integrity of the whole poem. For example, he considers from the lexical point of view the verses: 'Y el pueblo de Israel vagaba inquieto / En redor del gran monte / Mirando el horizonte,'[5] and observes:

Vagar vale tanto como caminar sin *rumbo fijo*, a la ventura; de donde infiero que *vagar en redor del gran monte* es contradictorio, porque *en rededor* or *al rededor* significa en torno de una cosa y caminar al rededor quiere decir: caminar con rumbo circular fijo, por eso se dice que los planetas giran o dan vueltas al rededor del sol, y, o el pueblo de Israel vagaba, esto es caminaba sin rumbo fijo, o caminaba *en redor* del gran monte y en este caso no vagaba porque llevaba rumbo fijo en su marcha.[6]

It is true that at times Contreras's interest in the 'infracción de los cánones literarios'[7] betrays an inflexible purist bent. Commenting, for example, on the verses 'De pronto perdió el Sol su luz brillante, / La tierra estremecióse en sus cimientos,'[8] he writes:

La expresión adverbial *de pronto* es propia del lenguaje de la prosa y el pronombre *se* enclítico o pospuesto a los verbos, es señal cierta de que el lenguaje no amolda sus miembros al lecho de Procusto representado en la poesía por el metro. Nunca o muy rara vez he visto usada esta preposición en los poetas clásicos, más injustificable cuando no hay necesidad de arrimar el pronombre al verbo.[9]

But despite his purist criteria Contreras makes valid comments about Darío's art and about the limits of effectiveness of such rhetorical devices as simile, personification, metonymy, and hyperbole,[10] and he judges that Darío sometimes strains those limits. On the other hand, he praises the poet's lyrical intonation, which he regards as comparable to Quintana's. Contreras emphasizes the instructive purpose of his essay when he concludes that

Rubén tiene imaginación fecunda, estro poético; pero a la inspiración debe añadir la reflexión si, cerrando los oídos a los vanos aplausos, quiere llegar a ser, no un poeta, sino el poeta de la América Central. Yo soy tal vez el primero que tiene la ruda franqueza de decírselo: si le admiro, le admiro con discernimiento y le digo lo que no es, para decirle lo que puede llegar a ser algún día, si quiere.[11]

Darío's reply to Contreras, his 'Epístola a Ricardo Contreras,'[12] shows that the youthful poet felt somewhat chastened; that, although Contreras's article deserved a reply,[13] much of the intrinsic criticism of his poem was irrefutable.

The fact that the kind of criticism done by Contreras can be taken to excess, that there is a fine line, easily transgressed, between valid, instructive criticism of a poet's imagery and idiosyncratic, picayune, literal-minded reading, is amply demonstrated by the critical work done on Darío's poetry by Matías Calandrelli. He analysed poems from *Prosas profanas* in essays that were published two years after the first edition of this book appeared. In his first essay he commented on 'Era un aire suave,' 'Sonatina,' 'Mía,' and 'Coloquio de los centauros.' He states his hostile views with regard to Darío as a poet at the beginning of the essay, complaining that Darío does not really seem to *feel* his poems and that in turn the reader is thwarted of what for Calandrelli is one of the indispensable effects of good poetry, the sensation of being overwhelmed. Of the marquise in 'Era un aire suave' he writes: 'No la vemos, ni concebimos, porque es figura descrita, con rasgos y lineamientos generales que se confunden con los de todas las hijas de Eva. No tiene vida ni personalidad propia.'[14] He sums up his comments on Darío's display in the poem by declaring 'Pobreza verdaderamente franciscana en la concepción poética, en las ideas, en las estrofas, en el verso!'[15] When Calandrelli moves from the sweepingly impressionistic to specific points about imagery, as he attempts to do in his comments on 'Sonatina,' his work can be subjected to more precise evaluation. He singles out for special comment the fourth verse of the fourth stanza, 'ir al sol por la escala luminosa de un rayo,' and two verses from the seventh stanza,

> Quién volara a la tierra donde un príncipe existe
> más brillante que el alba, más hermoso que Abril!

For Calandrelli the first quoted verse represents an impermissible and laughable unlikelihood. He writes: 'Aparte la ausencia completa de armonía del verso, dudamos que haya quién alcance a concebir cómo se pueda subir al sol por la escala de un rayo.'[16] He is quite pedagogical in his comments on the other quoted verses, stating that:

> Cuando se comparan dos o más términos, es menester que la imaginación descubra en ellos semejanza o diferencia de formas y caracteres, sin esfuerzo alguno. Compréndese que Abril pueda ser personificado y comparado luego con un joven ''más brillante que el alba''; pero no podemos comprender el acto de *despersonificar* al príncipe de marras para compararlo con los *treinta días del mes* !"[17]

Such comments, made with utmost confidence, reveal the inflexible, literal, line by line, non-contextual reading that represents a trend in the intrinsic criticism of Darío's poetry. Calandrelli does not take into account the tone of the whole poem, the fantasy that controls this tone, and therefore cannot comprehend the appropriateness of the 'impossible' imagery that springs from the dreams of the princess.

The classical canons from which Calandrelli draws his criteria are shown through his frequent references to Horace in his next essay, 'Manera de poetizar de Rubén Darío.'[18] In this article he examines 'El poeta pregunta por Stella,' 'Bouquet,' 'Sinfonía en gris mayor,' and 'Canto de la sangre.' He attacks the first poem for the capricious order of its metaphors, for its excess of epithets, and says of verses like 'Las místicas estrofas de cánticos celestes': 'No agregan nada porque nada significan. Son *flatus vocis*, sin sentido poético, ripios de gusto estético muy dudoso.'[19] He finds an unacceptable repetition of images and words in 'Bouquet,' and he calls 'Sinfonía en gris mayor' una composición sin objeto serio; está en una palabra, fuera de los límites de la poesía y del arte.'[20] Calandrelli crowns his effort with a poem of his own entitled 'Montes de oro,' which is intended to demonstrate that he himself, though not a poet, could produce work that was the equal of Darío's. In a sense Calandrelli's criticism resembles the method used by Rodó in the final part of the latter's essay on Darío. They both are spurred to creative effort by their reading of *Prosas profanas* and might be said to practise what is often called creative criticism. But whereas Rodó follows Darío admiringly, recreating some of his works, Calandrelli, offers his own limited talent as a match for Darío's.

More aesthetically distanced critical perspective on Darío's work was provided by Pedro Henríquez Ureña, whose early study of 1905 includes one of the first important assessments written of *Cantos de vida y esperanza*. In addition to his already mentioned observations on Darío's metrical innovations, he characterizes *Azul, ... Prosas profanas*, and *Cantos de vida y esperanza* on the basis of their language and imagery. He regards Darío as demonstrating from the time of *Azul ...* that he was 'realmente un maestro del idioma.'[21] Where Calandrelli attacks *Prosas profanas* for capricious and disordered imagery, Henríquez Ureña sees the book as displaying a virtue that was 'casi desconocida en castellano: la *nuance*, la gradación de matices.'[22] At the same time poems like 'Marcha triunfal' and 'A Roosevelt' are used by him to exemplify the forcefulness of Darío's *Cantos de vida y esperanza*. He cites Rodó's comments about the absence of any personal confession or baring of the soul in *Prosas profanas* and declares that, whereas Darío presents his states of soul only through symbolic pictures that needed interpretation such as Julián del Casal provided in his 'Páginas de vida,' in his later book, in poems such as 'Pórtico' Darío's *yo* becomes a subject of overt representation and he makes a profession of his faith. By commenting too on the Latinism and the Indigenism evident in the book, on the treatment of love and on the features of expression that distinguish Darío from his French models, Pedro Henríquez Ureña initiated, in the year of its publication, positive discussion of several of the most remarkable aspects of *Cantos de vida y esperanza*.

The most extensive practice of intrinsic criticism in early Darío criticism was carried out by Andrés González-Blanco. The first volume of his three-volume edition of Darío's *Obras escogidas* is devoted to a preliminary study of the works contained in the other two volumes and is entitled 'Rubén Darío su ideología, su estética, su técnica.' The study is divided into two parts 'El poeta' and 'La obra'; and it is especially in the second and longer part of the volume that analysis of Darío's works is carried out. González-Blanco has described his own critical practice, in terms that reveal his admiration for Anatole France, as 'ondulante sin contradicciones, impresionista sin banalidad, elegante sin afectación, erudita sin pedantería, elogiosa sin empalago, seria sin pedagogismos, amena sin frivolidad de *croniqueur*.'[23] These characteristics are amply displayed in González-Blanco's comments on Darío's works from the earliest poems to *El canto errante*. Instead of doing thorough and elaborate analyses of the works he selects for examination, the Spanish critic comments on some of their features and displays the wide range of critical and literary references at his command from Greek, Latin, German, French, English, and Spanish American sources. He nevertheless makes penetrating comments which have served well later students of Darío's works who are interested in the works themselves. One important but often overlooked aspect of González-Blanco's study is the emphasis he places on Darío's prose. He prepares the way for his comments on *Azul, España contemporánea, Peregrinaciones, La caravana pasa, Tierras solares, Opiniones, Parisiana* and, principally, *Los raros* by comparing the demands of prose writing with those of lyric poetry. He stresses the precision involved in the writing of good prose when he states concerning Darío's prose works:

> No puede realizarse esta labor sin un dominio absoluto del lenguaje; y este dominio del lenguaje implica la adquisición tenaz de cultura. Se puede ser un inspirado poeta sin estar al corriente de las ideas del siglo; se pueden producir bellos himnos, harmoniosas odas, sentimentales elegías y delicados epigramas sin saber gran cosa de ninguna disciplina científica; pero no se puede llegar a transformar un lenguaje y a crearse un estilo nuevo sin estar ayudado por una intensa cultura bien absorbida. Para ser poeta lírico no es necesario ser hombre muy leído, aunque ello no estorbe; pero ser buen prosista sin ser muy culto y aun muy libresco, es un sueño insensato.[24]

Within this view of the demanding nature of prose González-Blanco allows any unconventional usage that will enhance 'la disposición hábil y harmoniosa'[25] of the words in a composition; thus neologisms, archaic usage, and expressions coined from foreign sources are welcomed by him provided they are aptly used.[26] He was well prepared by all his critical precepts to appreciate Darío's prose and poetry. His attempts to assess explicitly many of Darío's prose works and poems as separate and whole works and to arrive at his view of Darío as a writer on the basis of such assessments provided a valuable early example of intrinsic criticism.

For many years following the publication of his book, González-Blanco's approach was not influential in Darío criticism. Darío's death, occurring only six years after González-Blanco's study appeared, gave rise to new trends. The tendency to review his life and to consider his works as events in his life became the primary one in the years immediately following 1916 and for a considerable period after that. This tendency led, as was shown in Chapter 1, to general characterizations of stories, poems, and even whole books. As was observed in other chapters, Darío's works have been studied too with the emphasis on a certain element like music, metrics, religion, love, mythology, indigenism, Hispanicism, Americanism, and so on. A consequence of such tendencies was the virtual absence for a long period of attempts to analyse and evaluate intrinsically as poems or stories Darío's creative works. In fact, only since the late nineteen-forties have Darío critics again made any effort at such detailed analysis, interpretation, and evaluation; and the effort became sustained only in the nineteen-sixties.

Darío's short stories received penetrating attention in Raimundo Lida's essay 'Los cuentos de Rubén Darío'[27] which serves as a preliminary study to Ernesto Mejía Sánchez's edition of Darío's stories. After brief comments on the persistence of Darío's narrative efforts, which predated his first and postdated his last book of poetry, and on the presence of poetry in Darío's prose, Lida proceeds to examine the stories. He divides his essay into four parts entitled 'Forma,' 'Poeta y mundo,' 'Maestría,' and 'Complejidad'; but this division hardly implies definite categories and, in fact, in all the sections of his essay Lida effectively considers aspects of expression in relation to meaning in Darío's works. Thus in discussing 'forma' he deals with internal structural features, such as contrast and irony, and relates them to the meaning of the works in which they appear. In the next section, the subject of the poet in the world, his treatment by society, and his attitude to his art are considered with reference to specific usage in specific stories. When he discusses Darío's 'maestría,' he focuses on features such as adjectivization, tension, and distension with regard to their function in certain stories. And he appraises Darío's 'complejidad' on the basis of the variety of expression found in the stories, on the symmetries and antitheses which harmonize to produce impressive works of narrative art. In concluding his essay Lida claims that 'El análisis, obligado a seguir uno por uno los hilos de esta compleja obra narrativa y a recogerlos en didácticos esquemas, corre el riesgo de no hacer justicia a la unidad del conjunto.'[28] His statement is modest when it is taken as a characterization of the method of his essay; for, as we have seen, his observations on Darío's stories are always rooted in the relation between various functions of language in the creation of meaning in different stories. It is true that he does not show 'la unidad del conjunto,' that is to say, of all the stories, but it may be doubted whether it is possible to demonstrate this unity in Darío's stories, whether the attempt to do this would be more successful in showing convincing unity than has the quest for oneness of theme in Darío's work discussed in Chapter 4. Another important study of Darío's prose, which deals with internal features of specific stories is Anderson Imbert's 'Rubén Darío and the Fantastic Element in Literature.'[29] It may be gathered from the study that the fantastic element in prose fiction, usually associated with post-Darío writers such as Borges and Anderson Imbert himself, was a feature of Darío's work. A study of the various categories of Darío's prose writing has been contributed by Raúl Silva Castro in his article 'Prosa periodística y artística en Rubén Darío.'[30] He examines Darío's journalistic work, mainly his articles written for La Nación of Buenos Aires; his poems in prose, which he considers to be very few in number, his narrative prose as practised in the novels and short stories and what Silva Castro calls Darío's artistic prose, the pieces found mainly in Azul which resemble recreations of paintings. Serious studies of this scope have also been done by Guillermo de Torre,[31] Max Henríquez Ureña,[32] Alejandro Reyes Huete,[33] and Eduardo Zepeda-Henríquez.[34] A not very favourable view of his achievement as a novelist has been presented in a study by Juan Loveluck.[35] In addition to these works of broad range are critical works devoted to the detailed examination of specific prose works. Such, for instance, are Allen W. Phillips's study of El oro de Mallorca,[36] Brenda Segall's analysis of 'El rey burgués,'[37] and Homero Castillo's examination of narrative techniques in 'El fardo.'[38]

Raimundo Lida's valuable contribution to the criticism of Darío's stories has been matched by his contribution to the study of Darío's poetry in his article 'Notas al casticismo de Rubén.'[39] The article deals with Darío's language in all the genres in which he worked, but the sections devoted to poetry are substantial and laden with insight into Darío's art. Lida's examination of language here does not yield a mere categorizing of Darío's usages; rather, he constantly demonstrates how language and other features such as metrics and rhyme serve Darío's aesthetic system. Furthermore, the tone of Lida's essay reflects the happy mastery with which Darío employed language in many innovative ways. Where Mario Benedetti notices the naturalness and unobtrusiveness of rhyme in the 'Epístola a la señora de Lugones,' Lida explores the subtleties of the verses' construction and in so doing reveals the consummate skill with which Darío achieves their multifaceted effects. The richness of these effects is such that no one aspect of them stands out for attention and they need the kind of scrutiny given them by Lida. He writes:

> con parecido humor se permite el poeta jugar con rimas hispano-extranjeras como: 'Barcas de pescadores sobre la mar tranquila/descubro desde la terraza de mi *villa*' ... y utilizar luego, con el mismo sentido y, sin duda, diverso sonido, la palabra española: 'Y hay villa de retiro espiritual famosa' ... o hacer que, con alguna violencia, consuenen lo todavía exótico y lo ya semi-hispanizado: 'y conforme el poeta, tengo un Cristo y un máuser./Así vive este hermano triste de Gaspar Hauser.'[40]

Such observations display fine sensitivity to the workings of language. A less acute reader of the verses may simply note that 'máuser,' for instance, was in use in Spain and find nothing remarkable about its employment here. An example of the internal study of a whole book has been provided by Allen W. Phillips in his article 'Releyendo *Prosas profanas*.'[41] On the basis of usage and meaning in the different poems he comes to positive conclusions about the quality of the book and not so positive ones about its relative place in Darío's work from the point of view of most contemporary readers who in Phillips's judgment would call the book 'el menos actual de los grandes libros de Darío.'[42]

The study of individual poems has been undertaken with increasing frequency in the last twenty years, notable analyses having been carried out of such poems as 'Primaveral,'[43] 'Estival,'[44] 'Invernal,'[45] 'Caupolicán,'[46] 'Era un aire suave ...,'[47] 'Coloquio de los centauros,'[48] 'El país de sol,'[49] 'Sinfonía en gris mayor,'[50] 'Yo soy aquel,'[51] 'Pegaso,'[52] 'Caracol,'[53] 'Lo fatal,'[54] the *Nocturnos*,[55] 'Canción de otoño en primavera,'[56] 'La gran cosmópolis,'[57] 'Los motivos del lobo,' 'Trébol,' 'La marcha triunfal,' 'Poema de otoño,' and 'Epístola a la señora de Lugones.'[58] Several different aims and methods may be applied to the study of individual poems, as is illustrated by the work done on 'Coloquio de los centauros.' Arturo Marasso's study of the poem[59] is devoted primarily to the tracing of sources and to showing the differences between

Darío's use of the myth in this poem and that of his sources. María Teresa Maiorana[60] goes fully into this latter aspect, showing elaborate variations of the myth and of the characterization of its principal characters that have occurred in literature. René L.F. Durand[61] sees the centaur as a traditional literary motif which has universal currency and which in turn serves as one of the basic vehicles for the conveyance of Darío's universality. He calls the poem 'una pieza maestra'[62] but, like Marasso and Maiorana, does not really analyse it, stating that 'sería inútil analizar aquí estos poemas harto conocidos en la patria del poeta.'[63] It was left for Arturo Echavarría to go beyond the essentially historical approaches to the poem in the second part of his essay and to consider its inner workings, to explain how the elements used in the poem combine to give it its particular meaning. This is essentially the method employed recently by critics such as Anderson Imbert, Benítez, Castillo, Darroch, Pagés Larraya, Predmore, and Segall. The root of the critical theory that is implicit in this approach is the simple fact that a writer is ultimately read and taken into account because he composes worthy works of literary art. The skill he displays in his compositions, the ability with which he uses language to show a range or even a facet of human emotion, is the basis of his reputation. This skill is determinable by scrutiny of the way in which he selects from the great storehouse of language the fundamental material which he fashions into a literary work, either by conforming with or by reacting against the methods of other practitioners of the art. The aesthetic principle governing this approach is that of coherence, the notion that the elements of the work – the matter treated, the language, the versification, the rhetorical devices, the tone – should cohere to produce a unity of effect. A cataloguing of the separate elements is not economically productive since their isolated treatment is not conducive to demonstrating their interrelation and their contribution to unity. Nor can a strictly line-by-line analysis of the works adequately reflect tension and dynamic flow of meaning in a poem. There is often, particularly in cases where irony or paradox is present, a need to reappraise the contribution of earlier sections of a work as later sections have their transforming effect on them.[64] The integral emphasis of the kind of intrinsic study recently undertaken is often not made evident from the titles of these studies; and it needs to be pointed out that a title like 'A Stylistic Analysis of ...' is sometimes used in studies concerned with the whole process of how, as Predmore following Amado Alonso[65] has put it, 'linguistic material is converted into a non-discursive vehicle of feeling and emotion.'[66] This is the meaning of style implied in Gianni Toti's plea for an anti-ideological and stylistic interpretation of Darío's work.[67] Style is not regarded as a subject to be discussed in isolation, confined to a separate chapter or other special section of a study of a writer's work. The question 'What is the function, in terms of the whole composition, of the author's particular usage?' is a crucial one. Also to be understood in a new way is the use of 'structural,' as in a possible title 'A Structural Analysis of ...' For the word in this sense comprehends not only the gross organization or overall design but also the fine details, the subtle devices, that contribute to the effect of the whole. By demonstrating through scrutiny the complexities and subtleties by which coherence is achieved or the flaws that detract from coherence, this kind of stylistic or structural analysis can serve as useful criticism of any literary work. The observations made in the course of the analysis reflect the core value of the literary work and raise points that may be elaborated on by critics who wish to emphasize a particular aspect of the poet's work. The correctness of the text studied is an indispensable pre-condition for the valid employment of intrinsic criticism. This is one of the reasons why the studies of textual variations in Darío's works done by such scholars as Alfonso Méndez Plancarte,[68] Alfredo Roggiano,[69] and Theodore S. Beardsley[70] are valuable indeed. Of some usefulness too are the indexes of subject matter, names and titles in Darío's complete poetry compiled by Helene Westbrook Harrison.[71]

I wish now to attempt to analyse structurally, according to the method I have been describing,[72] three of Darío's compositions. It would be useful to apply the method both to his prose and to his poetry, to his poetry that appears to be 'pure' and to that which appears to be 'social,' to his early as well as to his later poetry. Accordingly, I have selected the short story 'El rubí' and the poems 'Venus' and 'A Roosevelt.'

El rubí[73]

'El rubí' is structured on the principle of antithesis. This fact is observable both in the overall aspects of the arrangement of the story and in the subtle details of its elaboration. The central contrast is that between the natural and the artificial, between the capacity of nature to produce real beauty and the presumptuous fraudulence that marks the effort of those who would attempt to imitate her achievements. This contrast is elaborated by means of the harmonious functioning of point of view, characterization, setting, and flexibility in the use of language.

The position of nature is championed by the gnomes, mythical spirits of the earth and the legendary guardians of the mines. It is their subterranean caves, rather than the nineteenth-century Parisian world of science, that provide the principal setting for the story, a setting that abounds in precious exhibits of the authentic creations of nature. The narrator of the story not only speaks mostly from this setting but also comes gradually to represent and share the point of view of the gnomes. Like their spokesmen – Puck and the old gnome – he comes to present the point of view in the pole of the antithesis that favours the natural world and thus helps to give it ascendancy. The language in the story is also made to serve the cause of nature, sometimes through the use of irony. The first sentence presents the nucleus of what will be developed later to form the story. The strongly exclamatory tone of Puck's verification of the synthesizing of a ruby indicates his concerned reaction. The concern seems to be based partly on his fear of leading a superfluous existence, since his role in producing rubies would no longer be necessary, and partly on aesthetic grounds. The natural ruby with which he has lived familiarly is described in elevated terms as 'la púrpura cristalina de que están incrustados los muros de mi palacio' (p. 79). Puck's aesthetic reaction, then, seems to be caused by the evident disparity between such a product and its new provenance, 'el sabio parisiense' (p. 79) having extracted it 'del fondo de sus retortas, de sus matraces' (p. 79). The adverbial phrase 'del fondo,' in combination with the laboratory instruments which are alien to the gnome, serves to throw negative light on the source. To state in this way the discrepancy between product and origin indicates that the ruby that Puck has always known and the new ruby are not the same; and the rest of the story is devoted to specifying and giving the implications of this difference. The narrator confirms Puck's initial statement and gives some verifiable facts concerning the synthesizing of the ruby. This description of Chevreul corresponds to historical reality; Chevreul was a scientist and a centenarian, having lived from 1786 to 1889. And the 'sabio parisiense' of whom Puck spoke is identified by the narrator as Frémy, who did in fact succeed in synthesizing the ruby in 1877. But by describing Frémy as 'cuasi Althotas' (p. 79), the narrator robs him of any dignity that might have been given him by expressions 'sabio parisiense' or 'químico'; for Althotas, a character in Mémoires d'un médecin: Joseph Balsamo, a novel by Alexandre Dumas (père), is an alchemist notorious for butchering young girls so that their blood might be used for his elixirs.

Puck carries further the sarcasm that is now recognizable in his references to the scientists. He states that for all their Aristotelian philosophy, their necromancy and cabala, even the twelfth- and thirteenth-century sages Albert the Great, Averroes, and Raimundo Lulio did not presume to imitate nature's ruby as the nineteenth-century pseudo-scientist has done. The formula for fabricating the ruby being given after the negative attitude towards chemistry has been skilfully developed, the scientific

terminology, 'lengua diabólica' (p. 79), with which it is necessarily presented comes to serve as the antithesis of such artistic language as that
used by the narrator to describe the habitat of the gnomes. In the first
paragraph of the story he uses the word 'cueva' to refer to this habitat, but
he soon comes to show the regard that Puck had manifested for it in that
paragraph ('los muros de mi palacio') when he describes it in the following
paragraph:

> A aquellos resplandores podía verse la maravillosa mansión en todo su
> esplendor. En los muros, sobre pedazos de plata y oro, entre venas de
> lapislázuli, formaban caprichosos dibujos, como los arabescos de una
> mezquita, gran muchedumbre de piedras preciosas. Los diamantes, blan-
> cos y limpios como gotas de agua, emergían los iris de sus critalizaciones;
> cerca de calcedonias colgantes en estalactitas, las esmeraldas esparcían sus
> resplandores verdes, y los zafiros, en amontonamientos raros, en rami-
> lletes que pendían del cuarzo, semejaban grandes flores azules y tem-
> blorosas. (p. 80)

The names of the precious metals, which are traditionally used as vehicles
in the context of similes or metaphors to make prose ornamental, form the
principal subject or tenor of the passage. This being so, the narrator
enriches the passage by recourse to various other decorative vehicles:
'como los arabescos de una mezquita,' 'semejaban grandes flores azules y
temblorosas' (p. 80), or to a vehicle that suggests purity and simplicity:
'como gotas de agua' (p. 80). This concentrated richness and elaborateness
of description of definite shapes is, of course, one of the characteristics of
Parnassianism. But it is necessary to notice its function in the story,
which is to extol in elevated language the bounty of nature so that the
shortcomings of the world of science may form an evident contrast. The
narrator subsequently makes the antithesis explicit by juxtaposing the
two worlds: 'Puck había llevado el cuerpo del delito, el rubí falsificado, el
que estaba ahí, sobre la roca de oro como una profanación entre el
centelleo de todo aquel encanto' (p. 81). The phrase 'sabio parisiense' used
in the first sentence of the story receives further demoting treatment in
the course of the story. Paris is the place where Puck had found the
counterfeit ruby used decoratively by 'los rastacueros,' 'las cortesanas,'
'las primadonas' (p. 81) and other frivolous inhabitants of the city. Thus
the associations evoked by 'parisiense' are all negative. The narrator is
caught up in the spirit of the condemnation of the false ruby and exclaims
that it is '¡ ... obra de hombre, o de sabio, que es peor!' (p. 81). At the end
of the first part of the story a series of deprecations shouted at the false

ruby by the gnomes leads into exclamations extolling the qualities of the real ruby: It is important to observe the quality of these exclamations. '¡Pretender imitar un fragmento del iris!,' '¡El tesoro rubicundo de lo hondo del globo!' and '¡Hecho de rayos del sol poniente solidificados!' indicate the range of poetic imagination and the metaphorical language, enhanced by hyperbaton in the last instance, which spring spontaneously from the gnomes when their subject is the earth and its products. The aroused feeling of the assembled gnomes, who have displayed unanimity in different moods – curiosity, piquant humour, elegant patience, indignation – provides an effective background for the monologue by the oldest of the gnomes in the second part of the story.

His authority having been established through the way in which the narrator describes him: 'El gnomo más viejo, andando con sus piernas torcidas, su gran barba nevada, su aspecto de patriarca, su cara llena de arrugas' (p. 82), he gives his credentials, which have the primary effect of pointing to his experience and authenticity as a gnome. He pictures himself as having used the implements with which the gnomes described in the earlier part of the story were equipped. He has also shown on other occasions the spontaneous aesthetic response and the voluptuary nature that characterize the other gnomes: 'he dado un día un puñetazo a un muro de piedra, y caí a un lago donde violé a una ninfa' (p. 82). The real ruby was conspicuously excluded from all the earlier descriptions of precious metals; and the old gnome now lyrically recounts its origin in his monologue. His account is set in a world of joy, youthfulness, and harmony. It is spring in the open air; and the setting is ripe for the blossoming of love. The old gnome's account of his encounter with some women in this setting is remarkable for his manner of discovering and mentioning one by one, with erotic effect, different parts of their bodies among which flowers, fruits, and other prized objects of nature are harmoniously interspersed. The gnome's revelation that these were women and not nymphs, as would be expected in that world, is one of the instances of inversion that will have important ironic effect in terms of the whole story and is a device later used by Borges in his story 'Tlön, Uqbar, Orbis tertius,' for instance, where a characteristic of the real world is found surprisingly in the idealistic world of Tlön.[74] The group of women gives way to one who is the central figure in the rest of this episode. She becomes the beautiful woman among the precious metals carved from the earth by the gnome. In addition to being beautiful she is loved by man and gnome; and for the gnome the love enduring between her and her beloved is mysterious. As a result of her beauty, her state of loving and being loved, her attempt to flee, her fall and bleeding on the fragments of the

diamond, rubies have their origin. The gnomes, quick in their understanding of the processes of nature, beauty, and love, accept the old
gnome's account and now with a new seriousness that contrasts with their
playful gestures in the earlier part of the story, pour scorn on the ruby,
finally displaying their rage by crushing it. Laughter and contentment can
return only after the false ruby has been destroyed. But after the old
gnome's story the other gnomes do not simply revert to their former state.
The importance given to nature begins to reflect on the gnomes too, on
their stature and even on their physical size: 'Y celebraron con risas el
verse grandes en la sombra' (p. 85). Puck demonstrates the new spaciousness of his universe 'Ya Puck volaba afuera, en el abejeo del alba recién
nacida como de una pradera en flor' (p. 85). This new spaciousness is
symbolic of a broadened, confident mentality. What he knew before only
intuitively now becomes a confirmed, reassuring fact, based on the historical experience of the old, representative gnome. Awareness of the relationship between earth and woman is a key indicator of this process from
intuition to rational knowledge. Puck's first linking of the two through his
vision of Titania, who as a spirit of nature had functioned as the fairy
queen in Shakespeare's *Midsummer Night's Dream*, is intuitive and not
as firm as it will be later. It is made firmer and given new meaning by the
old gnome's story. Puck captures this meaning with delight. He understands now that work done by man independently of the productive
resources of nature and woman cannot match the beauty of work done
with these resources. This theme is made precise by the narrator in the
closing paragraph of the story. By doing so he shows clearly that he shares
and represents Puck's point of view and that of the other gnomes too; for,
given the emphasis throughout the story on the united reaction of the
gnomes, it may be assumed that Puck's reaction is a representative one.

The substance of the old gnome's story of the origin of the ruby is
conveyed by language that is the antithesis of that of Frémy. In the former
case language is expansive indicating the openness of nature, the rich
variety of objects, beings, and emotions. There is frequent usage of 'y,'
but this does not indicate rapid enumeration. Rather the conjunction links
whole sentences with new subjects, verbs, objects, and elaborate, and
often numerous, subordinate clauses. His story is developed with the
rhythm of repose that suggests the serene mystery of natural creativity.
Frémy's verbless, cacophonic formula, on the other hand, 'fusión por
veinte días, de una mezcla de sílice y de aluminado de plomo; coloración
con bicromato de potasa o con óxido de cobalto' (p. 80), provides no relief
from brusqueness, reflecting thus the business-like manner of a late
nineteenth-century metropolitan setting.

As a result of all this there is an ultimate irony in 'El rubí.' In the kind of world that represents one pole of contrast in the story, the sophisticated Parisian world of the late nineteenth century, there was implicit belief in the general progress that science had brought and would continue to bring. This world is peopled by known personages and is supported by real events. Yet despite its confidence and its instances of reality, when it is pitted against the mythical world of the gnomes it proves to be false. At the same time the world of fantasy is shown to be the authentic world that contains the eternal values of beauty. This meaning of 'El rubí' is effected by the harmonious functioning of point of view, characterization, tone, rhythm, and flexibility in the use of language.

Venus[75]

1	En la tranquila noche, mis nostalgias amargas sufría.
2	En busca de quietud, bajé al fresco y callado jardín.
3	En el obscuro cielo, Venus bella temblando lucía,
4	como incrustado en ébano un dorado y divino jazmín.
5	A mi alma enamorada, una reina oriental parecía
6	que esperaba a su amante, bajo el techo de su camarín,
7	o que, llevada en hombros, la profunda extensión recorría,
8	triunfante y luminosa, recostada sobre un palanquín.
9	'¡Oh reina rubia! – díjele –, mi alma quiere dejar su crisálida
10	y volar hacia ti, y tus labios de fuego besar;
11	y flotar en el nimbo que derrama en tu frente luz pálida,
12	y en siderales éxtasis no dejarte un momento de amar.'
13	El aire de la noche, refrescaba la atmósfera cálida.
14	Venus, desde el abismo, me miraba con triste mirar.

A reading of the poem indicates that equivocality (in the sense not only of dual but also of multiple possibilities of meaning) and decisive opposition are together prominent. And indeed the full effect of the poem can be appreciated only when the interdependence of these two elements is analysed. At the service of this interdependence is the poet's economical use of the multiple connotations of words.

Antithesis is most pronounced in the first quatrain where setting and object contrast. In the first two lines the poet[76] is at odds with his surroundings, 'tranquila noche' of the first hemistich serving as the antithetical setting to the poet and his 'nostalgias amargas.' The words 'quietud' and 'callado' of the second line reinforce and define the atmosphere of peacefulness first introduced by 'tranquila,' 'quietud' seeming here more strongly to connote the spiritual aspect and 'callado' the physical. In the original version of this poem published in 1889, instead of 'En la tranquila noche' Darío had written 'En una negra noche.'[77] Clearly, his revision, made when he included the sonnet in the second edition of *Azul*, enhances the effectiveness of the couplet by establishing from the outset the antithetical tension which, as will be shown, is so important for the rest of the poem.

The image 'Venus bella temblando lucía' of verses 3 and 4 is seen by the poet to contrast with its setting, 'el obscuro cielo.' The use of the image also indicates that Venus is being used both literally as planet and figuratively as goddess. And when the description is elaborated by the simile 'como incrustado en ébano un dorado y divino jazmín' it becomes clear that the attractive qualities of Venus are at once sensual and sacred, and thus parallel the physical-spiritual duality of 'tranquila' (as it was elaborated by 'quietud' and 'callado') to refer to the environment whose characteristics the poet desires to possess.

Through rhyme and metonymical relationship with 'jardín,' 'jazmín' links the two parts of the quatrain. This link is defined by other structural associations. The use of anaphora in the first and third lines suggests certain parallels in the construction of the two parts. As has been shown, the first and the third lines present first setting and then object in a relationship of contrast. In both parts of the quatrain the poles of the antithesis are, from the poet's viewpoint, the enviable and the unenviable. However, the parallel ends here, for the order of antithesis is inverted. In the first line the setting is the enviable element while the poet's condition is the unenviable element. In the third line this sequence is reversed in the relationship between Venus and her setting. The poet suffers in his setting and aspires to acquire qualities it possesses. Venus dominates hers, and the poet is aware of the contrast between his relationship to his setting and that of Venus to hers. The inversion of these relationships in the two parts of the quatrain is underscored by the link between 'jazmín,' a simile for Venus, and 'jardín,' representing the poet's setting. All this serves to create a wide gulf between the poet and Venus.

The imagery of the second quatrain, while maintaining links with that of the first, is developed to correspond with the poet's effort to possess the beauty he longs for. Contributing essentially to this is the use of exotic imagery. Thus exoticism is not to be treated here merely as one in a list of features of a poem, as so often happens in historical studies of Modernist poetry. To understand its usage in this poem as an example of a poet writing 'sobre océanos que no conoce,' to use Pablo Neruda's famous allusion to the nineteenth-century poets,[78] is not to appreciate its function in the creation of meaning in the sonnet. Exoticism, which was already suggested in the simile that forms the last line of the first quatrain 'ébano,' 'dorado jazmín,' is prominent in this second quatrain 'camarín,' and functions to sustain the idea of longing for the remote, the revered, and the sensual. The new simile 'una reina oriental parecía' makes the poet's hopes seem more terrestrial and thus more within human reach by emphasizing Venus's human form and activity. However, as 'una reina oriental' Venus still remains distant and unattainable in relation to the poet. In fact, the 'nostalgias amargas' he reveals in the first stanza now appear more serious in his new state of anxiety; for, in love with her, he now seems separated from her, not only by distance, but also by her apparent love for someone else and by her superior status.

The imagery and structure of the twelfth line of the sonnet, 'y en siderales éxtasis no dejarte un momento de amar,' create a formal problem with respect to the stanzaic arrangement of the sonnet. The rhyme scheme used by Darío suggests the division of the sonnet into the customary two quatrains and two tercets. With the quatrains rhyming ABAB ABAB the sonnet also represents a Modernist variation on the rhyme scheme of the traditional Spanish sonnet, whose quatrains rhyme ABBA. Yet this division seems arbitrary or even baseless when the form of the twelfth line is considered with regard to the other structural elements of the poem. Its relation to the third stanza is most intimate: together with the two preceding lines it is bound to the verb 'quiere' of the first line of the stanza; and this binding is reinforced by anaphora. The final, climactic statement of the poet's direct speech to Venus is made in this line. The adjective 'siderales' emphasizes the ethereal and distant environment in which the poet would possess her. In preparation for this, the poet employs synecdoche to represent himself: 'mi alma quiere dejar su crisálida.' To the soul in turn is applied the transformation metaphor signifying the development from chrysalis to winged imago with its dual suggestion of physical and spiritual refinement and, thus, of the means of access to Venus. The four lines, then, on the basis of their syntax and meaning can easily be regarded as a quatrain. The final two lines, as will be shown, form an important sense unit. For these reasons the sonnet would be best divided, like the so-called Shakespearean sonnet, into three quatrains and a couplet. The use of this stanzaic pattern would have served the poem well and would have been another effective Modernist innovation.

In the third quatrain, the poet moves from 'reina' as simile in the second quatrain to 'reina' as metaphor. Her environment is no longer earthly but celestial and emphasizes her ideality. At the same time, while the poet's own transformation makes him eligible to address her directly, the diction of his address is enhanced by multiple connotation to reveal simultaneously the sensual and spiritual aspects of Venus as both goddess and planet: e.g., 'siderales,' 'fuego,' 'luz,' 'nimbo,' 'rubia,' 'amar,' etc. This complexity of significance confirms the suggestion of 'dorado y divino' that the poet's vision is a synthesis of the divine and the sensual and that the object of his search is the ideal of sensual and spiritual Beauty. The meaning of this poem relates it closely to a predominant quest encountered in the works in *Azul*. The quest for a multiform ideal: an ideal of achievement, an ideal of expression, or the ideal environment in which the pursuit of beauty in art can be carried on, is often prominent in this book. In his thematic study of Darío's poetry, Pedro Salinas[79] considers 'Venus' to be prophetic of what he considers a subsequent emphasis on the opposition between the sensual and the ideal in Darío's poetry. He believes that the poem poses the question to which 'toda la lírica de Rubén será una lenta respuesta ... ¿es el amor gracia celestial o pérfido obsequio de los abismos y su dueño?'[80] It would seem nevertheless that opposition between the sensual and the ideal is not operative in 'Venus.' The two are neither antithetical nor mutually exclusive. The sensual and the spiritual are different aspects of the poet's ideal. Venus, as goddess of Beauty and Love, is the incarnation of the ideal of Beauty and, as planet, is sylleptically both an incarnation of this ideal and an image of its difficult, if not impossible, attainment.

The interrelated images by which the poet represents Venus show her developing from a sacred and carefully wrought object ('dorado y divino jazmín') to an adored being in a setting of exotic splendour ('reina oriental') to a celestial queen ('reina rubia'). At the same time the poet evolves from a troubled nostalgic searcher to a distantly yearning admirer, to an ecstatic, transfigured lover who seemingly achieves his goal. In the first image a generic difference confirms the distance between Venus and the poet. In the second, the distance is as between humans, but remains great geographically and socially. In the third, the distance is but seemingly overcome, for it is overcome only by a denial of his real situation. The verb 'quiere' testifies to the ever-present antithesis of reality and imagination.

Venus's reaction to the poet's wish, given in the last line of the poem, 'Venus, desde el abismo, me miraba con triste mirar,' can be more conclusively interpreted in the light of the pattern of antithesis and synthesis established earlier in the poem. Throughout the poem the voice and the vision are those of the poet, and the changing images he presents of Venus are intimately related to his feelings. His final vision of Venus is a sad one. She has listened to his declaration of love, and, whereas the goddess of mythology customarily regards her lovers as victims and laughs mockingly at them, the poet's Venus gives him a sad, concerned look. All this represents a continuation of the tendency to interiorize shown throughout the poem. The fact that the poet is making Venus's reaction a correlative of his own final despair is also substantiated by structural elements within the last two lines themselves. The first of these lines, 'El aire de la noche refrescaba la atmósfera cálida,' recalls the pleasant surroundings which were antithetical to the poet's emotional state in the first quatrain of the poem. But there antithesis occurred within the line, while, in the last couplet, it occurs in the contrast between the two lines. 'Abismo' is related to 'obscuro cielo' of the first quatrain, to 'profunda extensión' of the second, and to 'siderales' of the third; they all refer to Venus's setting and are related in terms of light and dark. As such, they are indicators of the poet's changing moods as his relationship to Venus varies in the four stanzas. The poet's increasing optimism is reflected by the movement towards brightness from 'obscuro cielo' to 'profunda extensión' to 'siderales.' Following this pattern, 'abismo' indicates a deterioration of the poet's mood. Together with Venus's sad look, it represents his final despair on recognizing that Beauty, as symbolized by both goddess and planet, is unattainable. The ideal and the actual aspects of his existence will not be correlated, and he perceives the sadness of this fact.

It is necessary to comment too on the function of metre in the poem. Andrés González-Blanco, among others, has been critical of the metre employed. He called it 'metro raro e inusitado en poesía castellana, que se reduce naturalmente a la combinación de un heptasílabo y de un decasílabo. Pero tiene el inconveniente de que no se soldan [sic] bien; se siente demasiado la ligadura forzada.'[81] It would seem, on the contrary, that Darío has used the seventeen-syllable line in such a way that it contributes importantly to the effect of the poem. It is precisely the pronounced caesura that rhythmically accentuates the antithetical structure of most of the lines. At the same time the effect of the caesura is diminished, sometimes through the use of punctuation, at other times through syntax, when the emphatic pause that might be introduced by caesura is inappropriate. See, for instance, the lines.

y en siderales éxtasis no dejaxte un momento de amar.
El aire de la noche, refrescaba la atmósfera cálida.[82]

'Venus,' then, is a poem of well-managed complexity. The poem's meaning is derived from the careful use of opposition and synthesis. Darío has known how to employ the kind of diction that functions perfectly in the isolated image and, at the same time, acquires new connotations as the poem develops. The rhythm of his lines contributes essentially to the poem's meaning; and, although the rhyme scheme might not be the most suitable to convey the sense of the poem, rhyme is sometimes used with dynamic effect. Darío's achievement in this poem is compelling evidence that already in 1890 he was displaying the ability of a major poet. The failure to attain Beauty which is dramatized in this poem in a sense contrasts ironically with the success of the poem itself: for in the poem 'Venus' Darío clearly captures the beauty of a poetic creation.

A Roosevelt[83]

1	Es con voz de la Biblia, o verso de Walt Whitman,
2	que habría de llegar hasta ti, Cazador,
3	primitivo y moderno, sencillo y complicado,
4	con un algo de Wáshington y cuatro de Nemrod.
5	Eres los Estados Unidos,
6	eres el futuro invasor
7	de la América ingenua que tiene sangre indígena,
8	que aún reza a Jesucristo y aún habla en español.
9	Eres soberbio y fuerte ejemplar de tu raza;
10	eres culto, eres hábil; te opones a Tolstoy.
11	Y domando caballos, o asesinando tigres,
12	eres un Alejandro-Nabucodonosor.
13	(Eres un profesor de Energía,
14	como dicen los locos de hoy.)
15	Crees que la vida es incendio,
16	que el progreso es erupción,
17	que en donde pones la bala
18	el porvenir pones.
19	No.
20	Los Estados Unidos son potentes y grandes.
21	Cuando ellos se estremecen hay un hondo temblor
22	que pasa por las vértebras enormes de los Andes.
23	Si clamáis, se oye como el rugir del león.

24   Ya Hugo a Grant lo dijo: Las estrellas son vuestras.
25   (Apenas brilla, alzándose, el argentino sol
26   y la estrella chilena se levanta …) Sois ricos.
27   Juntáis al culto de Hércules el culto de Mammón;
28   y alumbrando el camino de la fácil conquista,
29   la Libertad levanta su antorcha en Nueva-York.

30   Mas la América nuestra, que tenía poetas
31   desde los viejos tiempos de Netzahualcoyotl,
32   que ha guardado las huellas de los pies del gran Baco,
33   que el alfabeto pánico en un tiempo aprendió;
34   que consultó los astros, que conoció la Atlántida
35   cuyo nombre nos llega resonando en Platón,
36   que desde los remotos momentos de su vida
37   vive de luz, de fuego, de perfume, de amor,
38   la América del grande Moctezuma, del Inca,
39   la América fragante de Cristóbal Colón,
40   la América católica, la América española,
41   la América en que dijo el noble Guatemoc:
42   'Yo no estoy en un lecho de rosas'; esa América
43   que tiembla de huracanes y que vive de amor;
44   hombres de ojos sajones y alma bárbara, vive.
45   Y sueña. Y ama, y vibra, y es la hija del Sol.
46   Tened cuidado. ¡Vive la América española!
47   Hay mil cachorros sueltos del León Español.
48   Se necesitaría, Roosevelt ser, por Dios mismo,
49   el Riflero terrible y el fuerte Cazador,
50   para poder tenernos en vuestras férreas garras.
51   Y, pues contáis con todo, falta una cosa: ¡Dios!

Few of Darío's poems have surpassed the fame won by this ode 'A Roosevelt.'[84] Dealing with a subject that was a burning issue in 1904 when it was written, the poem became popular immediately. And it has continued to be cited as an example of a literary manifestation of a great socio-political problem that was rooted in the relations between the United States and Spanish America: the menace of United States imperialism. It seems to me that in spite of its popularity and of the numerous commentaries that have been dedicated to it, another analysis and further interpretation of the poem might still be attempted. I believe that a detailed examination of the work will bring to light certain contradictions in the second part of this two-part poem, where the characterization of Spanish America is developed, and that a careful study of these contradictions will help to explain the poem's complex unity.

The dramatic situation is established in the first stanza of the poem. The poet addresses Roosevelt whom he sees as a threat to 'la América ingenua.' He presents him as 'Cazador,' referring, literally, to his passion for hunting, and, symbolically, to his politics of aggressive expansionism. The invocation, 'voz de la Biblia, o verso de Walt Whitman,' explains the solemn, sermonizing tone which he finds appropriate for addressing the complex Roosevelt, who displays the character traits of Nimrod, the legendary hunter, the symbol of tyranny. The United States is then personified explicitly in Roosevelt; and the character of Spanish America, as it will be developed later in the poem, is summarized in the second part of the stanza:

> Eres los Estados Unidos,
> eres el futuro invasor
> de la América ingenua que tiene sangre indígena,
> que aún reza a Jesucristo y aún habla en español.

The contrast between the two peoples is underlined in the second stanza as Roosevelt is given traits directly opposed to those suggested by 'ingenua.' He is 'soberbio' and 'hábil.' By rejecting Tolstoy he reveals his opposition to what is simple and peaceful, while Spanish America comes to be identified with these attributes. Roosevelt's love for hunting is presented hyperbolically with the joint reference to the great Greek and Babylonian conquerors. His attitude of blatant aggression is defined in three lines of parallel construction before being repudiated by the defiant 'No,' which, although it completes the romance metre of the stanza, receives special emphasis by being placed in a separate line. The gradual shortening of the lines from fourteen syllables at the beginning of the poem to ten and then eight syllables, with the consequent quickening of the rhythm, enhances the climactic quality of the 'No.' Also, as a separate sentence it acquires its own emphatic stress and makes the assonance in 'o' stand out. All this contributes to the solemn sermonizing tone of the poem. The alexandrines reappear in the following stanza where the poet describes, with images of awesome power, the United States in relation to Spanish America:

> Los Estados Unidos son potentes y grandes.
> Cuando ellos se estremecen hay un hondo temblor
> que pasa por las vértebras enormes de los Andes.
> Si clamáis, se oye como el rugir del león.

Referring to Hugo's reproach of General Grant, he declares that United States imperialism is threatening the young republics to the south. Physical strength ('el culto de Hércules'), greed ('el culto de Mammón'), and cynical propaganda ('alumbrando el camino de la fácil conquista,/ la libertad levanta su antorcha en Nueva York') are identified as combining in the hostile effort.[85]

In the final part of the poem the poet elaborates the definition of Spanish America given in the first stanza. The America that will confront the United States possesses the double heritage of the indigenous and the Spanish:

> la América del Grande Moctezuma, del Inca,
> la América fragante de Cristóbal Colón,
> la América católica, la América española,
> la América en que dijo el noble Guatemoc:
> 'Yo no estoy en un lecho de rosas.'

And nevertheless the meaning of these lines can be seen to be somewhat ambiguous when the logical argument of the whole poem is considered. The poet challenges Roosevelt at the beginning of the poem, since by representing and personifying the United States he is 'el futuro invasor de la América ingenua.' When the poet refers to the Spanish factor in the second part of the poem, he in fact invokes, if the whole historical allusion is to be considered, another invader of 'la América ingenua.' In the reference to Guatemoc, juxtaposed as it is with the verse 'la América católica, la América española,' the ambiguity is intensified since Guatemoc's statement 'Yo no estoy en un lecho de rosas' was directed, according to the legend, at one of his compatriots while the two were being tortured by the Spanish invaders. He wanted thereby to indicate his wish that his compatriot not betray his country. These are important complexities that must be understood before the contribution of this part to the meaning of the poem and to the place of the poem itself in Darío's work can be evaluated.

The first fifteen verses of this second part of the poem establish the traditional idealism of the Spanish American people. The first of the attributes that the poet finds in Spanish America is that, in contrast to the United States, 'tenía poetas desde los viejos tiempos de Netzahualcoyotl.' The interest in social idealism suggested by the reference to the Texcocan poet king (who was not a 'rey-burgués' and therefore was not representative of a materialist ideal) is maintained in the allusion to America's knowledge of Atlantis, Plato's ideal commonwealth. The refer-

ences to Spanish America's devotion to the teachings of Bacchus concerning the attractiveness of poetry and to music, happiness, and the message
of the Muses and the stars show the idealism of its artistic tradition, which
is at the same time sensual and spiritual, aesthetic and religious. This
description of Spanish American idealism continues as the poet declares
that America 'vive de luz, de fuego, de amor.' Verses 38–41 strengthen
this characterization. Their anaphorical structure indicates that the adjectives have a special significance and that this significance, suggested by the
explicitly evaluative adjectives 'grande,' 'fragante,' and 'noble' unites
these lines to the elevated idealist spirit of the preceding ones. Guatemoc's
statement ought to be interpreted in accordance with this spirit. Moctezuma, the Inca, Catholicism, the love of poetry, Columbus, and
Guatemoc represent the search here for a heroic ideal; and the words 'Yo
no estoy en un lecho de rosas' do not allude to the tortures but rather, and
only, to the heroism of Guatemoc. That is to say the historical meaning of
the allusion and the meaning required by the structure of the poem are
different.[86] Despite the fact that the lines lack logical force when the
political relationship between the Spanish invaders and Guatemoc is
considered, they serve effectively to yield meaning consistent with the
rest of the second part of the poem. The political context being noticeable,
the factor of idealism, by superseding it, becomes all the more pronounced.

In the first fifteen verses of the last part of the poem there are, as I have
indicated, anaphorical groups containing alliterative adjectival phrases
that sing of the glorious heritage of Spanish America. The passage culmi-
nates with dramatic force in the fifteenth verse where the United States,
called 'hombres de ojos sajones y alma bárbara,' is told that this heritage
still lives in Spanish America. Owing to the numerous elaborative phrases
occurring between 'Mas la América nuestra' and 'vive,' this concluding
verb comes to acquire considerable climactic effect.[87] 'Vive' is followed by
a series of verbs indicating the deeds that make America invulnerable to
Roosevelt who, at the end of the poem, as at the beginning, personifies the
United States. The last line of the poem,

> Y, pues contáis con todo, falta una cosa: ¡Dios!,

recapitulates in the symbol 'Dios'[88] the essential difference between the
peoples of Spanish America and those of the United States: the lack of
what from the point of view of Spanish America, as it is represented in the
poem, is the ultimate of spiritual ideals. The preponderance of rhetorical
figures and the climactic structure of this part of the poem create a level of

expression that is more elevated than that found in the first part of the poem where the United States is characterized. The difference between the levels of expression is in itself indicative of the discrepancy between the portrayed ideological vision of the two peoples.

When the extent of the preoccupation with the ideal in 'A Roosevelt' is shown in this way, the relationship between this poem and a significant part of Darío's poetry becomes evident; and a way is opened to the interpretation of those of his compositions that are usually placed under the heading of political poetry. The poem's similarity to 'Salutación del optimista' and 'Los cisnes' has often been observed, as has its contrast with 'Salutación al águila' (1906),[89] in regard to the attitude shown towards the United States. But on examining the poems it is clear that an artistic constant based on a perception of the ideal is always present. This is as true for Darío's presentation of the United States in 'Salutación al águila' as it is for his interpretation of Spanish America in 'A Roosevelt.' In 'Salutación al águila' he treats the United States favourably and this makes it qualify for entrance into the ideal state of Panamericanism which he presents in the poem. The whole course of Darío's poetic career indicates that for him artistic unity based on the desire for or the manifestation of an ideal was more important than the cogency of political arguments. This explains his remark concerning 'A Roosevelt' in his essay on Manuel Ugarte: 'Yo mismo, hace ya bastante tiempo, lancé a Mr Roosevelt, el fuerte cazador, un trompetazo, por otra parte, inofensivo'[90] and his explanation in his 'Epístola a la señora de Leopoldo Lugones' of the circumstances of his writing of the 'Salutación al águila' in Rio de Janeiro: 'Yo pan-americanicé/ con un vago temor y con muy poca fe/ ... encontré también un gran núcleo cordial/de almas llenas de amor, de ensueño, de ideal.'[91]

The role given to the indigenous element in Darío's conception of the ideal needs special examination. In 1896 he had declared that 'Si hay poesía en nuestra América, ella está en las cosas viejas: en Palenke y Utatlán, en el indio legendario y el inca sensual y fino, y en el gran Moctezuma de la silla de oro.'[92] It is not surprising, then, that when Darío came to characterize Spanish America as an ideal, images from the indigenous world should predominate.[93] It is perhaps due chiefly to his characterization of Spanish America in this way that he can with certainty be called 'el poeta de América.'[94] Since Darío, Spanish American poets have paid increasing attention to indigenous subjects and have been demonstrating too that in them 'hay poesía.'

Thus in the poem 'A Roosevelt,' Spanish America and the United States are put in sharp contrast and the poem, having been written in a period of great apprehension concerning the designs of the United States, lends itself to being classified as political. But the elements that constitute it: the hymn-like musicality of its praise for Spanish America resounding above the solemn, sermonized description of the aggressive United States and the sacrifice of logical rigour of the political arguments for the coherent structuring of images that represent the ideal, all this places the poem within the mainstream of Darío's poetry and explains the statement made in the preface to *Cantos de vida y esperanza* that the poem 'queda escrita sobre las alas de los inmaculados cisnes.'[95]

CHAPTER SIX

General Assessments

Many works have been written with the express purpose of assessing Darío's place as a writer, of estimating his lasting value. Sometimes these works are in the form of essays that develop their arguments with evidence that reveals several aspects of the poet's work. At other times opinions are given in less extensive statements that may well be called testimonies. In the first category are the essay 'El caracol y la sirena' by the renowned poet and essayist Octavio Paz,[1] the essays collected by Ernesto Mejía Sánchez for the volume *Rubén Darío en Oxford*[2] and other studies by Arturo Torres-Ríoseco,[3] Raimundo Lida,[4] and Edgardo Buitrago.[5] Many other critics and poets have contributed statements which come under the second category. Both categories may be usefully examined in this concluding chapter.

Viewing Darío's career first in the context of Modernism, Paz calls him, without much elaboration, 'el menos actual de los grandes modernistas.'[6] He adds, however, 'No es una influencia viva sino un término de referencia: un punto de partida o llegada, un límite que hay que alcanzar o traspasar. Ser o no ser como él: de ambas maneras Darío está presente en el espíritu de los poetas contemporáneos. Es el fundador.'[7] When he later compares Darío with other poets of the late nineteenth century he clarifies his opinion, saying of him: 'Darío no es únicamente el más amplio y rico de los poetas modernistas: es uno de nuestros grandes poetas modernos. Es el origen.'[8] Later in his essay Paz, in the course of a chronological examination of Darío's career, indicates some of the bases for his view of Darío's position as a poet. In writing of *Azul*, for instance, Paz offers succinctly his reasons for considering 'Venus' a great poem. He notices, in considering *Prosas profanas*, the Pythagorean character of Darío's use of music and declares, coinciding with Gullón,[9] that 'El erotismo de Darío es una visión mágica del mundo.'[10] A related idea, one that was developed almost simultaneously by Trueblood,[11] is to be found in his discussion of *Cantos de vida y esperanza* where he gives special importance to the relation between man and nature. Paz writes of Darío:

> La originalidad de nuestro poeta consiste en que, casi sin proponérselo, resucita una antigua manera de ver y sentir a la realidad. Al redescubrir la solidaridad entre el hombre y la naturaleza, fundamento de las primeras civilizaciones y religión primordial de los hombres, Darío abre a nuestra poesía un mundo de correspondencias y asociaciones. Esta vena de erotismo mágico se prolonga en varios grandes poetas hispanoamericanos como Pablo Neruda.[12]

Paz finally points to Darío's meditation on death in his latest poetry and ends his essay with Darío's death in 1916. His essay, then, combines biography, literary history, thematic and intrinsic considerations to give a measured picture of Darío's place in literature.

A more sweeping and less favourable view of Darío's work is given by Cecil Maurice Bowra in his essay 'Rubén Darío.' He constantly compares Darío with other poets – Verlaine, Mallarmé, Coleridge, Keats – on the terms of those poets, perhaps because he possesses a more penetrating understanding of them than he does of Darío. 'El defecto central de este estudio' Torres-Ríoseco has written of Bowra's essay, 'consiste en el conocimiento incompleto que el crítico inglés tiene de la poesía de Rubén Darío, que creemos basado en *Prosas profanas* y en algunas selecciones de antología.'[13] Commenting on the question of Darío's sincerity, for example, Bowra writes:

> When Darío speaks of sincerity, he reminds us of the great change which came over such poets as W.B. Yeats and Alexander Blok when they gave up their first, entrancing dreams to face naked facts. Darío's intention resembles theirs, but he differs from them because his decision demands a much less violent break with his earlier outlook. For him dreams are still a part of truth so long as the poet speaks truthfully of them. In his career there is no such abrupt division as there is in that of Yeats or Blok. None the less he knew that dreams were not enough and must not be indulged in entirely for their own sake. They must be tempered by truth, and this in his own way he tried to do.[14]

With Darío, as has been shown in Chapter 1, sincerity has nothing to do with any tempering of dream with truth, nor did any such tempering mark the dividing line between periods of insincerity and sincerity. Rather sincerity meant being constantly true to his concept that the finest poetic expression should be used in his poetry, whatever its subject might be. Aspects of Bowra's biographical criticism of Darío betray his belief that given certain biographical circumstances in Darío's life he does not expect him to perform as a fully developed poet. And Bowra seems determined that his expectations should not be frustrated. For how else could he write of Darío in terms such as 'his untutored simplicity and his complete lack of irony.'[15] Such a view of Darío comes from what Bowra calls the 'right perspective'; that is, 'we must remember that he was a stranger from an undeveloped land, that he had Indian blood in his veins and lacked the complexity and the sophistication which would belong to a European of his gifts and tastes.'[16] Bowra's essay purports to demonstrate that Darío's achievement' may seem in retrospect not to deserve its first renown';[17] and the Spanish poet Luis Cernuda[18] accepts his arguments declaring that Bowra does not go far enough. What particularly invalidates Darío's work for Cernuda is the fact that Darío followed French models in his poetry. But any inclination to consider Cernuda's opinions seriously is dispelled by his admission that at the time of writing his essay he had not read Darío's poetry for forty years. Gastón Baquero[19] agrees with Cernuda, adding complaints about Darío's alienation from his condition of being Spanish American. A refutation of Cernuda's position was provided by Ernesto Mejía Sánchez in his essay 'Rubén Darío, poeta del siglo xx.'[20] In answer to Cernuda's charge that Darío's inability to remain important as a poet is evidenced by the fact that no one now imitates him, Mejía Sánchez argues that a poet lives on by what is not imitable in his work. More significantly, he reveals techniques, in poems like 'Soneto autumnal al marqués de Bradomín' and 'La gran cosmópolis,' which have attained high regard in the works of other twentieth-century poets in Europe and America.[21] Torres-Ríoseco's reply to Bowra, cited above, does not constitute his definitive statement on the question of Darío's lasting value. This comes in his article 'Nueva evaluación de Rubén Darío,' which sums up views similar to those expressed in some of his earlier publications. As early as 1931,[22] in his article 'Rubén Darío y la crítica' he had stated that Darío was a classic poet. In 1967 he reaffirmed this view, putting Darío on a level with the two or three greatest poets to have written in Spanish. This essay concludes with the statement:

> Darío fue esencialmente un poeta serio: un hombre enteramente dedicado

a su arte; por eso dijo: 'que ser sincero es ser potente.' La poesía fue para él un magisterio, el más alto magisterio a que puede aspirar el hombre. Por eso yo creo que es hora de considerarle no como el primer modernista, sino como el primer poeta clásico de nuestro continente.[23]

It was Pedro Henríquez Ureña who, in his article 'Rubén Darío'[24] which appeared in the form of an obituary in 1916, as far as is known first put Darío on a par with Góngora and Quevedo for his achievement in Hispanic poetry. This comparison has been made repeatedly since that time, as will be shown later. A review of the evaluations done by Paz, Bowra, Cernuda, Torres-Ríoseco, Mejía Sánchez, Juan Marinello (in 1959), and Manuel Pedro González was made by Edgardo Buitrago in his article 'Consideraciones polémicas acerca de la vigencia y actualidad de Rubén Darío.' In his own positive evaluation of Darío which follows his review he stresses Darío's particular Americanist vision, in which the indigenous aspect was of great significance.

Positive assessment of Darío's work with regard to his lasting contribution to Spanish literature was made in memorable terms by Enrique Díez-Canedo. His statement is included in Juan González Olmedilla's *La ofrenda de España a Rubén Darío*,[25] a book that contains warm acknowledgments by many leading Spanish writers of Spain's debt to Darío. Díez-Canedo's statement touches on several important aspects of Darío's achievement. He believes that just as Verlaine did for poetry in his time

> Rubén Darío abrió también las ventanas a los poetas españoles. Les dio a conocer los poetas extranjeros que él amaba; leyó con ellos los poetas primitivos españoles; les libertó de la rigidez de una versificación atada por inflexibles reglas; les dio la preocupación de la forma, transformando el período oratorio, que hace impresión cuando se redondea en la expresión cortada, rica en sugestiones, valiosa por sí misma: algo de exotismo; algo de arcaísmo; algo de preciosismo. Y, con todo eso, les trajo el don de una exquisita sensibilidad para lo nuevo ... algo ha cambiado en la poesía española desde que Rubén Darío apareció, y por su nombre ha de empezar el capítulo de nuestra historia literaria en que se estudia la poesía de los comienzos del siglo xx.[26]

Testimonies to Darío's importance from fellow practitioners of his art have been abundant, and they bear a special significance. They have been written in various forms by both Spanish and Spanish American poets. Antonio Machado, for example, contributed the poems 'Al maestro Rubén Darío' and 'A la muerte de Rubén Darío,'[27] Juan Ramón Jiménez, the poem 'Rubén Darío,'[28] César Vallejo, the poem 'Retablo,'[29] Pablo Neruda and Federico García Lorca, the poetic dialogue 'Discurso al alimón sobre Rubén Darío,'[30] and Neruda, the poem 'R.D.'[31] Two other poets, one Chilean, the other Spanish, have made statements concerning Darío's lasting value which, in addition to those by Borges and Benedetti cited in Chapter 3, deserve to be quoted. Vicente Huidobro, *creacionista*, wrote in 1924, when the Vanguardist movement was in force:

> Estos señores que se creen representar la España moderna han tomado moda de reírse de Rubén Darío, como si en castellano desde Góngora hasta nosotros hubiera otro poeta fuera de Rubén Darío.
>
> Los que conocemos las bases del arte y de la poesía modernos, los que podemos contarnos entre sus engendradores, como Picasso, Juan Gris, yo, Pablo Gargallo (hablo de los que pueden leer a Darío en su lengua), sabemos lo que significa el poeta y por eso hablamos de él en otra forma. Los falsos modernos lo denigran.
>
> Pobre Rubén, puedes dormir tranquilo; cuando todos ellos hayan desaparecido aún tu nombre seguirá escrito entre dos estrellas.[32]

And writing in 1967, the year in which Bowra's opinion that Darío's achievement 'may seem in retrospect not to deserve its first renown' was drowned in a torrent of tributes, Gerardo Diego declared:

> le considero el más alto poeta de lengua española después – cronológicamente – de Lope y de Góngora. Ninguno, ni Bécquer, ni Antonio Machado, ni Juan Ramón, ni los que siguen le iguala.[33]

From the 1880s to the 1970s Darío has had his detractors and his commenders. There has never been a period in which opposite reactions to his work could not easily be found. This is not surprising, given the nature of poetry in general, of his poetry in particular, and the plural concepts of literary criticism. Darío's fortune with the critics to 1966 has been well summarized by Raimundo Lida in the final paragraph of his essay 'Rubén y su herencia,' where he writes:

> Y lo viviente y actual de Rubén se nos muestra en su capacidad de seguir produciendo, no sólo confusiones de lejanía, sino apasionados errores de proximidad. Que a medio siglo de su muerte Rubén pueda suscitar todavía desprecios y elogios injustos, que hasta pueda impacientar a algunos verdaderos poetas, todo eso nos dice cuán cerca de nosotros está. Su legado no es bloque unitario e inerte al que convengan cultos igualmente muer-

tos. La modernidad de Darío, como la de Martí, es, en nuestros tiempos, más tangible que nunca. Rubén sigue provocando herejías, discrepancias y ambigüedades: sigue siendo un gran poeta aún hoy inexplorado y difícil, aún hoy pregunta viva.[34]

Enough has been done since 1966 when Lida wrote his comments to make the present state of Darío criticism considerably brighter than Lida pictured it. Many among the multitude of studies brought out by the recent centennial celebrations sharpen the focus on parts of the spectrum of approaches employed by earlier Darío critics and in so doing have usefully elucidated Darío's production.

The effort that has gone into the critical study of Darío's work has been enormous. During his life time studies were produced that are of lasting importance. Critics such as Ricardo Contreras and José Enrique Rodó examined carefully and explicitly the works on which they based their conclusions. After his death the tendency to interpret and evaluate the work itself yielded to the practice of biography, the consideration of his socio-political position, the fixing of his place in literary history, and the elaboration of certain elements in his work. And now, the process of analysing the poems and short stories as whole compositions is being developed in a way that no doubt would have pleased Ricardo Contreras. Some of the studies that form this great body of criticism lend themselves to use as illustrations of the weaknesses of certain critical approaches. But there have always been critics who have displayed a systematic, analytical attitude and whose work, undertaken with serious and informed notions about literature, is based on carefully weighed evidence. The growing number of Darío critics will doubtless continue to shed valuable light on his poetry and prose, that is, on the real basis of his literary significance. The task attempted in this study, of examining the findings and of assessing the strengths and weaknesses of the principal methodologies, may help to indicate the critical orientations that can be used, either singly or in concert, to continue the creditable work that has been done in the past.

Appendix:
Rubén Darío as a
Literary Critic

In a book that examines the chief critical methods employed in studies of
Darío's work it seems necessary to make a few observations concerning an
aspect of his work that has received scant critical attention: his view and
practice of literary criticism.[1] I will draw my observations from his
principal books of criticism and from those aspects of his literary manifes-
toes which bear on his critical practice.[2]

In the 'Palabras liminares' to *Prosas profanas* Darío states that in
reaction to both his creative work, *Azul*, and his critical work, *Los raros*,
he had been asked to present a literary manifesto, a project that he
considered to be 'ni fructuoso ni oportuno.'[3] He gives the following as one
of the reasons for his negative reaction: 'Porque proclamando, como
proclamo, una estética acrática, la imposición de un modelo o de un código
implicaría una contradicción.'[4] Further basis for his reluctance to propose
precepts for artistic and critical conduct is given in the fifth section of the
'Dilucidaciones' which introduce *El canto errante*. There he writes:

> Pienso que el don del arte es aquél que de modo superior hace que nos
> reconozcamos íntima y exteriormente ante la vida. El poeta tiene la visión
> directa e introspectiva de la vida y una supervisión que va más allá de lo
> que está sujeto a las leyes del general conocimiento ... Cuando dije que mi
> poesía era 'mía en mí,' sostuve la primera condición de mi existir.[5]

These comments indicate that for Darío literary creation is personal and
therefore diverse in its manifestations. That being so, the critic in his

approach to literature should maintain a flexibility that would allow him to consider the work of different authors without dogmatic preconceptions of what literature should be; and on the basis of Darío's critical performance it can be observed that the absence of a definite code led him to represent several possible critical theories. In spite of this, certain fairly insistent procedures result from his premises.

The first consequence is Darío's recourse to the biographical approach. He dealt with the important writers of his time, paying special attention to those of Latin America, Spain, France, and North America; and one of the ways he found of dealing with so diverse a body of writers and of writings was not unrelated to Sainte-Beuve's methodology. Darío tended to consider the literary production in conjunction with its author, to proceed from an examination of those features of a writer's outward life that are easily perceived to an intimate probing into the inner, spiritual man, in so far as this goal can be arrived at through an examination of the writer's work.

The procedure may be observed throughout Darío's work; but his essay 'Nuevos poetas de España' from the book *Opiniones* illustrates it economically and is a convenient starting point for the examination of his practice. The essay, Darío declares, is prompted by Enrique Gómez Carrillo's question '¿Qué piensa usted sobre el estado actual de la poesía en España?'[6] Darío calls the question 'compleja, porque no hay una poesía actual española, sino muchos poetas españoles,'[7] thus recalling, by his emphasis on the individual poets, his dictum, 'no hay escuelas; hay poetas.'[8] Among the poets he examines in the essay is Juan Ramón Jiménez of whom he repeats an assessment he had made earlier:

> lejos del desdoro de la imitación y ajeno a la indigencia del calco, ha aprendido a ser él mismo – *être soi-même* – y dice su alma en versos sencillos como lirios y musicales como aguas de fuente. Este poeta está enfermo, vive en un sanatorio, en Madrid. Así, en su poesía no busquéis salud gozosa ni rosas de risa. Cuando más, a veces, una sonrisa, una sonrisa de convaleciente,
>
> > convalescente de squisitti mali ...,
>
> pero en la cual se insinúa uno de los más grandes misterios de la vida.[9]

Summing up the first part of his essay 'Jose Martí, poeta' – an essay considered by Martí's compatriot Juan Marinello to be the finest written on Martí as a poet[10] – he writes after listing and characterizing briefly Martí's poetic works: 'Viviendo y muriendo, hizo de su vida y de su muerte un poema.'[11] In another essay, 'Julián del Casal,' from yet another collection, *Páginas de arte*, the same tendency of having the poetry reflect the personality is shown. At the beginning of the essay he recalls a visit to a cemetery in Havana; and among the happy company with which he made the visit only Casal was sad until they reached the cemetery, when 'Casal se puso a hablar lleno de animación, tal como un pájaro que se sintiese en su propio bosque. ¡Desdichado ruiseñor del bosque de la muerte!'[12] Later in his essay Darío relates this biographical characteristic to Casal's literary works: 'esa nostalgia de otra existencia se advierte a medida que uno va leyendo la producción de Casal. Surge ya en *Hojas al viento* ; crece en las tristes rosas de *Nieve* ; reina en sus últimos retratos, cuentos y poesías.'[13] Darío's biographical method is also exemplified in *Los raros*. The essays, 'Paul Verlaine' and 'José Martí,' both written as obituaries, are, especially the former, concise biographies that always manifest Darío's concept of the unity of life and work. While in the essay entitled 'El conde de Lautréamont,' an extreme of this concept is touched when, in commenting on Lautréamont's book, *Cantos de Maldoror*, with its radical revolt against the human condition, he goes so far as to infer the character of the author from the work. He writes:

> Se trata de un loco, ciertamente. Pero recordad que el *deus* enloquecía a las pitonisas, y que la fiebre divina de los profetas producía cosas semejantes: y que el autor 'vivió' eso, y que no se trata de una obra literaria,' sino del grito, del aullido de un ser sublime martirizado por Satanás.'[14]

Darío repeatedly expressed the opinion in his well-known prefaces to his poetic collections that poetry should remain apart from the socio-political field. In the final paragraph of the preface to *Cantos de vida y esperanza* he explains that an exception is made to this view in that collection. But even so, as the final metaphor of the preface – 'mi protesta queda escrita sobre las alas de los inmaculados cisnes,'[15] – makes clear, the emphasis on beauty, the beauty of fitting expression and of lofty concepts, would not be abandoned. This attitude is reflected in many of Darío's articles concerning literary criticism. Among those written for *La Nación* between 1893 and 1897, some of which constituted *Los raros*,[16] and those of 1899 to 1900 which were later published as the volume *España contemporánea* (1901),[17] several are to be found which contain important statements of his views on this aspect of criticism. These essays, along with later ones appearing in *Opiniones*,[18] in *Cabezas*,[19] in his *Semblanzas*,[20] in his *Páginas de arte*[21] as well as other writings, give evidence of Darío's fundamental reluctance to concede a happy compatibility between literature and politics or to regard socio-political activity as even approaching the equal of literary pursuit. He does not refrain from expressing this strongly even in his obituary to José Martí in *Los raros*. Near the end of the essay, and after extolling Martí's literary production, he writes:

> Y ahora, maestro y autor y amigo, perdona que te guardemos rencor los que te amábamos y admirábamos, por haber ido a exponer y a perder el tesoro de tu talento ... Martínez Campos, que ha ordenado exponer tu cadáver, sigue leyendo sus dos autores preferidos: 'Cervantes' ... y 'Ohnet.' Cuba quizá tarde en cumplir contigo como debe. La juventud americana te saluda y te llora; pero ¡oh, Maestro, qué has hecho ...!22

The brief essay, 'Manuel Ugarte' (*Cabezas*), written near the end of his career, is devoted mainly to Darío's views on the Argentinian writer's book *El porvenir de la América latina*.23 Book and author receive high praise from Darío for the treatment of a topic that he himself had treated poetically – 'el acecho de los hombres del Norte' – and for the 'erudición, método y, aunque el autor no lo quiera, literatura.'24 No doubt the last mentioned quality, 'literatura,' is weighted positively and heavily in Darío's assessment; for when he considers the book on the basis of its ideological argument he makes no more elevated judgment than to state: 'El libro es interesante, muy interesante.'25

In his essay entitled 'La crítica' (*España contemporánea*), he quotes approvingly the attack made by Leopoldo Alas (Clarín) on unworthy practices in contemporary Spanish criticism and adds: 'yo encuentro iguales o más lamentables tachas en la crítica que quisiera tender a sociológica.'26 But perhaps his most explicit views on the relationship between poetry and socio-political activity are presented in the following paragraph from his essay, 'De un libro de páginas íntimas: Rafael Núñez':

> Poeta político ... no entiendo eso; o más bien no lo quiero entender. Yo creo que no es otro el objeto, la atmósfera, el alimento, la vida de la poesía que el culto de la eterna y divina belleza; que los filósofos se ocupen del misterio de la vida y de todas las profundidades de lo incognoscible; que los señores políticos se entiendan con la suerte de los pueblos y arreglen esas complicadísimas máquinas que se llaman gobiernos; que los señores militares degüellen, defiendan o conquisten. Perfectamente. Tú, luminoso y rubio dios, has enseñado a tus elegidos estos asuntos en verdad muy interesantes: que las rosas son lindas; que los diamantes, el oro, el mármol y la seda son preciosos; y que nada hay igual en este mundo a la ventana en donde la mujer amada, Sol, Amalia, Estela, Florinda, meditabunda y tierna, contempla en una hora tranquila un vuelo de

palomas bajo el cielo azul. En conclusión, el poeta no debe sino tener, como único objeto, la ascensión a su inmortal sublime paraíso: el Arte.[27]

Although the paragraph was written before 1900, it remains representative of Darío's view of art: that it exists in harmony with what is valued, rare, lofty, and universally desired, and that in dealing with it the artist must be free of the encumbrances that attachment to causes or schools may bring. Hence his introduction to *Opiniones* which he repeated so often with slight variations:

> En este libro, como en todos los míos, no pretendo enseñarnada, pues me complazco en reconocerme el ser menos pedagógico de la tierra. Van aquí mis opiniones y mis sentires sobre cosas vistas e ideas acariciadas. Todo expresado de la manera más noble que he podido, pues no me avengo con bajos pensamientos ni vulgares palabras. No busco el que nadie piense como yo, ni se manifieste como yo. ¡Libertad, libertad, mis amigos! Y no os dejéis poner librea de ninguna clase.[28]

Hence, too, his account given in his biography of Pedro Balmaceda, *A. de Gilbert*,[29] of how he tried to dissuade his friend Pedro from being guided too closely by Hippolyte Taine in his literary opinions.

Greatest praise in Darío's essays is reserved for artists; and there are several statements of his view that politicians and politics exist on a plane inferior to that of art. In his essay, 'Un suicidio romántico,' he writes: 'para mí, todos los presidentes, todas las políticas, todas las patrias, no valen uno sólo de los rayos del arte, prodigioso y divino.'[30] Yet those better known as politicians who also involve themselves in literary matters win his congratulations. Gladstone, Bismark, Napoleon Bonaparte, from Europe and Bartolomé Mitre, García Moreno, and Don Pedro II from Latin America are among those on whom he comments approvingly in his essay 'La vida literaria' (*Juicios*).[31] In the essay 'Los diplomáticos poetas' (*Algunos juicios*),[32] another aspect of the relation between poetry and politics is discovered. Darío in discussing there the dual role of poet and diplomat exercised by Amado Nervo suggests that Nervo is, above all, a poet, for whom 'el peso del uniforme no impide el vuelo.'[33] This leads him to propose a benefit that the lesser office of diplomat holds for the poet, the benefit of providing diversion, relaxation from the arduous effort demanded by poetry:

> El poeta verdadero vive de su propia meditación, y la persecución de lo absoluto es causa de inenarrables angustias. Hay que hacerse un alma de

notorio o de sportsman para librarse de las malas consecuencias que traen
las incursiones y exploraciones dentro del propio espíritu. La diplomacia
también es bastante útil para el caso.[34]

Noticeable at the same time is the tone ranging from strongly sarcastic
to mockingly ironical with which he refers, in his *Vida*[35] and elsewhere, to
most of the politicians with whom he came into contact. An attitude of
amused condescension marks too his reporting of mass political activity,
as can be seen for example, in his article 'Un "meeting" político' (*España
contemporánea*).[36] Playful irony also characterizes his essay 'Un poeta
socialista: Leopoldo Lugones.'[37] He describes the young Lugones as 'un
fanático,' 'un revolucionario,' in the sense that he wants 'la revolución
social.' 'Yo soy su amigo': Darío continues, 'y a mi vez, convencido e
inabordable aristo, cuando llega a mi casa, tengo cuidado de guardar bajo
tres llaves mis princesas y príncipes, mis duques y duquesas, mis caba-
lleros y pajes.'[38] Darío sees him as wanting to revolutionize poetry too, but
gives faint praise to the literary work of Lugones which had appeared by
1896,[39] work that Darío evidently considered to be not sufficiently
meritorious to earn Lugones a place among 'Los raros.'

In the already mentioned essay 'La crítica,' devoted to the state of
criticism in Spain in 1899, Darío gives several further indications of his
tenets with regard to literary theory and criticism. He decried the lack of
vibrancy, of daring, of 'mentales especulaciones,' of specialization. 'Aquí
no hay más especialistas que los revisteros de toros; los cuales revisteros
también hacen crítica teatral, o lo que gustéis, con la mayor tranquilidad
propia del público.'[40] Menéndez y Pelayo, in the cloister of the Biblioteca
Nacional where he carries out antiquarian studies of rigorous erudition,
shuns the current literary production and the task of interpreting and
evaluating what is new. His contacts are consequently with a few scholars
who must be found outside Spain and who are necessarily removed from
the internal, contemporary Spanish situation.

Juan Valera is praised not so much for his critical ideology as for the
eloquence with which he expresses his ideas. His broad culture contributes to the distinction that marks his writings and lends reliability to his
opinions. By remarking at the end of his discussion of Valera on the wide
similarity he perceives between him and Anatole France, Darío, in effect,
classifies Valera as an impressionist whose opinions, if not always based
on sound critical principles, are worth reading for the mastery with which
he expounds them. Darío considers it unfortunate that Valera in 1899 no
longer writes criticism. Federico Balart, too, has been compared to
Anatole France and Jules Lemaître, but Darío would deny any important

similarity. Rather than seeming enticingly impressionistic, he strikes Darío as being authoritarian. The impressionist critic, then, to be acceptable to Darío, must have the right force of expression. His writings must show the sophistication and gracefulness that can keep his opinions from appearing to be authoritarian, which, for Darío, is a major sin, a sign of the absence of an adequate understanding of art.

In accounting for Leopoldo Alas's descent to mediocrity in his critical efforts, Darío has recourse to Hippolyte Taine's concept of 'le milieu' of which he had warned the young Balmaceda to be careful. He declares, in short, that the intellectual mediocrity at large in the environment has caused Alas to substitute small talk for criticism:

> Leopoldo Alas ... ha sufrido la imposición de un público poco afecto a producciones que exijan la menor elevación intelectual ... Clarín, pues, actualmente no escribe crítica, como no sea para el extranjero. ¡Aquí lo que pagan bien son paliques, pues paliques![44]

Darío tentatively mentions two young critics, Martínez Ruiz (Azorín) and Ramiro de Maeztu, promising to write more about them on another occasion. He makes enthusiastic comments about Llanas Aguilaniedo, a third young writer, whose fame has not endured. In discussing the work of this writer, Darío shows that he himself regards criticism as a serious undertaking for which Llanas displays promise because 'es un estudioso y un reflexivo. Comprende lo grave que encierra el trabajo de pensar y de juzgar.'[42] This comment is followed by one that is revealing in several important ways: 'Hay una luz individual que él ha descubierto dentro de su propio espíritu, y siguiendo el consejo de Emerson, la persigue.'[43] The immediate purpose of the comment is to provide some insight into Aguilaniedo's literary procedure. It must be noticed, however, that the comment is also self-revealing in the sense that it certainly corresponds to Darío's often expressed view of his own creative *modus operandi*: 'Cuando dije que mi poesía era *mía*, *en mí*, sostuve la primera condición de mi existir' ('Prefacio' to *Cantos de vida y esperanza*[44] and 'Dilucidaciones' to *El canto errante*).[45] The comment also serves to explain further Darío's employment of the specific critical procedure, referred to above in the discussion of his biographical method, of uniting the man with the work and thus discovering the individuality of the figure studied. And finally, the comment also spotlights Darío's kinship with Ralph Waldo Emerson's view of the importance of conceptual exploration and renewal for which freedom and flexibility are basic pre-conditions.

The broad cultural knowledge which Darío admired in Juan Valera and aspects of the erudition which he noticed in Menéndez y Pelayo are represented in Darío's critical writings. His knowledge, however, is usually at the service of a contemporary question that has attracted his interest. In his essay 'Eugenio de Castro' (*Los raros*),[46] he displays a sure grasp of the history of Portuguese literature, and refers to French, Italian, Spanish, Latin, Greek, Biblical, English, Argentinian, and Cuban literatures in order to elaborate his study of the symbolist poet. He follows a similar procedure in his study of the Brazilian poet-diplomat, Fontaura Xavier (*Semblanzas*);[47] and he writes of erudite topics with evident relish in his essay 'Homenaje a Menéndez Pelayo' (*Cabezas*).[48] Whenever Darío traces the history of literary movements, as he does in several essays in *Los raros*, he does so while keeping his main focus on the individual artist being studied. His reluctant following of the tradition of tracing a writer's literary precursors is shown in the ironic manner in which he writes about this aspect in his later essay on Leopoldo Lugones (*Cabezas*):

> Su genealogía mental – ¡por Dios, siempre descendemos, o ascendemos, de alguien, y ha existido el Adán literario! – ¿le emparenta con cuales antecesores? Pero ningún espíritu encuentro más fraternal para el suyo que el de Edgar Poe – tanto en todo va buscando su equilibrio nuestra balanza continental.[49]

The conviction that literary activity is distinct from other intellectual activity is expressed by Darío at several stages of his career. The concept seems to represent an ideal for him which, if practised, would eliminate the kind of dilettantism against which he had inveighed in his essay 'La crítica.' He states the claim for this specialization most clearly in his article on Eugênio de Castro:

> Lo cierto es, sin embargo, que la literatura es sólo para los literatos, como las matemáticas son sólo para los matemáticos y la química para los químicos. Así como en religión sólo valen las fes puras, en arte sólo valen las opiniones de conciencia, y para tener una concienzuda opinión artística es necesario ser un artista.[50]

And more than being a distinct activity there is little doubt that Darío considered literary activity to be the loftiest of activities – 'el don del arte es un don superior'[51] and that he assumed that criticism carried out by 'una concienzuda opinión artística' would avoid the contrasts of obsequiousness on the one hand and hostility on non-literary grounds on the other which he found to bedevil so much of what passed for criticism in his own time.

Some indication of his own reaction to criticism of his work may be fitting here. He did show annoyance at the false academicians, the conservative grammarians, *ceux qui ne comprennent pas*. In the 'Dilucidaciones' introducing the *Canto errante* he declares: 'He comprendido la inanidad de la crítica. Un diplomático os censura por lo menos alabable que tenéis ... Este enemigo os cubre de flores pidiéndoos por lo bajo una limosna.'[52] He was also convinced that while there would always be poets and poetry 'lo que siempre faltará será la abundancia de los comprendedores.'[53] Darío, nevertheless, accepted with grace criticism that seemed well founded. He paid José Enrique Rodó high compliments on his criticism of *Prosas profanas*, declaring that 'ha hecho el autor de *Motivos de Proteo* una encantadora exégesis.'[54] He used Rodó's criticism, though unsigned through a printer's error as he explained, as the introduction to the second edition of the work (Paris, 1901). Also, as he reports, in the 'Dilucidaciones,' when Menéndez y Pelayo corrected an impression concerning the originality of a verse form used in the poem 'Pórtico,' 'yo aprobé. Porque siempre apruebo lo correcto, lo justo y lo bien intencionado.'[55] He regarded Paul Groussac who, as we have seen, was particularly critical of *Azul* and slightly less so of *Los raros* as one of his masters; and he described Manuel Gondra who furiously attacked *Prosas profanas*, as 'el culto y noble Gondra.'[56]

But when all of Darío's critical theories and practices are considered it might be said that he distinguished readily between what he considered to be ideal and what he considered to be practicable, and was easily prepared to accept the practicable. He preferred that criticism be free from overt socio-political involvement, that it not be authoritarian, that it not exclude the contemporary production from its scope of interest, that unity of life and work be explored, that the critic put erudition and broad culture at the service of art. Two qualities, however, kept him from the didacticism or firmness that would make precepts of his preferences: his basic belief in freedom and non-alignment and his generosity. Secure in his ability and devoted to literature, he always seemed to have an intelligent awareness of the possible value of critical orientations that were not his, and in him there was nothing small minded or vindictive. Darío imposed one unyielding condition on those who would engage in literary activity of any kind. He required that whatever they wrote be endowed with what he called, in assessing the critical writing of Juan Valera, 'distinción.'[57] The writing itself, the style of expression, should be a contribution to literary art. In short, criticism, too, should be written 'sobre las alas de los inmaculados cisnes.'[58]

The point has been often made that the bases of Darío's view of artists and their work change radically from *Los raros* to *Opiniones*. Torres Bodet, for instance, states that the artists discussed in *Los raros* were predominantly 'figuras que se destacaban más por lo insólito que por lo auténtico, y por lo episódico más que por lo perdurable ... En *Opiniones*, la situación cambia por completo.'[59] In making his point Torres Bodet is forced to regard several writers as exceptions to his statement concerning *Los raros* – Poe, Ibsen, Verlaine, José Martí, Eugênio de Castro, Villiers de L'Isle-Adam, Léon Bloy and el conde de Lautréamont. Leconte de Lisle, and Paul Adam, as well as Jean Moréas who is also dealt with in *Opiniones*, could certainly have been added to his list of exceptions. That is to say eleven of the twenty figures studied in the collection may attract attention for their 'authentic' and 'lasting' quality. On the other hand, Isadora Duncan and Henri de Groux of *Opiniones* contribute much that is 'unusual' and 'episodic.' *Opiniones* does contain a new indication, in the essay on Zola, that popularity may be an important constituent of literary glory. Describing Zola's funeral procession, he emphasizes the participation of a miner, a blacksmith, a farmer, and summarizes: '¡Esa es la gloria! Iban obreros de blusa, y niños y niñas con sus padres.'[60] But even this concept of an appreciative base that is represented in all the strata of society is avoided in Darío's later essays. Indeed the major critical notions remain the same in *Los raros* and in *Opiniones* as they do to the end of Darío's career. His basic biographical approach, his lack of faith in sociopolitical orientations, his view of the seriousness of the critical task, his belief that literary activity is the supreme activity, and his insistence that all expression in criticism as in creative writing should be of the highest order, these were the qualities that remained constant throughout his career as a literary critic. His involvement in criticism reflected a predominant interest in 'los raros' and for him 'los raros' always meant the exceptional, the distinguished, the free.[61]

Bibliography

WORKS BY RUBÉN DARÍO

Epístolas y poemas. Managua: Tipografía Nacional, 1885
Abrojos. Santiago de Chile: Imprenta Cervantes, 1887
Certamen Varela. Santiago de Chile: Imprenta Cervantes, 1887 ('Canto épico a
  las glorias de Chile,' pp. 52–66; 'Rimas,' pp. 186–96)
Azul ... Valparaíso: Imprenta y Litografía Excelsior, 1888
A. de Gilbert. San Salvador: Imprenta Nacional, 1889
Azul ... 2nd ed., enlarged. Guatemala, Imprenta de 'La Unión,' 1890
Los raros. Buenos Aires: Talleres de 'La Vasconia,' 1896
Prosas profanas y otros poemas. Buenos Aires: Imprenta Pablo E. Coni e Hijos,
  1896
España contemporánea. Paris: Garnier Hermanos, 1901
Peregrinaciones. Prologue by Justo Sierra. Paris: Librería de la Vda. de Charles
  Bouret, 1901
Prosas profanas y otros poemas. 2nd ed., enlarged. Paris: Librería de Charles
  Bouret, 1901
La caravana pasa. París: Garnier Hermanos, 1902
Tierras solares. Madrid: Leonardo Williams Editor, 1904
Cantos de vida y esperanza. Los Cisnes y otros poemas. Madrid: Tipografía de la
  Revista de Archivos, Bibliotecas y Museos, 1905
Los raros. 2nd ed., enlarged. Barcelona: Casa Editorial Maucci, 1905
Azul ... Definitive edition. Buenos Aires: Biblioteca de 'La Nación,' 1905
Opiniones. Madrid: Librería de Fernando Fe [1906]
Parisiana. Madrid: Librería de Fernando Fe [1907]
El canto errante. Madrid: M. Pérez Villavicencio Editor, 1907
El viaje a Nicaragua e Intermezzo tropical. Madrid: Biblioteca 'Ateneo,' 1909
Poema del otoño y otros poemas. Madrid: Biblioteca 'Ateneo,' 1910
Letras. Paris: Garnier Hermanos [1911]

Todo al vuelo. Madrid: Renacimiento, 1912
Canto a la Argentina y otros poemas. Madrid: Biblioteca Corona, 1914
La vida de Rubén Darío escrita por él mismo. Barcelona: Casa Editorial Maucci
  [1915]
Obras completas. 5 vols. Edited by Sanmiguel Raimúndez and Emilio Gascó
  Contell. Madrid: Afrodisio Aguado, 1950–5

COLLECTIONS

Cuentos completos. Edited by Ernesto Mejía Sánchez. Preliminary study by
  Raimundo Lida. Mexico: Fondo de Cultura Económica, 1950
Escritos dispersos de Rubén Darío. 1. Edited by Pedro Luis Barcia. La Plata:
  Facultad de Humanidades y Ciencias de Educación de la Universidad Nacional de
  la Plata, 1968
Escritos inéditos. Edited by E.K. Mapes. New York: Instituto de las Españas en los
  Estados Unidos, 1938
*Obras desconocidas de Rubén Darío, escritas en Chile y no recogidas en ninguno
  de sus libros*. Edited by Raúl Silva Castro. Santiago de Chile: Universidad de
  Chile, 1934
Páginas desconocidas de Rubén Darío. Edited by Roberto Ibáñez. Montevideo:
  Biblioteca de Marcha, 1970
Poemas escogidos. Prologue by Leopoldo Lugones. Mexico: Lectura Selecta, 1919
Poesías completas. Edited by Alfonso Méndez Plancarte and Antonio Oliver
  Belmás. Madrid: Aguilar, 1967

SOME RECENT BIBLIOGRAPHIES

Anderson, Robert Roland. *Spanish American Modernism: A Selected Bibliog-
  raphy*. Tucson: University of Arizona Press, 1970, pp. 24–61
Hebblethwaite, Frank P. 'Una bibliografía de Rubén Darío (1945–1966).' *Revista
  Interamericana de Bibliografía*, vol. 17, no. 2, April–June, 1967, 202–21
Jirón Terán, José.   *Bibliografía general de Rubén Darío (julio 1883–enero 1967)*.
  Managua: Publicaciones del Centenario de Rubén Darío, 1967
Mota, Francisco. 'Ensayo de bibliografía cubana de y sobre Rubén Darío.' *L/L*,
  Boletín del Instituto de Literatura y Lingüística, vol. 1, no. 2, April–December,
  1967, 279–302
Woodbridge, Hensley C. 'Rubén Darío: A Critical Bibliography.' *Hispania*, vol.
  50, no. 4, December 1967, 982–95; and vol. 51, no. 1, March 1968, 95–110

WORKS ON DARÍO

Abreu Gómez, Emilio. *Rubén Darío: crítico literario*. Washington: Union
  Panamericana, 1951, pp. 11–16
Agramonte, Pedro. 'Vivencia americana de Darío.' *La Torre*, Año 15, nos. 55–6,
  January–June 1967, 323–71
Aguado-Andreut, Salvador. *Por el mundo poético de Rubén Darío*. Guatemala:
  Editorial Universitaria, 1966
Aguirre, Angel Manuel. 'Relaciones amistosas entre Rubén Darío y Juan Ramón
  Jiménez.' *Quaderni Ibero-Americani*, no. 37, December 1969, 42–6

Albornoz, Aurora de. ' "A Roosevelt" un poema muy actual de Rubén Darío.'
  Cuadernos Americanos, vol. 107, no. 4, September–December 1961, 255–8
Alegría, Fernando. Walt Whitman en Hispanoamérica. Mexico: Studium, 1954,
  pp. 250–75
Alegría, J.C. et al. Rubén Darío y Ecuador. Quito: Casa de Cultura Ecuatoriana,
  1968
Alemán Bolaños, Gustavo. La juventud de Rubén Darío (1890–1893).
  Guatemala: Sánchez y De Guisse, 1923
Alonso, Amado. 'Estilística de las fuentes literarias: Rubén Darío y Miguel
  Angel.' Estudios sobre Rubén Darío. Edited by Ernesto Mejía Sánchez. Mexico:
  Fondo de Cultura Económica, 1968, pp. 368–79
Alvarez Henríquez, Dictino. Cartas de Rubén Darío. Madrid: Taurus, 1963
Anderson Imbert, Enrique. Crítica interna. Madrid: Taurus, 1960
– La originalidad de Rubén Darío. Buenos Aires: Centro Editor de América
  Latina, 1967
– Review of La poesía de Rubén Darío by Pedro Salinas. Nueva Revista de
  Filología Hispánica, vol. III, no. 1, January–March 1949, 91–3
– 'Rubén Darío and the Fantastic Element in Literature.' Translated by Anne
  Bonner. Rubén Darío Centennial Studies. Edited by Miguel González and
  George D. Schade. Austin: University of Texas, 1970, pp. 97–117
Argüello, Santiago. Modernismo y modernistas. Guatemala: Tipografía Na-
  cional, 1935
Armijo, Roberto. Rubén Darío y su intuición del mundo. San Salvador: Editorial
  Universitaria de El Salvador, 1968
Arrieta, Rafael Alberto. 'Rubén Darío y la Argentina.' La Torre, Año 15, nos.
  55–6, January–June 1967, 373–94
Arrom, José Juan. 'El oro, la pluma y la piedra preciosa: Indagaciones sobre el
  trasfondo indígena de la poesía de Darío.' Hispania, vol. 50, no. 4, December
  1967, 971–81
Augier, Angel. Cuba y Rubén Darío. Havana: Academia de Ciencias de Cuba,
  Instituto de Literatura y Lingüística, 1968
Avila, Mary. 'Principios cristianos en los cuentos de Rubén Darío.' Revista
  Iberoamericana, vol. 24, no. 47, January–June 1959, 28–39
Avrett, Robert. 'Música y efectos melódicos en "Sinfonía en gris mayor." '
  Seminario-Archivo Rubén Darío, no. 3, 1960, 33–7
Balseiro, José Agustín. Seis estudios sobre Rubén Darío. Madrid: Editorial Gre-
  dos, 1967
Baquero, Gastón. Darío, Cernuda y otros temas poéticos. Madrid: Editorial
  Nacional, 1969
Barreda-Tomás, Pedro. 'Elementos religiosos en la poesía de Rubén Darío.'
  Homenaje a Rubén Darío (1867–1967), Memoria del XIII Congreso del
  Instituto Internacional de Literatura Iberoamericana. Edited by Aníbal
  Sánchez-Reulet, Los Angeles: Centro Latinamericano, University of Califor-
  nia, Los Angeles, 1970, pp. 139–48
Bazil, Osvaldo. 'Mujeres de Rubén Darío.' El Mercurio (Santiago de Chile), 1
  February 1942
– Vidas de iluminación. La huella de Martí en Rubén Darío. Como era Rubén
  Darío. Havana: Imp. de Julio A. Arrogo y Cía, 1932

Bellini, Giuseppe. 'Rubén Darío e Italia.' *Revista Iberoamericana*, vol. 33, no. 64, July–December 1967, 367–86
Beltrán Guerrero, Luis. *Rubén Darío y Venezuela*. Caracas: Instituto Nacional de Cultura y Bellas Artes, 1967
Benedetti, Mario. *Genio y figura de José Enrique Rodó*. Buenos Aires: Eudeba, 1966
– *Letras del continente mestizo*. Montevideo: Arca Editorial, 1967, pp. 22–34
– 'Señor de los tristes.' *Casa de las Américas*, no. 42, May–June 1967, 78–80
Benítez, Rubén. 'La celebración del amor en "Primaveral" de Darío: Voz poética y tono.' *Insula*, Año 22, nos. 248–9, July–August 1967, 6, 28
– 'La expresión de la frivolidad en "Era un aire suave ... "' '*Homenaje a Rubén Darío (1867–1967)*. Edited by Aníbal Sánchez-Reulet, Los Angeles: Centro Latinoamericano, Universidad de California, Los Angeles, 1970, pp. 90–105
– 'La expresión de lo primitivo en "Estival" de Darío.' *Revista Iberoamericana*, vol. 33, no. 64, July–December 1967, 237–50
Blanco-Fombona, Rufino. *El modernismo y los poetas modernistas*. Madrid: Editorial Mundo Latino, 1929
Bonilla, Abelardo. *América y el pensamiento poético de Rubén Darío*. San José: Editorial Costa Rica, 1967
Borges, Jorge Luis. 'Mensaje en honor de Rubén Darío.' *El Despertador Americano* (Mexico), vol. 1, no. 2, May 1967, 9
Borghini, Vittorio. *Rubén Darío e il modernismo*. Genova: Pubblicazioni Dell' Instituto Universitario di Magistero, 1955
Boti, Regino E. *Martí en Darío*. Havana: Imprenta Siglo xx, 1925
Bowra, Cecil Maurice. *Inspiration and Poetry*. London: Macmillan & Co., 1955, pp. 242–64
Bowra, Cecil Maurice, Arturo Torres-Ríoseco, Luis Cernuda, and Ernesto Mejía Sánchez. *Rubén Darío en Oxford*. Managua: Academia Nicaragüense de la Lengua, 1966
Boyd, Lola E. '"Lo de dentro" en Rubén Darío.' *Hispania*, vol. 45, no. 4, December 1962, 651–7
Buitrago, Edgardo. 'Consideraciones polémicas acerca de la vigencia y actualidad de Rubén Darío.' *Repertorio Centroamericano* (San José), Año 3, nos. 7–8, May 1967, 6–19
Cabezas, Juan Antonio. *Rubén Darío: un poeta y una vida*. Madrid: Ediciones Morata, 1944
Calandrelli, Matías. 'Manera de poetizar de Rubén Darío.' *Revista de Derecho, Historia y Letras*, vol. 1, no. 2, November 1898, 54–69
– 'Prosas profanas y otros poemas de Rubén Darío.' *Revista de Derecho, Historia y Letras*, vol. 1, no. 1, October 1898, 514–29
Campos, Jorge. 'Rubén Darío y sus biógrafos.' *Insula*, Año 16, no. 170, January 1961, 11
Cano, José Luis. 'Rubén Darío y Andalucía.' *Azul* (Managua), February 1956, pp. 16–19
Capdevila, Arturo. *Rubén Darío: 'Un bardo rei.'* Buenos Aires: Espasa Calpe, 1946
Cardwell, Richard A. 'Darío and *El arte puro*: The Enigma of Life and the Beguilement of Art.' *Bulletin of Hispanic Studies*, vol. 47, 1970, 37–51

Carlos, Alberto. '*El alba de oro* en "Canción de otoño en primavera."' *Homenaje
a Rubén Darío (1867–1967)*, Memoria del XIII Congresso del Instituto Internacional de Literatura Iberoamericana. Edited by Aníbal Sánchez-Reulet. Los
Angeles: Centro Latinoamericano, University of California, Los Angeles, 1970
pp. 82–9
– '"Divagación": La geografía erótica de Rubén Darío.' *Revista Iberoamericana*,
vol. 33, no. 64, July 1967, 293–313
Carreño, Eduardo. 'Rubén Darío y la gramática.' *Revista Nacional de Cultura*,
vol. 3, no. 31, January–February 1942, 74–8
Carilla, Emilio. *Una etapa decisiva de Darío: Rubén Darío en la Argentina.*
Madrid: Editorial Gredos, 1967
Castagnino, Raúl H. '"No soy más que un hombre de arte."' *Rubén Darío:
Estudios reunidos en conmemoración del centenario (1867–1967)*. Edited by
Juan Carlos Ghiano. La Plata: Universidad Nacional de La Plata, 1968, pp.
128–37
Castañón Díaz, Jesús. 'Anotaciones de un lector para una fuente más de "Lo fatal"
de Rubén Darío.' *Estudios* (Madrid), Año 20, no. 65, April–June 1964, 325–6
Castillo, Homero. 'Caupolicán, en el modernismo de Darío.' *Revista
Iberoamericana*, vol. 19, no. 37, October–December 1953, 111–18
– 'Recursos narrativos en "El fardo."' *Atenea*, Año 44, nos. 415–16, January–
June 1967, 29–37
Castro, Humberto de. *Rubén Darío y su época*. Bogotá: Sociedad Editora de los
Andes, 1967
Concha, Jaime. 'El tema del alma en Rubén Darío.' *Atenea*, Año 44, nos. 415–16,
January–June 1967, 39–62
Contreras, Francisco. *Rubén Darío: su vida y su obra*. Barcelona: Editorial
Agencia Mundial de Librería, 1930
Cossío, José María de. 'El modelo estrófico de los "Layes, decires y canciones" de
Rubén Darío.' *Revista de Filología Española*, vol. 19, no. 2, July–September
1932, 283–7
Crema, Edoardo. 'Rodó y Rubén Darío.' *Revista Nacional de Cultura*, no. 178,
December 1966, 72–80
Crispo Acosta, Osvaldo. *Rubén Darío y José Enrique Rodó*. Montevideo: Agencia
General de Librería y Publicaciones, 1924
Cuadra, Pablo Antonio. 'Pequeña invectiva contra la rojería española.' *Lectura*
(Mexico), vol. 25, 1 November 1941, 14–22
Cupo, Oscar. 'Fuentes inéditas de *Cantos de vida y esperanza*.' *Revista del
Profesorado* (Buenos Aires), March–June 1940, 39–46
Darío III, Rubén. *Tres mujeres en la vida de Rubén Darío*. Buenos Aires: Editorial
Nova, 1966
– *Rubén Darío y los mercaderes del templo*. Buenos Aires: Editorial Nova, 1967
Darroch, Ann B. 'Rubén Darío's "Sinfonía en gris mayor": A New Interpreta-
tion.' *Hispania*, vol. 53, no. 2, May 1970, 46–52
Davison, Ned J. *The Concept of Modernism in Hispanic Criticism*. Boulder:
Pruett Press, 1966
Delgado, Jaime. 'Rubén Darío, poeta transatlántico.' *Cuadernos Hispano-
americanos*, nos. 212–213, August–September 1967, 289–331
Devoto, Daniel. 'García Lorca y Darío.' *Asomante*, vol. 23, no. 2, April–June
1967, 22–31

Díaz Arrieta, Hernán. 'El sentimiento religioso en la obra de Rubén Darío.' *La Torre*, Año 15, nos. 55–56, January–June 1967, 255–72
Díaz-Plaja, Guillermo. *Modernismo frente a noventa y ocho*. Madrid: Espasa Calpe, 1951
– '*Rubén Darío, la vida, la obra; notas críticas*. Barcelona: Sociedad General de Publicaciones, 1930
– 'Rubén Darío y Cataluña.' *La Torre*, Año 15, nos. 55–6, January–June 1967, 181–94
Diccionario enciclopédico hispanoamericano. Barcelona: Montaner y Simón, 1890
Diego, Gerardo. 'Carta.' *La Estafeta Literaria*, nos. 360–1, 14 January 1967, 41
– 'Ritmo y espíritu en Rubén Darío.' *Cuadernos Hispanoamericanos*, nos. 212–13, August–September 1967, 247–64
Diez estudios sobre Rubén Darío. Edited by Juan Loveluck. Santiago de Chile: Empresa Editora Zig Zag, 1967
Díez-Canedo, Enrique. *Juan Ramón Jiménez en su obra*. Mexico: El Colegio de México, 1944
Durand, René L.F. 'El motivo del centauro y la universalidad de Rubén Darío.' *La Torre*, Año 15, nos. 55–6, January–June 1967, 71–97
– *La Négritude dans l'œuvre poétique de Rubén Darío*. Dakar: Centre de Hautes Etudes Afro-Ibero-Americanes de L'Université de Dakar, 1970
Echavarría, Arturo. 'Estructura y sentido poético del "Coloquio de los centauros."' *La Torre*, Año 17, no. 65, July–September 1969, 95–130
Ellis, Keith. 'Un análisis estructural del poema "Venus" de Rubén Darío.' *Revista Iberoamericana*, vol. 33, no. 64, July–December 1967, 251–7
– 'Un análisis del poema "A Roosevelt."' *Cuadernos Hispanoamericanos*, nos. 212–213, August–September 1967, 523–8
Ellison, Fred P. 'Rubén Darío and Brazil.' *Hispania*, vol. 47, no. 1, March 1964, 24–34
– 'Rubén Darío y Portugal.' *Hispanófila* (Madrid), vol. 2, no. 4, September 1958, 23–33
Englekirk, John. *Edgar Allan Poe in Hispanic Literature*. New York: Instituto de las Españas en los Estados Unidos, 1934, pp. 165–210
Estudios sobre Rubén Darío. Edited by Ernesto Mejía Sánchez. Mexico: Fondo de Cultura Económica, 1968
Ferrer-Canales, José. 'La vendimia cívica.' *Homenaje a Rubén Darío* (*1867–1967*). Edited by Aníbal Sánchez Reulet. Los Angeles: Centro Latinoamericano, University of California, Los Angeles, 1970, pp. 180–9
Figueira, Gastón. 'Dos críticos de Darío.' *La Torre*, Año 15, nos. 55–6, January–June 1967, 217–28.
Fiore, Dolores Ackel. *Rubén Darío in Search of Inspiration* (*Greco-Roman Mythology in his Stories and Poetry*). New York: Las Américas Publishing Co., 1963
Flores López, Santos. *Psicología y tendencia poética en la obra de Rubén Darío*. Managua: Academia Nicaragüense de la Lengua, 1958
Florit, Eugenio. 'Modernist Prefigurement in the Early Works of Rubén Darío.' Translated by John Wilcox. *Rubén Darío Centennial Studies*. Edited by Miguel González-Gerth and George D. Schade. Austin: University of Texas, 1970
Forcadas, Alberto. 'El romancero español, Lope de Vega, Góngora y Quevedo, y

sus posibles resonancias en "Sonatina" de Rubén Darío.' *Quaderni Ibero-americani*, no. 41, December 1972, 1–6

Gaibisso, Alicia Haydée. 'Darío y las letras lusobrasileñas.' *Rubén Darío: estudios reunidos en conmemoración del centenario (1867–1967)*. Edited by Juan Carlos Ghiano. La Plata: Universidad Nacional de la Plata, 1968, pp. 497–509

García Calderón, Ventura. 'Los primeros versos de Rubén Darío.' *Revue Hispanique*, vol. 40, no. 97, June 1917, 47–53

García de Castro, Ramón. 'Rubén Darío y Asturias.' *Papeles de Son Armadans*, vol. 12, nos. 137–8, August–September 1967, 305–17

García Girón, Edmundo. 'La adjetivación modernista en Rubén Darío.' *Nueva Revista de Filología Hispánica*, vol. 13, nos. 3–4, July–December 1959, 345–51

García Lorca, Federico. *Obras completas*. Madrid: Aguilar, 1962, pp. 1717–21

Garciasol, Ramón de. *La lección de Rubén Darío*. Madrid: Taurus, 1960

Gardes, Roxana. 'Lo raro en *Los raros*.' *Rubén Darío: Estudios reunidos en conmemoración del centenario (1867–1967)*. La Plata: Universidad Nacional de La Plata, 1968, pp. 179–92

Gershator, David. 'Rubén Darío's Reflections on Manhattan: Two Poems.' *Romance Notes*, vol. 11, no. 1, Autumn 1967, 30–5

Ghiano, Juan Carlos. 'El modernismo entre América y España.' *Ramón M. del Valle-Inclán, 1866–1966*. La Plata: Universidad Nacional de la Plata, Facultad de Humanidades y Ciencias de la Educación, 1966, pp. 163–93

– 'La versión autobiográfica de Darío.' *Rubén Darío: estudios reunidos en conmemoración del centenario (1867–1967)*. Edited by Juan Carlos Ghiano. La Plata: Universidad Nacional de La Plata, 1968, pp. 29–63

Ghiraldo, Alberto. *El archivo de Rubén Darío*. Santiago de Chile: Editorial Bolívar, 1940. Second edition. Buenos Aires: Editorial Losada, 1943

Gicovate, Bernardo. *Conceptos fundamentales de literatura comparada: Iniciación de la poesía modernista*. San Juan: Asomante, 1962

– 'Dante y Darío.' *Hispania*, vol. 40, no. 1, March 1951, 29–33

– 'Lectura de un poema de Darío.' *Asomante*, vol. 23, no. 1, January–March 1967, 38–42

– 'El modernismo y su historia.' *Hispanic Review*, vol. 32, no. 2, July 1964, 217–26

Giordano, Jaime. *La edad del ensueño: Sobre la imaginación poética de Rubén Darío*. Santiago de Chile: Editorial Universitaria, 1971

Glickman, Robert Jay. 'El joven Rubén Darío en confrontación con la vida.' *Homenaje a Rubén Darío (1867–1967)*, Memoria del XIII Congreso del Instituto Internacional de Literatura Iberoamericana. Edited by Aníbal Sánchez-Reulet, Los Angeles: Centro Latinamericano, University of California, Los Angeles, 1970, pp. 169–79

Goldberg, Isaac. *Studies in Spanish-American Literature*. New York: Brentano's Publishers, 1920, pp. 101–83

Gómez Carrillo, Enrique. *De Marsella a Tokio*. Prologue by Rubén Darío. Paris: Garnier Hermanos, 1912

– *Treinta años de mi vida: Libro I, El despertar del alma*. Buenos Aires: Casa Vaccaro, 1918

– *Treinta años de mi vida: Libro III, La miseria de Madrid*. Buenos Aires: Casa Vaccaro, 1921

Gómez Paz, Julieta. 'Rubén Darío y Rosalía de Castro.' *Asomante*, no. 2, April–June 1967, 44–9

Gondra, Manuel. *Hombres y letrados de América*. Edited by J. Natalicio
González. Asunción: Editorial Guaranía, 1942, 201–40
González, Manuel Pedro. 'Deslindes indeclinables.' *Casa de las Americas*, no. 42,
May–June 1967, 36–51
– *Notas en torno al modernismo*. Mexico: Universidad Nacional Autónoma de
México, Dirección General de Publicaciones, 1958
– Review of *La poesía de Rubén Darío* by Pedro Salinas. *Hispanic Review*, vol.
17, no. 1, January 1949, 260–3
González-Blanco, Andrés. *Rubén Darío: Obras escogidas*. Madrid: Librería de los
Sucesores de Hernando, 1910
González Olmedilla, Juan. *La ofrenda de España a Rubén Darío*. Madrid: Editor-
ial América, 1916
González-Rodas, Publio. 'Rubén Darío y el conde de Lautréamont.' *Revista
Iberoamericana*, vol. 37, no. 75, April-June 1971, 375–89
Groussac, Paul. 'Los raros.' *Nosotros*, vol. 21, February 1916, 151–7
– 'Prosas profanas.' *Nosotros*, vol. 21, February 1916, 158–61
Gullón, Ricardo. *Direcciones del modernismo*. Madrid: Editorial Gredos, 1963
– 'Rubén Darío, España y los españoles.' *Asomante*, vol. 23, no. 1,
January–March 1967, 15–23
– 'Rubén Darío y el erotismo.' *Papeles de Son Armadans*, vol. 12, nos. 137–8,
August–September 1967, 143–58
– 'Pitagorismo y modernismo.' *Mundo Nuevo*, no. 7, January 1967, 22–32
Hamilton, Carlos D. 'Rubén Darío en la Isla de Oro.' *Cuadernos His-
panoamericanos*, nos. 212–13, August–September 1967, 556–73
Harrison, Helene Westbrook. *An Analytical Index of the Complete Poetical
Works of Rubén Darío*. Washington, D.C.: Microcard Editions, 1970
Henríquez Ureña, Max. *Breve historia del modernismo*. Mexico: Fondo de Cul-
tura Económica, 1962
– 'Las influencias francesas en la literatura hispanoamericana.' *Revista
Iberoamericana*, vol. 2, no. 4, November 1940, 401–17
– *El retorno de los galeones y otros ensayos*. Mexico: Ediciones Galaxia y
Ediciones de Andrea, 1963
– *Rodó y Rubén Darío*. Havana: Sociedad Editorial Cuba Contemporánea, 1918
– 'En torno a las prosas de Rubén Darío.' *La Torre*, Año 15, nos. 55 and 56,
January–June 1967, 155–77
Henríquez Ureña, Pedro. *Antología de la versificación rítmica*. San José: El
Convivio, 1918
– 'Carta a Alfonso Reyes sobre Rubén Darío.' In Ernesto Mejía Sánchez, *Cues-
tiones rubendarianas*, Madrid: Ediciones de la Revista de Occidente, 1970, 53–9
– *Literary Currents in Hispanic America*. Cambridge: Harvard University Press,
1949
– 'El modelo estrófico de los "Layes, decires y canciones" de Rubén Darío.'
Revista de Filología Española, vol. 19, no. 4, October–December 1932, 421–2
– *Obra crítica*. Edited by Emma Susana Speratti Piñero. Mexico: Fondo de
Cultura Económica, 1960, 95–105
– 'Rubén Darío.' *El Fígaro* (Havana), 16 February 1916
– 'Rubén Darío y el siglo XV.' *Revue Hispanique*, vol. 50, no. 118, December
1920, 324–7
– *La versificación irregular en la poesía española*. Madrid: Publicaciones de la
Revista de Filología Española, 1920

Huerta, Eleazar. 'Perfiles de Rubén Darío.' *Atenea*, Año 44, nos. 415–16, January–June 1967, 133–46

Huidobro, Vicente. *Obras completas*. Edited by Braulio Arenas. Santiago de Chile: Editorial Zig Zag, 1964, I, 728

Hurtado Chamorro, Alejandro. *La mitología griega en Rubén Darío*. Avila: Editorial La Muralla, 1967

Ibarra, Fernando. 'Clarín y Rubén Darío: historia de una incomprensión.' *Hispanic Review*. vol. 41, no. 3, Summer 1973, 524–40

Irving, Evelyn Uhrhan. 'Narciso Tondreau: Close Friend of Rubén Darío in Chile.' *Hispania*, vol. 52, no. 5, December 1969, 864–7

– 'Rubén Darío's First Days in Guatemala.' *Hispania*, vol. 46, no. 2, May 1963, 319–22

– 'Rubén Darío in Guatemala.' *Kentucky Foreign Language Quarterly*, vol. 10, no. 1, March 1963, 14–19

Irving, Thomas. 'San Marcos de Colón: Rastros de la niñez de Rubén Darío.' *Revista Iberoamericana*, vol. 20, no. 40, April–September 1955, 311–22

Jackson, Richard L. 'La presencia negra en la obra de Rubén Darío.' *Revista Iberoamericana*, vol. 33, no. 64, July–December 1967, 395–417

Jiménez, Juan Ramón. *Antología poética*. Madrid: Editorial Magisterio Español, 1968, 105–6

– *El modernismo: notas de un curso (1953)*. Mexico: Aguilar, 1962

Kelin, Fiodor. 'Rubén Darío.' *Estudios sobre Rubén Darío*. Edited by Ernesto Mejía Sánchez. Mexico: Fondo de Cultura Económica, 1968, 181–5

Larrea, Juan. 'Rubén Darío contra Bolívar?' *Repertorio Americano*, no. 906, 11 January 1941, 17–20

– 'Vaticinio de Rubén Darío.' *Cuadernos Americanos*. vol. 1, no. 4, October–December 1942, 213–38

Lazar, Moshé. '*Eros y cronos* en la poesía de Rubén Darío: proyección poética de una dualidad.' Translated by Fidel Coloma. *Revista conservadora del pensamiento centroamericano*, vol. 15, no. 71, August 1966, 1–17

Lázaro, Angel. 'El indigenismo de Rubén Darío.' *Managua (Diario nicaragüense)*, 22 March 1960

Leal, Luis. 'Darío en México.' *Estudios sobre Rubén Darío*. Edited by Ernesto Mejía Sánchez. Mexico: Fondo de Cultura Económica, 1968, 118–24

Ledesma, Roberto. *Genio y figura de Rubén Darío*. Buenos Aires: Editorial Universitaria de Buenos Aires, 1964

Levy, Kurt L. Review of *Rubén Darío: 'bajo el divino imperio de la música'* by Erika Lorenz. *Modern Language Quarterly*, vol. 18, no. 3, September 1957, 226–67

Libro de oro. Semana de centenario de Rubén Darío. Managua: Editorial Nicaragüense, 1967

Lida, Raimundo. 'Desde Rubén.' *Asomante*, vol. 23, no. 2, April–June 1967, 7–21

– 'Notas al casticismo de Rubén.' *Revista Iberoamericana*, vol. 33, no. 64, July–December 1967, 333–58

– 'Rubén y su herencia.' *La Torre*, Año 15, nos. 55–6, January–June 1967, 287–308

Lihn, Enrique. 'Varadero de Rubén Darío.' *Casa de las Américas*, no. 42, May–June 1967, 21–38

López Estrada, Francisco. *Rubén Darío y la edad media (Una perspectiva poco conocida sobre la vida y la obra del escritor)*. Barcelona: Editorial Planeta, 1971

López Morilla, Juan. 'El *Azul* de Rubén Darío. ¿Galicismo mental o lingüistico?' *Revista Hispánica Moderna*, vol. 10, no. 1, January 1944, 9–14

Lorenz, Erika. *Rubén Darío: 'bajo el divino imperio de la música.'* Translated by Fidel Coloma González. Managua: Ediciones de la Academia Nicaragüense de la Lengua, 1960

Loveluck, Juan. 'Rubén Darío y el modernismo en *La Biblioteca.*' *La Torre*, Año 15, nos. 55–6, January–June 1967, 229–51

– 'Rubén Darío y sus primeros críticos (1888–1900).' *Revista Iberoamericana*, vol. 33, no. 64, July-December 1967, 209–35

Machado, Manuel and Antonio. *Obras completas*. Madrid: Editorial Plenitud, 1962, 851–2

Maiorana, María Teresa. *Rubén Darío y el mito del centauro*. Buenos Aires: Casa Editora Coni, 1961

Maldonado de Guevara, Francisco. 'La función del alejandrino francés en el alejandrino español de Rubén Darío.' *Revista de Literatura*, vol. 4, no. 7, July–December 1953, 9–58

– 'Un soneto de Rubén Darío.' *Seminario-Archivo Rubén Darío*, no. 1, 1961, 5–12

Mapes, Erwin K. *L'influence française dans l'œuvre de Rubén Darío*. Paris: Libraire Ancienne Honoré Champion, 1925

– 'Innovation and French Influence in the Metrics of Rubén Darío.' *Publications of the Modern Language Association of America*, vol. 49, no. 1, January 1934, 310–26

– 'Los primeros alejandrinos de Rubén Darío.' *Revista Hispánica Moderna*, vol. 1, no. 4, July 1935, 241–59

– Review of *La dramática vida de Rubén Darío* (first edition) by Edelberto Torres. *Hispanic Review*, vol. 21, no. 2, April 1953, 249–51

Marasso, Arturo. 'La poesía "Lo fatal" de Rubén Darío.' *Revista de Educación* (Buenos Aires), Año 4, no. 2, February 1959, 348–56

– *Rubén Darío y su creación poética*. Buenos Aires: Editorial Kapelusz, 1954

Marinello, Juan. *José Martí, escritor americano*. Mexico: Editorial Grijablo, 1958

– *Sobre el modernismo: Polémica y definición*. Mexico: Universidad Nacional Autónoma de México. Dirección General de Publicaciones, 1959

– 'Rubén Darío: Meditación de centenario.' *L/L*, Año 1, no. 2, April–December 1967, 15–32

Marrero Suárez, Vicente. *Nuestro Rubén*. Madrid: Ediciones Cultura Hispánica, 1970

Martín, Carlos. *América en Rubén Darío*. Madrid: Editorial Gredos, 1972

Mejía Sánchez, Ernesto. 'El caso Martí-Whitman-Darío.' *Casa de las Américas*, no. 42, May–June 1967, 52–7

– *Cuestiones rubendarianas*. Madrid: Ediciones de la Revista de Occidente, 1970

– 'Las humanidades de Rubén Darío. Años de aprendizaje.' *Libro jubilar de Alfonso Reyes*. Mexico: Universidad Nacional Autónoma de México, 1956, 243–63

– *Los primeros cuentos de Rubén Darío*. Mexico: Universidad Nacional Autónoma de México, 1962

Mendes Campos, Mario. *Ruben Dario e o Modernismo Hispano-Americano*.

Belo Horizonte: Publicações da Secretaria da Educação de Estado de Minas
   Gerais, 1968
Miró, Rodrigo. 'Rubén Darío en Panamá.' *Estudios sobre Rubén Darío*. Edited by
   Ernesto Mejía Sánchez. Mexico: Fondo de Cultura Económica, 1968, 279–83
Monguió, Luis. 'El origen de unos versos de "A Roosevelt."' *Hispania*, vol. 38,
   no. 3, September 1955, 424–5
– 'Sobre la caracterización del Modernismo.' *Revista Iberoamericana*, vol. 7, no.
   13, November 1943, 69–80
Montagne, Edmundo. 'Rubén Darío en Costa Rica.' *El Hogar* (San José), 13
   February 1920
Morales, Angel Luis. *La angustia metafísica en la poesía de Rubén Darío*. Río
   Piedras: Biblioteca de Extramuros, Universidad de Puerto Rico, 1967
Navarro, Joaquina. 'Ritmo y sentido en "Canción de otoño en primavera."'
   Thesaurus, vol. 24, no. 3, September–December 1969, 408–16
Navarro Tomás, Tomás. 'La cantidad silábica en unos versos de Rubén Darío.'
   Revista de Filología Española, vol. 9, no. 1, January–March 1922, 1–29
– *Estudios de fonología española*. Syracuse: Syracuse University Press, 1946,
   178–90
– 'Ritmo y armonía en los versos de Darío.' *La Torre*, Año 15, nos. 55–6,
   January–June 1967, 49–69
Neale-Silva, Eduardo. 'Rubén Darío y la plasticidad.' *Atenea*, Año 44, nos.
   415–16, January–June 1967, 193–208
Neruda, Pablo. *Obras completas*. Buenos Aires: Editorial Losada, 1962
– 'R.D.' *Homenaje a Rubén Darío (1867–1967)*. Edited by Aníbal
   Sánchez-Reulet. Los Angeles: Centro Latinoamericano, University of Califor-
   nia, Los Angeles, 1970, pp. 296–8
Núñez, Estuardo. 'La imaginería oriental exotista en Rubén Darío.' *Homenaje a
   Rubén Darío*. Lima: Universidad Nacional Mayor de San Marcos, Instituto de
   Literatura, 1967, 52–61
Núñez, Zulma. 'Rubén Darío recordado por su hijo.' *Argentina Libre*, 6 February
   1941, p. 9
Oliver Belmás, Antonio. 'Los americanismos en Rubén Darío.' *Papeles de Son
   Armadans*, vol. 12, nos. 137–8, August–September 1967, 287–304
– 'La dislocación acentual en la poesía de Rubén Darío.' *Cuadernos His-
   panoamericanos*, nos. 212–13, August–September 1967, 405–9
– 'El hispanismo mental de Rubén Darío.' *La Torre*, Año 15, nos. 55–6, January–
   June 1967, 195–202
– *Este otro Rubén Darío*. Barcelona: Editorial Aedos, 1960
– 'Lo social en Rubén Darío.' *Asomante*, vol. 23, no. 1, January–March 1967,
   58–62
Onís, Federico de. *España en América*. Río Piedras: Ediciones de la Universidad de
   Puerto Rico, 1955
Ory, Eduardo de. *Rubén Darío*. Cádiz: Tipografía Comercial, 1917
Oyarzún, Luis, Eleazar Huerta, Jaime Concha, Raúl Silva Castro, Fernando
   Alegría, Mario Rodríguez Fernández, Hugo Montes, and Luis Iñigo Madrigal.
   Darío. Santiago: Departamento de Extensión, Universidad de Chile, 1968
Pagés Larraya, Antonio. 'Estructura y sentido en un soneto de Darío.' *Hispania*,
   vol. 53, no. 2, May 1970, 181–8
– 'Revelación y mito en un soneto de Darío.' *Revista Iberoamericana*, vol 35, no.
   69, September–December 1969, 441–58

Pantorba, Bernardino de. *La vida y el verbo de Rubén Darío*. Madrid: Compañia Bibliográfica Española, 1967

Paz, Octavio. *Cuadrivio*. Mexico: Editorial Joaquín Mortiz, 1965, 9–65

Paz Castillo, Fernando. *Con Rubén Darío*. Caracas: Instituto de Bellas Artes, 1967

Pedro, Valentín de. *Vida de Rubén Darío*. Buenos Aires: Compañía General Fabril Editora, 1961

Pemán, José María. 'En respuesta a la salutación de Rubén Darío.' *Domingo* (Mexico), 14 July 1940

Pereira Rodríguez, José. 'Cuando Rubén Darío vino al Uruguay.' *Seminario-Archivo de Rubén Darío*, no. 5, 1961, 21–5

Pérez, Ramón Andrés. *Permanencia de Rubén Darío*. Charlotte, N.C.: Heritage Printers, 1967

Phillips, Allen W. 'El oro de Mallorca: Textos desconocidos y breve comentario sobre la novela autobiográfica de Darío.' *Revista Iberoamericana*, vol. 33, no. 64, July–December 1967, 444–92

– 'Releyendo *Prosas profanas*.' *Insula*, Año 22, nos. 248–9, July–August 1967, 11–12

– 'Rubén Darío and Valle Inclán: The Story of a Literary Friendship.' Translated by Esther W. Phillips. *Rubén Darío Centennial Studies*. Edited by Miguel González-Gerth and George D. Schade. Austin: University of Texas, 1970, 49–83

– 'Rubén Darío y sus juicios sobre el modernismo.' *Revista Iberoamericana*, vol. 24, no. 47, January–June 1959, 41–64

– 'Sobre "Sinfonía en gris mayor" de Rubén Darío.' *Cuadernos Americanos*, vol. 113, no. 6, November–December 1960, 217–24

Picado, Teodoro. *Rubén Darío en Costa Rica (1891–1892)*. San José: G. Monge, 1919–20

Pineda, Rafael. 'Darío y América.' *Insula*, Año 16, no. 170, January 1961, 13

Pinilla Ecijo, Mercedes. 'La métrica en Rubén Darío.' Dissertation. University of Madrid, 1957

Polidori, Erminio. 'Rubén Darío en Mallorca.' *Actas del Congreso Internacional de Hispanistas*, III. Mexico: El Colegio de México, 1970, 695–714

Portuondo, José Antonio. 'Cronología del modernismo.' *L/L*, Año 1, no. 2, April–December 1967, 9–14

– *El heroísmo intelectual*. Mexico: Tezontle, 1955

– 'Martí y Darío: polos del modernismo.' *Casa de las Américas*, no. 42, May-June 1967, 68–72

– Review of *Rubén Darío en Oxford* by C.M. Bowra *et al. L/L*, Año 1, no. 2, April–December 1967, 307–9

Predmore, M.P. 'A Stylistic Analysis of "Lo fatal."' *Hispanic Review*, vol. 39, no. 4, October 1971, 443–8

Pucciani, Oreste. 'An Interview with Jean-Paul Sartre.' *Tulane Drama Review*, vol. 5, no. 3, March 1961, 12–18

Pueyo Casáus, María Pilar. 'Dante y Rubén Darío.' *Seminario–Archivo de Rubén Darío*, no. 10, 1965, 113–18

Punte, María Luisa. 'El poema prólogo a *Cantos de vida y esperanza*.' *Rubén Darío: Estudios reunidos en conmemoración del centenario (1867–1967)*. Edited by Juan Carlos Ghiano. La Plata: Universidad Nacional de la Plata, 1968, pp. 168–75

Rama, Angel. *Rubén Darío y el modernismo*. Caracas: Ediciones de la Biblioteca de la Universidad Central de Venezuela, 1970
Rangel Baez, C. 'The Poetry of Ideas in Darío and Nervo.' *Inter America*, vol. 8, no. 1, October 1924, 29–38
Reichardt, Dieter. 'Rubén Darío y Alemania.' *Papeles* (Caracas), no. 4, May–July 1967, 173–82
Reyes, Alfonso, 'Rubén Darío en México.' *Estudios sobre Rubén Darío*. Edited by Ernesto Mejía Sánchez. Mexico: Fondo de Cultura Económica, 1968, 14–26
– *Obras completas*, vol. xiv. Edited by Ernesto Mejía Sánchez. Mexico: Fondo de Cultura Económica, 1962
– 'Tres puntos de exegética literaria.' *Revista de Literatura Mexicana*, vol. 1, no. 1, July–September 1940, 8–23
Reyes Huete, Alejandro. *Darío en su prosa*. Granada, Nicaragua: Editorial Hospicio, 1960
Rodó, José Enrique. *Obras completas*. Edited by Emir Rodríguez Monegal. Madrid: Aguilar, 1967
Rodríguez Demorizi, Emilio. *Rubén Darío y sus amigos dominicanos*. Bogotá: Ediciones Espiral, 1948
Rodríguez Monegal, Emir. 'Encuentros con Rubén Darío.' *Mundo Nuevo*, no. 7, January 1967, 5–21
Rull, Enrique. 'El símbolo de psique en la poesía de Rubén Darío.' *Revista de Literatura*, vol 27, nos. 53–4, January–June 1965, 33–50
Saavedra Molina, Julio. 'Los hexámetros castellanos y en particular los de Rubén Darío.' *Anales de la Universidad de Chile*, vol. 93, no. 18, April–June 1935, 5–90
– 'El verso que no cultivó Rubén Darío.' *Anales de la Universidad de Chile*, vol. 91, no. 12, October–December 1933, 33–61
Sainz de Robles, Federico Carlos. 'El postizo afrancesamiento de Rubén Darío.' *La Torre*, Año 15, nos. 55–6, January–June 1967, 203–14
Salgado, María. 'El retrato como crítica literaria en *Los raros*.' *Romance Notes*, vol. 11, no. 1, Autumn 1969, 30–5
Salinas, Pedro. *La poesía de Rubén Darío : Ensayo sobre el tema y los temas del poeta*. Buenos Aires: Editorial Losada, 1948
Sánchez, Juan Francisco. 'De la métrica en Rubén Darío.' *Anales de la Universidad de Santo Domingo*, vol. 19, nos. 69–70, 1954, 65–94
Sánchez-Castañer, Francisco. 'Andalucía y Rubén Darío.' *Literatura de la emancipación hispanoamericana y otros ensayos*. Memoria del xv Congreso del Instituto Internacional de Literatura Iberoamericana. Lima: Universidad Nacional Mayor de San Marcos, Dirección Universitaria de Biblioteca y Publicaciones, 1972, pp. 132–7
– 'Huellas épicas en la poesía de Rubén Darío.' *Revista de la Universidad de Madrid*, vol. 19, no. 75, 1970, 221–47
Schrader, Ludwig. 'Rubén Darío, crítico en *Los raros*.' *El ensayo y la crítica en Hispanoamérica*, Memoria del xiv Congreso Internacional de Literatura Iberoamericana. Edited by Kurt L. Levy and Keith Ellis. Toronto, 1970, pp. 95–9
Schulman, Ivan A. *Génesis del modernismo*. Mexico: El Colegio de México, 1966
Schulman, Ivan and Manuel Pedro González. *Martí, Darío y el modernismo*. Madrid: Editorial Gredos, 1969

Segall, Brenda. 'The Function of Irony in "El rey burgués."' *Hispania*, vol. 49, no. 2, May 1966, 223–7

Sequeira, Diego Manuel. *Rubén Darío criollo: o raíz y médula de su creación poética*. Buenos Aires: Editorial Guillermo Kraft, 1945

– *Rubén Darío criollo en El Salvador*. León: Editorial Hospicio, 1965

Silva Castro, Raúl. '?Es posible definir el modernismo?' *Cuadernos Americanos*, vol. 141, July–August 1965, 172–9

– *Rubén Darío a los veinte años* (second edition). Santiago de Chile: Editorial Andrés Bello, 1966

Skyrme, Raymond. 'The Meaning and Function of Music in Rubén Darío: A Comparative Approach.' Dissertation. University of Michigan, 1969

Sol, Ildo. *Rubén Darío y las mujeres*. Managua: Editorial La Estrella de Nicaragua, 1948

Soto Vergés, Rafael. 'Rubén y el neoclasicismo.' *Cuadernos Hispanoamericanos*, nos. 212–13, August–September 1967, 462–71

Suárez Wilson, Reyna. 'Los prólogos de Darío.' *Rubén Darío: Estudios reunidos en conmemoración del centenario (1867–1967)*. La Plata: Universidad Nacional de La Plata, 1968, pp. 128–37

Taupin, Sidonia C. ' ¿Había leído Darío a Lautréamont cuando lo incluyó en *Los raros*?' *Comparative Literature*, vol. 11, no. 2, Spring 1959, 165–70

Tomás McNamee, Catalina. *El pensamiento católico de Rubén Darío* (Extracto de la tesis doctoral del mismo título). Madrid: Facultad de Filosofía y Letras de la Universidad de Madrid, 1967

Torre, Antonio M de la. 'Consideraciones sobre la actitud político-social de Rubén Darío.' *Revista Iberoamericana*, vol. 19, no. 38, January 1954, 261–72

Torre, Guillermo de. 'Rubén Darío, prosista.' *La Torre*, Año 15, nos. 55 and 56, January–June 1967, 135–54

–*Vigencia de Rubén Darío y otras páginas*. Madrid: Ediciones Guadarrama, 1969

Torres, Edelberto. *La dramática vida de Rubén Darío* (third edition). Mexico: Editorial Grijalbo, 1958

– 'Introducción a la poesía social de Rubén Darío.' *Humanismo* (Mexico), Año 6, nos. 50–1, July–October 1958, 74–87

Torres Bodet, Jaime. *Rubén Darío: Abismo y cima*. Mexico: Universidad Nacional Autónoma de México, 1966

Torres-Ríoseco, Arturo. 'Nueva evaluación de Rubén Darío.' *La Torre*, Año 15, nos. 55–6, January–June 1967, 121–31

– *Nueva historia de la gran literatura iberoamericana*. Buenos Aires: Emecé Editores, 1960

– *Precursores del modernismo*. New York: Las Américas Publishing Co., 1963

– 'Casticismo en la obra de Darío: Resurrecciones e innovaciones métricas.' *Revista Americana de Buenos Aires*, February 1922, 117–47

– *Rubén Darío. Casticismo y americanismo*. Cambridge, Mass: Harvard University Press, 1931

– 'Rubén Darío y la crítica.' *Hispania*, vol. 14, no. 1, February 1931, 99–106

– *Vida y poesía de Rubén Darío*. Buenos Aires, Emecé Editores, 1944

Toti, Gianni. 'Hipótesis cuadricontinental.' *Casa de las Américas*, Año 7, no. 42, May–June, 1967, 59–67

Trend, John Brand. '*Res metricae* de Rubén Darío' *Libro jubilar de Alfonso Reyes*.
    Mexico: Universidad Nacional Autónoma de México, 1956, 383–90
Trueblood, Alan S. 'Rubén Darío: The Sea and the Jungle.' *Comparative Litera-
    ture Studies*. vol. 4, no. 4, December 1967, 425–56
Turner, John. 'Sobre el uso de los tiempos verbales en Rubén Darío.' *Revista
    Hispánica Moderna*, vol. 30, nos. 3–4, July–October 1964, 205–14
Vallejo, César. *Los heraldos negros*. Buenos Aires: Editorial Losada, 1961, 88
Vanegas, Juan de Dios and Alfonso Valle. *Nacimiento y primera infancia de
    Rubén Darío*. Managua: Ediciones del Club del Libro Nicaragüense, 1962
Vargas Vila, José María. *Rubén Darío*. Madrid: V.H. de Sanz Calleja, Editores,
    1917
Watland, Charles D. *Poet-errant: A Biography of Rubén Darío*. New York:
    Philosophical Library, 1965
Ycaza Tigerino, Julio. *Los Nocturnos de Rubén Darío y otros ensayos*. Managua:
    Imprenta Granada, 1954
Ycaza Tigerino, Julio and Eduardo Zepeda-Henríquez. *Estudio de la poética de
    Rubén Darío*. Managua: Comisión Nacional del Centenario, 1967, 7–52
Yurkievich, Saúl. 'Rubén Darío, precursor de la vanguardia. *Literatura de la
    emancipación hispanoamericana y otros ensayos*. 'Memoria del XV Congreso
    del Instituto Internacional de Literatura Iberoamericana. Lima: Universidad
    Nacional Mayor de San Marcos, Dirección Universitaria de Biblioteca y Pub-
    licaciones, 1972, 117–31
Zardoya, Concha. 'Rubén Darío y la fuente.' *Asomante*, vol. 23, no. 1,
    January–March 1967, 7–14
– 'Rubén Darío y "La poesía castellana."' *Papeles de Son Armadans*, vol. 12,
    nos. 137–8, August–September 1967, 229–71

OTHER WORKS

Abrams, Meyer. *A Glossary of Literary Terms*. New York: Rinehart and Co.,
    1957
Ayala, Francisco. *Hacia una semblanza de Quevedo*. Santander: Editorial Bedia,
    1969
Bachelard, Gaston. *Lautréamont*. Paris: J. Coti, 1939
Borges, Jorge Luis. *Discusión*. Buenos Aires: Emecé, 1957
– *Otras inquisiciones*. Buenos Aires: Emecé, 1960
Bowra, Cecil Maurice. *Poetry and Politics 1900–1960*. Cambridge: Cambridge
    University Press, 1966
Brecht, Bertolt. 'Theatre for Learning.' *Tulane Drama Review*, vol. 6, no. 1,
    September 1960, 18–25
Coleridge, Samuel Taylor. *Biographia literaria*. London: George Bell & Sons,
    1894
Dahlström, Carl W.L. 'The Analysis of the Literary Situation.' *Publications of
    the Modern Language Association*, vol. 51, no. 3, September 1936, 872–89
Dictionary of World Literary Terms. Edited by Joseph T. Shipley. Boston: The
    Writer, Inc., 1970
Edel, Leon. *Literary Biography* (The Alexander Lectures 1955–6). Toronto:
    University of Toronto Press, 1957
Eliot, T.S. *Selected Essays 1917–1932*. New York: Harcourt Brace, 1932

– *Selected Prose*. Edited by John Hayward. Harmondsworth: Penguin Books, 1959

Ellis, Keith. 'Cervantes and Ayala's *El rapto*: The Art of Reworking a Story.' *Publications of the Modern Language Association of America*, vol. 84, no. 1, January 1969, 14–19

–'Concerning the Question of Influence.' *Hispania*, vol. 55, no. 2, May 1972, 340–2

– 'Poema xx': A Structural Approach.' *Romance Notes*, vol. 11, no. 3, Spring 1970, 507–17

Encyclopedia of Poetry and Poetics. Edited by Alex Preminger, Princeton: Princeton University Press, 1965

Garaudy, Roger. *D'Un Réalisme sans rivages*. Paris: Libraire Plon, 1963

Jakobson, Roman and Lévi-Strauss, Claude. '"Les Chats" de Charles Baudelaire.' *L'Homme*, vol. 2, no. 1, January–April 1967, 5–21

Johnson, Samuel. *Johnson on Shakespeare*. Edited by Walter Raleigh. London: Oxford University Press, 1925

Kayser, Wolfgang. *Interpretación y análisis de la obra literaria*. Madrid: Editorial Gredos, 1958

Literatura hispanoamericana. Edited by Enrique Anderson Imbert and Eugenio Florit. New York: Holt, Rinehart & Winston, 1960

Lukács, Georg. *The Meaning of Contemporary Realism*. Translated by John and Necke Mander. London: Merlin Press, 1962

Mao Tse-tung. *An Anthology of his Writings*. Edited by Anne Fremantle. New York: New American Library of World Literature, 1962

Mariátegui, José Carlos. *Siete ensayos de interpretación de la realidad peruana*. Lima: Biblioteca Amauta, 1928

Martin, Wallace. 'The Hermeneutic Circle and the Art of Interpretation.' *Comparative Literature*, vol. 24, no. 2, Spring 1972, 97–117

Michelangelo. *Rime*. Florence: Renascimento del Libro, 1944

Peña, Lynherst. 'Trends of Literary Criticism in Spanish America (1900–1950).' Dissertation. University of Toronto, 1970

Richards, I.A. *Science and Poetry*. London: Kegan Paul, 1926

Riffaterre, Michael. "Describing Poetic Structures: Two Approaches to Baudelaire's 'Les Chats'." *Structuralism, Yale French Studies*, Nos. 36–37, October 1966, pp. 200–242.

Sainte-Beuve, Charles. *Nouveaux Lundis*. Paris: Michel Lévy Frères, 1865

Strachey, Giles Lytton. *Eminent Victorians*. London: Chatto & Windus, 1948

Valdés, Mario. *Death in the Literature of Unamuno*. Urbana: University of Illinois Press, 1962

Wellek, René and Austin Warren. *Theory of Literature*. New York: Harcourt, Brace, 1949.

Wimsatt, Jr., William Kurtz. *The Verbal Icon*. Lexington: University of Kentucky Press, 1954.

Wimsatt Jr., W.K. and Cleanth Brooks. *Literary Criticism: A Short History*. New York: Alfred A. Knopf, 1962.

Notes

CHAPTER ONE

1 Giles Lytton Strachey, *Eminent Victorians*, London: Chatto & Windus, 1948, p. vi
2 Quoted by W.K. Wimsatt and Cleanth Brooks, *Literary Criticism: A Short History*, New York: Alfred A. Knopf, 1962, p. 535. The original French text may be consulted in Sainte-Beuve, *Nouveaux Lundis*, III, Paris: Michel Lévy Frères, 1865, pp. 15, 28.
3 Rubén Darío, *Obras completas*, 1, Madrid: Afrodisio Aguado, 1950, pp. 179–92
4 *Obras completas*, IV, 872–82
5 *Obras completas*, V, 861–5
6 *Obras completas*, II, 622–9
7 *Obras completas*, V, 901–3
8 See Allen W. Phillips, 'El oro de Mallorca : Textos desconocidos y breve comentario sobre la novela autobiográfica de Darío,' *Revista Iberoamericana*, vol. 33, no. 64, July–December 1967, pp. 444–92 ; and *Páginas desconocidas de Rubén Darío*, edited by Roberto Ibáñez, Montevideo: Biblioteca de Marcha, 1970, pp. 180–219
9 *Obras completas*, V, 1021–30
10 *Obras completas*, I, 17
11 Ibid., p. 123
12 Ibid., p. 98
13 Ibid., pp. 61, 140. For an excellent article on Darío's view of his own career see Juan Carlos Ghiano (ed.), 'La versión autobiográfica de Darío,' in *Rubén Darío: estudios reunidos en conmemoración del centenario (1867–1967)*, La Plata: Universidad Nacional de La Plata, 1968, pp. 29–63
14 Enrique Gómez Carrillo, *Obras completas*, XVII, Madrid: Editorial Mundo Latino, pp. 195–202. For the first biography of Darío, published in the *Diccionario enciclopédico hispanoamericano*, VII, Barcelona: Montaner y Simón, 1890, pp. 99–100, see Ernesto Mejía Sánchez, *Cuestiones rubendarianas*, Madrid: Ediciones de la Revista de Occidente, 1970, pp. 32–3.
15 See, for example, Carlos D. Hamilton, 'Rubén Darío en la Isla de Oro,' *Cuadernos*

Hispanoamericanos, Nos. 212–13, August–September 1967, pp. 556–73, for evidence to the contrary.

16 Enrique Gómez Carrillo, *Treinta años de mi vida*: Libro I, *El despertar del alma*, Buenos Aires: Casa Vaccaro [1918], p. 217

17 *Treinta años de mi vida*: Libro III, *La miseria de Madrid*, Buenos Aires: Casa Vaccaro, 1921, p. 119

18 *El despertar del alma*, p. 222

19 *Rubén Darío*, Cádiz: Tipografía Comercial [1917]

20 *Rubén Darío*, Madrid: V.H. de Sanz Calleja, Editores, 1917

21 *Rubén Darío: su vida y su obra*, Barcelona: Editorial Agencia Mundial de Librería, 1930

22 *Vida y poesía de Rubén Darío*, Buenos Aires, Emecé Editores, 1944

23 Cambridge, Mass.: Harvard University Press, 1931

24 Santiago de Chile: Editorial Bolívar, 1940

25 Buenos Aires: Editorial Losada, 1943

26 Madrid: Ediciones Morata, 1944. Cabezas's procedure is quite similar to that of Arturo Capdevila in his *Rubén Darío*: '*Un bardo rei*,' Buenos Aires: Espasa Calpe, 1946.

27 *Cabezas*, p. 113

28 *La dramática vida de Rubén Darío*, Guatemala: Editorial del Ministro de Educación Pública, 1952, p. 9

29 *La dramática vida de Rubén Darío* (third edition), Mexico: Editorial Grijalbo, 1958

30 In his review of the book in *Hispanic Review*, vol. 21, no. 2, April 1953, 249–51

31 See, for example, his account of Darío's writing of 'Salutación del optimista,' *La dramática vida* (first edition), p. 291.

32 Barcelona: Grijalbo, 1966

33 *Este otro Rubén Darío*, Barcelona: Editorial Aedos, 1960, p. 452

34 *Poet-errant: A Biography of Rubén Darío*, New York: Philosophical Library, 1965

35 *Rubén Darío: Abismo y cima*, Mexico: Universidad Nacional Autónoma de México, 1966

36 Buenos Aires: Centro Editor de América Latina, 1967

37 For other volumes devoted to Darío's life and works, see Valentín de Pedro, *Vida de Rubén Darío*, Buenos Aires: Compañía de General Fabril Editora, 1961; and Bernardino de Pantorba, *La vida y el verbo de Rubén Darío*, Madrid: Compañía Bibliográfica Española, 1967.

38 Juan de Dios Vanegas and Alfonso Valle, *Nacimiento y primera infancia de Rubén Darío*, Managua: Ediciones del Club del Libro Nicaragüense, 1962. For studies that assert Darío's Nicaraguan identity, see Julio Ycaza Tigerino, 'Lo étnico y lo telúrico,' in his *Estudio de la poética de Rubén Darío*, Managua: Comisión Nacional del Centenario, 1967, pp. 255–300; and Ernesto Mejía Sánchez, 'El nicaragüense Rubén Darío,' *Cuestiones rubendarianas*, pp. 9–31; and 'En su Nicaragua natal,' ibid., pp. 129–36.

39 *Rubén Darío criollo: o raíz y médula de su creación poética*, Buenos Aires: Editorial Guillermo Kraft Ltd., 1945; and *Rubén Darío criollo en El Salvador*, León: Editorial Hospicio, 1965

40 *La juventud de Rubén Darío (1890–1893)*, Guatemala: Sánchez y De Guisse, 1923; Second edition, Guatemala: Editorial Universitaria, 1958

41 'San Marcos de Colón: Rastros de la niñez de Rubén Darío,' *Revista Iberoamericana*, vol. 20, no. 40, April–September 1955, 311–22

42 'Rubén Darío's First Days in Guatemala,' *Hispania*, vol. 46, no. 2, May 1963, 319–22; and, 'Rubén Darío in Guatemala,' *Kentucky Foreign Language Quarterly*, vol. 10, no. 1, March 1963, 14–19

43 'Las humanidades de Rubén Darío: Años de aprendizaje,' *Libro jubilar de Alfonso Reyes*, Mexico: Universidad Nacional Autónoma de México, 1956, pp. 243–63; *Los primeros cuentos de Rubén Darío*, Mexico: Studium, 1951, and 'Darío y Centroamérica,' *Revista Iberoamericana*, vol. 33, no. 64, July–December 1967, 189–208. These works have been reprinted in Mejía Sánchez's *Cuestiones rubendarianas*, pp. 137–60 and pp. 161–268, respectively.

44 *Rubén Darío a los veinte años* (second edition), Santiago de Chile: Editorial Andrés Bello, 1966

45 'Los primeros versos de Rubén Darío,' *Revue Hispanique*, vol. 40, no. 97, June 1917, 47–53. See also Robert Jay Glickman, 'El joven Rubén Darío en confrontación con la vida,' in *Homenaje a Rubén Darío (1867–1967)*, Memoria del xiii Congreso del Instituto Internacional de Literatura Iberoamericana, edited by Aníbal Sánchez-Reulet, Los Angeles: Centro Latinoamericano, University of California, Los Angeles, 1970, pp. 169–79.

46 Emilio Carilla, *Una etapa decisiva de Darío: Rubén Darío en la Argentina*, Madrid: Editorial Gredos, 1967; Rafael Alberto Arrieta, 'Rubén Darío y la Argentina,' *La Torre*, nos. 55–6, January–June 1967, 373–94; Pedro Luis Barcia, 'Rubén Darío en la Argentina,' *Escritos dispersos de Rubén Darío*, edited by Pedro Luis Barcia, La Plata: Facultad de Humanidades y Ciencias de la Educación de la Universidad Nacional de La Plata, 1968, pp. 11–81; and Arturo Capdevila, *Rubén Darío: 'Un bardo rei,'* Buenos Aires: Espasa Calpe, 1946, pp. 81–129

47 *Rubén Darío en Costa Rica (1891–1892)*, edited by Teodoro Picado, San José: G. Monge, 1919–1920 (see especially Picado's introduction on pages v–viii); and Edmundo Montagne, 'Rubén Darío en Costa Rica,' *El Hogar* (San José), 13 February 1920

48 Angel Augier, *Cuba y Rubén Darío*, Havana: Academia de Ciencias de Cuba, Instituto de Literatura y Lingüística, 1968; also published in *L/L, Boletín del Instituto de Literatura y Lingüística*, Año 1, no. 2, April–December 1967, 87–278. This number also contains an important 'Ensayo de una bibliografía cubana de y sobre Rubén Darío,' 279–302, by Francisco Mota.

49 Emilio Rodríguez Demorizi, *Rubén Darío y sus amigos dominicanos*, Bogotá: Ediciones Espiral, 1948

50 J.C. Alegría, *et al.*, *Rubén Darío y Ecuador*, Quito: Casa de la Cultura Ecuatoriana, 1968

51 Alfonso Reyes, 'Rubén Darío en México,' *Estudios sobre Rubén Darío*, edited by Ernesto Mejía Sánchez, Mexico: Fondo de Cultura Económica, 1968, pp. 14–26; and Luis Leal, 'Darío en México,' *Estudios sobre Rubén Darío*, pp. 118–24. See also Darío's 'Diario,' *Obras completas*, I, 179–92.

52 Rodrigo Miró, 'Rubén Darío en Panamá,' *Estudios sobre Rubén Darío*, pp. 279–83

53 José Pereira Rodríguez, 'Cuando Rubén Darío vino al Uruguay,' *Seminario-Archivo de Rubén Darío*, No. 5, 1961, pp. 21–5

54 Luis Beltrán Guerrero, *Rubén Darío y Venezuela*, Caracas: Instituto Nacional de Cultura y Bellas Artes, 1967

55 Fred P. Ellison, 'Rubén Darío and Brazil,' *Hispania*, vol. 47, no. 1, March 1964, 24–34

56 Fred P. Ellison, 'Rubén Darío y Portugal,' *Hispanófila* (Madrid), vol. 2, no. 4, September 1958, 23–33. For a study dealing with Darío's literary relations with both Portuguese and Brazilian writers see Alicia Haydée Gaibisso, 'Darío y las letras lusobrasileñas,' *Rubén Darío: estudios reunidos en conmemoración del centenario*, pp. 497–509.

57 José Augustín Balseiro, 'Rubén Darío y Estados Unidos,' *Seis estudios sobre Rubén Darío*, Madrid: Editorial Gredos, 1967, pp. 117–43. See also Pedro Henríquez Ureña,

'Carta a Alfonso Reyes sobre Rubén Darío' in Ernesto Mejía Sánchez, *Cuestiones rubendarianas*, pp. 53–9, for an account of Darío's last visit to New York.
58 José Augustín Balseiro, 'Rubén Darío y España,' *Seis estudios*, pp. 17–56
59 Guillermo Díaz Plaja, 'Rubén Darío y Cataluña,' *La Torre*, nos 55–6, January–June 1967, 181–94
60 Ramón García de Castro, 'Rubén Darío y Asturias,' *Papeles de Son Armadans*, vol. 12, nos. 137–8, August–September 1967, 305–17
61 José Luis Cano, 'Rubén Darío y Andalucía,' *Azul* (Managua), February 1956, pp. 16–19; and Francisco Sánchez-Castañer, 'Andalucía y Rubén Darío,' *Memoria del xv Congreso del Instituto Internacional de Literature Iberoamericana*, Lima: Universidad Nacional Mayor de San Marcos, Dirección Universitaria de Biblioteca y Publicaciones, 1972, pp. 132–7
62 Carlos D. Hamilton, 'Rubén Darío en la Isla de Oro,' *Cuadernos Hispanoamericanos*, nos. 212–13, August–September 1967, 556–73; and Erminio Polidori, 'Rubén Darío en Mallorca,' *Actas del Congreso Internacional de Hispanistas*, iii, Mexico: El Colegio de México, 1970, pp. 695–714
63 Guiseppe Bellini, 'Rubén Darío e Italia,' *Revista Iberoamericana*, vol. 33, no. 64, July–December 1967, 367–86
64 Osvaldo Bazil, 'Mujeres de Rubén Darío,' *El Mercurio* (Santiago de Chile), 1 February 1942; Ildo Sol, *Rubén Darío y las mujeres*, Managua: Editorial La Estrella de Nicaragua, 1948; and two books by Rubén Darío iii, *Tres mujeres en la vida de Rubén Darío*, Buenos Aires: Editorial Nova, 1966; and *Rubén Darío y los mercaderes del templo*, Buenos Aires: Editorial Nova, 1967
65 For bibliography dealing with these topics and for further bibliography dealing with the topics discussed above, see Hensley C. Woodbridge, 'Rubén Darío: A Critical Bibliography,' *Hispania*, vol. 50, no. 4, December 1967, 982–95, and vol. 51, no. 1, March 1968, 95–110. I have attempted to give important items that have appeared since his bibliography was published and others that were not mentioned by him. Little of importance can be added at this time to his bibliography of Darío's relations with such figures as José Martí, Julián del Casal, Paul Groussac, Ricardo Jaimes Freyre, Amado Nervo, Juan Ramón Jiménez, Antonio and Manuel Machado, Menéndez Pelayo, Miguel de Unamuno and Juan Valera, for which Dictino Alvarez Hernández's *Cartas de Rubén Darío*, Madrid: Taurus, 1963, provides useful source material. Aspects of Darío's relations with José Enrique Rodó are discussed in my following chapter. For recent articles dealing with his relations with Pedro Balmaceda, Valle Inclán, Narciso Tondreau, Heliodoro Valle, Juan Ramón and Clarin, respectively, see Eduardo Neale-Silva, 'Rubén Darío y la plasticidad,' *Atenea*, Año 44, nos. 415–16, January-June 1967, 193–208; Allen W. Phillips, 'Rubén Darío and Valle Inclán: The Story of a Literary Friendship,' translated by Esther W. Phillips, in *Rubén Darío Centennial Studies*, edited by Miguel González-Gerth and George D. Schade, Austin: University of Texas, 1970, pp. 49–83; Evelyn Uhrhan Irving, 'Narciso Tondreau: Close Friend of Rubén Darío in Chile,' *Hispania*, vol. 52, no. 5, December 1969, 864–9, Ernesto Mejía Sánchez, 'Rafael Heliodoro Valle,' *Cuestiones rubendarianas*, pp. 61–78; Angel Manuel Aguirre, 'Relaciones amistosas entre Rubén Darío y Juan Ramón Jiménez,' *Quaderni Ibero-Americani*, no. 37, December 1969, 42–6; and Fernando Ibarra, 'Clarín y Rubén Darío: historia de una incomprensión,' *Hispanic Review*, vol. 41, no. 3, Summer 1973, 524–40
66 *Obras completas*, i, 18
67 All works by Darío mentioned here will be included in the bibliography.
68 For documentary evidence supporting these much disputed dates see Angel Augier,

'Cuba y Rubén Darío,' *L/L*, vol. 1, no. 2, April–December 1967, 155.

69 See the chapter entitled 'Las funciones' in his *Este otro Rubén Darío* as well as his article 'Lo social en Rubén Darío,' *Asomante*, vol. 23, no. 1, January–March 1967, 58–62.

70 *Obras completas*, I, 45–6

71 Ibid., pp. 53–4

72 See, for instance, the account of this return given in Charles Watland, *Poet Errant*, pp. 210–15.

73 *El despertar del alma*, p. 222

74 Rubén Darío, *Obras completas*, I, 223–4

75 *Literary Biography* (Alexander Lectures 1955–6), Toronto: University of Toronto Press, 1957, pp. 50–1

76 *Theory of Literature*, New York: Harcourt, Brace, 1949, pp. 70–2

77 'Tres puntos de exegética literaria,' *Obras completas de Alfonso Reyes*, XIV, edited by Ernesto Mejía Sánchez, Mexico: Fondo de Cultura Económica, 1962, pp. 249–66. Reyes's essay first appeared in the *Revista de Literatura Mexicana*, vol. 1, no. 1, July–September 1940, 8–23.

78 This will be discussed further in a later chapter dealing with intrinsic approaches to the criticism of Darío's work.

79 A measure of the expectation of sincerity or truthfulness from the nineteenth-century poets is Enrique Anderson Imbert's observation that the statement from *Martín Fierro*, 'Las coplas me van brotando/como agua de manantial,' is not true. He adduces as evidence the numerous corrections shown in José Hernández's manuscript. In doing so he understands the statement to be made biographically by Hernández rather than fictionally by Martín Fierro. See *Literatura hispanoamericana*, edited by Enrique Anderson Imbert and Eugenio Florit, New York: Holt, Rinehart and Winston, 1960, p. 295.

80 *Obras completas*, V, 761–4

81 Ibid., pp. 859–60

82 Ibid., pp. 945–60

83 *Obras completas*, IV, 874

84 'Sincerity' had for Martí a meaning that was closer to 'truthful,' 'good' in a social sense.

85 *Poesías completas*, edited by Alfonso Méndez Plancarte and Antonio Oliver Belmás, Madrid: Aguilar, 1967, p. 627

86 Ibid., p. 657

87 Ghiraldo, *El archivo*, p. 172

88 For some of the problems that were caused for his early biographers, in particular Francisco Contreras (*Rubén Darío*), and Guillermo Díaz Plaja (*Rubén Darío, la vida, la obra; notas críticas*, Barcelona: Sociedad General de Publicaciones, 1930), see Arturo Torres-Ríoseco, 'Rubén Darío y la crítica,' *Hispania*, vol. 14, no. 1, February 1931, 99–106.

89 See his *Obras completas*, I, 27, 42–3.

90 Leon Edel states forthrightly some of the problems involved in the application of Freudian psychology to literary figures when he writes: 'The other side of the picture has been inevitably the venture, on the part of critics and biographers, upon psychoanalytic ground, where they have been no less inexpert than the psychoanalysts on *our* ground. The use of the psycho-analytic tool involves high skills, some quasi-scientific: a deep saturation in the problems of the mind and of the emotions, and a grasp of certain phenomena – such as "projection" or "distortion" or "malevolent transformation". We have thus a common problem: that of certain individuals who are perfectly competent in their proper field but who seem prepared to blazon forth their

incompetence on ground where they do not belong.' *Literary Biography*, p. 57

91 Juan Antonio Cabezas, *Rubén Darío*, p. 24. For more speculative psychological commentary on Darío see Santos Flores López, *Psicología y tendencia poética en la obra de Rubén Darío*, Managua: Academia Nicaragüense de la Lengua, 1958.

92 'Rubén Darío,' *Inspiration and Poetry*, London: Macmillan and Co., 1955, pp. 245, 264

93 'Rubén Darío visto por un inglés,' in Cecil Maurice Bowra *et al.*, *Rubén Darío en Oxford*, Managua: Academia Nicaragüense de la Lengua, 1966, pp. 55–6. The article appeared originally in *La Nueva Democracia*, vol. 39, no. 3, June–September 1959, 33–5.

94 'El indigenismo de Rubén Darío,' *Managua* (Diario nicaragüense), 22 March 1960

95 'Rubén Darío y sus biógrafos,' *Insula*, Año 16, no. 170, January 1961, 11

96 The article appeared originally in *Hispania*, vol. 50, no. 4, December 1967, 971–81, and later, in less complete form, in *Homenaje a Rubén Darío (1867–1967)*, edited by Aníbal Sánchez-Reulet, Los Angeles: Centro Latinoamericano, University of California, Los Angeles, 1970, pp. 121–6.

97 I quote from the version published in *Hispania*, vol. 50, no. 4, December 1967, 971–2.

98 For a case in point see the discussion of the 'I' in Ayala's prologue in my article 'Cervantes and Ayala's *El rapto*: The Art of Reworking a Story,' *Publications of the Modern Language Association of America*, vol. 84, no. 1, January 1969, 14–19.

CHAPTER TWO

1 Another member of the Asociación de Mayo who gave particular emphasis to literary liberalism was Juan Bautista Alberdi. He was also keenly interested in the moral and social attitudes conveyed by the literary work.

2 See Fernando Alegría, *Breve historia de la novela hispanoamericana*, Mexico: Studium, 1959, pp. 31–2. José Enrique Rodó, *Obras completas*, edited by Emir Rodríguez Monegal, Madrid: Aguilar, 1967, p. 771, describes the literary works of Gutiérrez in terms that underline their distance from the field of combat against Rosas. Rodó calls them: 'la delicada leyenda de *Caicobé*, la hermosa página de idealización histórica que intituló *El capitán de Patricios* y la pastoral criolla de *Los amores del payador*.'

3 José Enrique Rodó, *Obras completas*, p. 169

4 '*Los raros*,' *Nosotros*, vol. 21, February 1916, 152. Groussac's articles were reprinted in this volume which was published in honour of Darío a month after the latter's death.

5 Ibid., 156

6 '*Prosas profanas*,' *Nosotros*, vol. 21, February 1916, 158

7 Ibid., 160

8 Ibid., 159

9 For an excellent study of the criticism of Darío's work done by Eduardo de la Barra, Paul Groussac, Manuel Gondra, and José Enrique Rodó, see Juan Loveluck, 'Rubén Darío y sus primeros críticos (1888–1900),' *Revista Iberoamericana*, vol. 33, no. 64, July–December 1967, 209–35.

10 *Hombres y letrados de América*, Asunción: Editorial Guaranía, 1942, pp. 201–40

11 Ibid., pp. 204–5

12 Rubén Darío, *Poesías completas*, Madrid: Aguilar, 1967, p. 545

13 Ibid.

14 Gondra, p. 208

15 *Poesías completas*, p. 546

16 Ibid., p. 211

17 The speech is published with the title 'Alberdi' in *Hombres y letrados de América*, pp. 241–8.

18 Ibid., pp. 211–12.

19 For detailed and perceptive comments on these articles and on Rodó's work in general see Emir Rodríguez Monegal's 'Introducción general' to his above-mentioned edition of Rodó's *Obras completas*.

20 Ibid., p. 799

21 Ibid.

22 Ibid., pp. 1323–4

23 Ibid., p. 1324

24 Ibid.

25 Ibid., p. 869

26 Ibid.

27 Ibid., p. 191. From Rodó's correspondence with Darío's secretary, Luis Berisso, dated 4 March 1898, we learn that Rodó completed his study by that date.

28 Ibid., p. 169

29 Ibid.

30 Ibid., p. 170

31 Ibid., p. 169

32 Ibid., p. 170

33 Ibid., p. 169

34 Ibid., p. 170

35 Ibid.

36 Ibid., p. 773

37 Ibid.

38 Ibid., p. 822. In his essay on Darío he mentions another of his own qualities that enables him to appreciate the poet's work when he writes: 'Presumo tener entre las pocas excelencias de mi espíritu, la virtud, literariamente cardinal, de la amplitud' (Ibid., p. 175).

39 Ibid., p. 175

40 Ibid., p. 191

41 For a useful study of the nineteenth-century critical background and of Rodó as a literary critic, see Lynherst Peña, 'Trends of Literary Criticism in Spanish America (1900–1950),' Dissertation, University of Toronto, 1970, pp. 7–27.

42 'Rodó y Rubén Darío,' *Revista Nacional de Cultura*, no. 178, December 1966, 72–80. Crema and others have mentioned their inability to consult the very rare work by Max Henríquez Ureña, *Rodó y Rubén Darío*, Havana: Sociedad Editorial Cuba Contemporánea, 1918. This book deals hardly at all with literary relationships between Rodó and Darío. It is, rather, a two-part study: one dealing with Rodó's career, the second with Darío's. In drawing attention to Rodó's eclecticism, Henríquez Ureña mentions Rodó's study of *Prosas profanas* and quotes his statement 'Yo soy un modernista también' (pp. 28–9). In the section of the book devoted to Darío, Henríquez Ureña writes 'José Enrique Rodó saludó la aparición de *Prosas profanas* con un estudio insuperable, que más tarde recogió Rubén Darío como prólogo para una nueva edición de su libro' (p. 113). He goes on to quote two long passages from Rodó's essay. Apart from this, there is no linking of the two writers in Henríquez Ureña's book.

43 He does not mention Rodó's 'En la muerte de Rubén Darío,' *Nosotros*, vol. 21, February 1916, 127–8.

44 José Enrique Rodó, p. 869

45 See Crema, pp. 77–8. Crispo Acosta himself, in his book *Rubén Darío y José Enrique Rodó*, Montevideo: Agencia General de Librería y Publicaciones, 1924, pp. 174–5, has explained satisfactorily, in terms of professional pride and devotion to poetry, aspects of the attitude Rodó displayed in his essay. Crispo Acosta writes: 'entregado a la emoción poética, no ve que el arte de *Prosas profanas* oculta un alma desemejante a la suya en todo lo que no es arte. No se contenta con dar sobre la poesía que estudia, una información exacta; no le basta comprenderla y gustarla; necesita hacerla suya en propia y doble recreación; y como en competencia con el artista a quien está analizando, reproduce, con maestría experta, en la fina prosa de sus comentarios, la elegancia alada, el sutil primor y la gracia de los versos.'

46 I believe that my interpretation of Rodó's essay pictures him as more favourable to Darío than, for example, Loveluck, 'Rubén Darío y sus primeros críticos,' has judged him to be.

47 Justo Sierra, prologue to Rubén Darío, *Peregrinaciones*, Paris: Librería de la Vda. de Charles Bouret, 1901, pp. 18–19

48 Federico de Onís, 'Rubén Darío,' *España en América*, Río Piedras: Ediciones de la Universidad de Puerto Rico, 1955, pp. 203–4

49 José Enrique Rodó, p. 170

50 Ibid., p. 191

51 Mario Benedetti, *Genio y figura de José Enrique Rodó*, Buenos Aires: Eudeba, 1966, p. 43

52 'Señor de los tristes,' *Casa de las Américas*, no. 42, May–June 1967, 78–80. Curiously, in an article bearing this same title, modified in the same year as this one was read in Cuba to serve as the introduction to an anthology of Darío's poems, Benedetti is considerably more sympathetic to Darío. He judges his work from 1905 onward to show deep American sentiment, to be unambiguous in its presentation of personal emotional states and to exemplify poetic techniques that are useful to poetic practice of the present day. This version of Benedetti's essay is reprinted in his *Letras del continente mestizo*, Montevideo: Arca Editorial, 1968, pp. 22–34.

53 'Darío y América,' *Insula*, Año 16, no. 170, January 1961, 13

54 'Varadero de Rubén Darío,' *Casa de las Américas*, no. 42, May–June 1967, 21–38

55 *L/L*, Año 1, no. 2, April–December 1967, 9–14

56 Julius Petersen: 'Las generaciones literarias,' en *Filosofía de la ciencia literaria*, edited by Emil Ermatinger, Mexico: Fondo de Cultura Económica, 1946, p. 192

57 *L/L*, Año 1, no. 2, April–December 1967, 9

58 Ibid.

59 Ibid., p. 10

60 Ibid.

61 This essay, like those of other writers mentioned earlier, was read as part of the program 'Encuentro con Rubén Darío' held in January 1967 in Varadero, Cuba. The papers were published in *Casa de las Américas*, no. 42, May–June 1967, Portuondo's article being on pages 68–72.

62 *Conferencias de historia habanera*, Primera Serie, *Habaneros ilustres*, III, Havana: Municipio de la Habana, 1937

63 Centenario de Rubén Darío,' *L/L*, Año 1, no. 2, April–December 1967, 7

64 Ibid. In his review of C.M. Bowra *et al.*, *Rubén Darío en Oxford*, Managua: Academia Nicaragüense de la Lengua, 1966, Portuondo also called for closer analysis of the works of Darío, analysis that would reveal more scientifically than has been done the contradictions imposed on the writer by a difficult period in the political and economic history of Latin America (*L/L*, Año 1, no. 2, April–December 1967, 307–9).

65 'Meditación de centenario,' *L/L*, Año 1, no. 2, April–December 1967, 21

66 Ibid., 30

67 Ibid., 23–4

68 For a perceptive study of Portuondo as a literary theorist and critic see Lynherst Peña, pp. 78–97.

69 Portuondo's high regard for Darío's poetry is almost as anomalous superficially as is that of another Marxist critic, the Peruvian José Carlos Mariátegui for the poetry of José María Eguren. (See the essay 'El proceso de la literatura' in Mariátegui's *Siete ensayos de interpretación de la realidad peruana*, Lima: Biblioteca Amauta, 1928.) Mariátegui had declared earlier in the same book that: 'Para una interpretación profunda del espíritu de una literatura, la mera erudición no es suficiente. Sirven más la sensibilidad política y la clarividencia histórica' (p. 191). He judges, however, that Eguren wrote excellent poetry even though he states that 'Eguren habría necesitado siempre evadirse de su época, de la realidad. El arte es una evasión cuando el artista no puede aceptar ni traducir la época y la realidad que le tocan' (p. 235).

70 Fiodor Kelin's 'Rubén Darío' appeared originally in *Literatura Soviética* (Moscow), no. 3, 1959, 125–9 and was published later in *Estudios sobre Rubén Darío*, edited by Ernesto Sánchez Mejía, Mexico: Fondo de Cultura Económica, 1968, pp. 181–5. My references are to the later text.

71 Ibid., p. 181

72 Ibid., p. 182

73 Ibid. (italics added)

74 Ibid.

75 In the speculative political area a polemic arose, shortly after the Spanish Civil War had ended, on the question of whether Darío, had he been alive during the struggle, would have been pro- or anti-Republican. Juan Larrea interpreted two articles, José María Pemán's 'A la salutación de Rubén Darío,' *Domingo*, 14 July 1940, and Pablo Antonio Cuadra's 'Pequeña invectiva contra la Rojería española,' *Lectura*, vol. 25, 1 November 1941, 14–22, to mean that their authors judged that Darío would have been anti-Republican. Larrea refuted this judgment and insisted in two articles, ' ¿Rubén Darío contra Bolívar?,' *Repertorio Americano*, no. 906, 11 January 1941, 17–20, and 'Vaticinio de Rubén Darío,' *Cuadernos Americanos*, vol. 1, no. 4, October–December 1942, 213–38, that Darío would have been pro-Republican. In his article 'Consideraciones sobre la actitud político-social de Rubén Darío,' *Revista Iberoamericana*, no. 19, no. 38, January 1954, 261–72, Antonio M. de la Torre approaches the subject with a broad perspective, stressing Darío's constant interest in social problems and popular causes. He also defended Darío against Blanco Fombona's accusation that 'En política no sólo fue conservador ... sino servil ... Jamás amó la libertad, ni en el fondo, a nuestra América' (*El modernismo y los poetas modernistas*, Madrid: Editorial Mundo Latino, 1929, pp. 165–6) and against Leopoldo Lugones's statement that 'Fue siempre católico y con ello, monárquico de convicción' (Rubén Darío, *Poemas escogidos*, prologue by Leopoldo Lugones, Mexico: Lectura Selecta, 1919, pp. 16–17).

76 Arturo Torres-Ríoseco, *Nueva historia de la gran literatura iberoamericana*, Buenos Aires: Emecé Editores, 1960, p. 10

77 Reprinted in Enrique Anderson Imbert, *Crítica interna*, Madrid: Taurus, 1960, p. 184

78 I quote from the second edition (1957), p. 228.

79 Ibid., p. 286

80 *Humanismo* (Mexico), Año 6, nos. 50–1, July–October 1958, 74–87

81 The work appeared originally in *El Heraldo* (Costa Rica), 17 March 1892, and was recently republished in *Poesía revolucionaria nicaragüense* (no editor named), Managua: Ediciones Patria y Libertad, 1968, pp. 109–10. It reads in part: 'El mundo anda muy mal, la sociedad se desquicia. El siglo que viene al mundo verá la mayor de las revoluciones que han ensangrentado la tierra. El pez grande se come al chico, pero pronto tendremos el desquite. El pauperismo reina, y el trabajador lleva sobre sus hombros la montaña de una maldición. Nada vale sino el oro miserable ... Yo quisiera una tempestad de sangre; yo quisiera que sonara ya la hora de la rehabilitación, de la justicia social, ¿No se llama democracia a esa quisicosa política que cantan los poetas y alaban los oradores? pues maldita sea esa democracia.'

82 'Lo social en Rubén Darío,' *Asomante*, vol. 23, no. 1, January–March 1967, 58

83 'La vendimia cívica,' *Homenaje a Rubén Darío (1867–1967)*, *Memoria* del xiii Congreso Internacional de Literatura Iberoamericana, edited by Aníbal Sánchez Reulet, Los Angeles: Centro Latinoamericano, University of California, Los Angeles, 1970, p. 180

84 'Vivencia americana de Darío,' *La Torre*, Año 15, nos. 55–6, January–June 1967, 323–71

85 *Cuadernos Hispanoamericanos*, nos. 212–13, August–September 1967, 289–331. Carlos Martín's *América en Rubén Darío* (Madrid: Editorial Gredos, 1972), is a recent work which deals more comprehensively with the whole range of topics related to Darío and America than any previously published. He considers Darío as a Spanish American in a new era of the life of the area. He outlines Spanish American traits in Darío's personality and his promotion of the cultural characteristics of the region, gives evidence of his representation of the language and landscape of Spanish America and of his continental view and supports the idea that Darío displayed substantial interest in socio-political questions affecting Spanish America. He also explores relations between Darío and prominent Spanish Americans such as Martí and Montalvo.

86 Ibid., 316. For a study of Darío's poetry in terms of its political and social setting see Washington Delgado, 'Situación social de la poesía de Rubén Darío,' *Homenaje a Rubén Darío*, Lima: Universidad Nacional Mayor de San Marcos, Instituto de Literatura, 1967, pp. 36–51.

87 *El heroísmo intelectual*, Mexico: Tezontle, 1955, p. 135

88 Borges's essay 'El escritor argentino y la tradición,' *Discusión*, Buenos Aires: Emecé, 1957, pp. 151–62, contains views that are at odds with Portuondo's. Borges refuses to oblige the Spanish American writer to represent Spanish American social reality and situates him rather in the broad stream of Western Literature. Such views are, however, less popular in Spanish American criticism than those expressed above.

89 Oreste Pucciani, 'An interview with Jean-Paul Sartre,' *Tulane Drama Review*, vol. 5, no. 3, March 1961, 13

90 *D'Un Réalisme sans rivages*, Paris: Libraire Plon, 1963, pp. 153–4

91 See Georg Lukács, *The Meaning of Contemporary Realism*, translated by John and Necke Mander, London: Merlin Press, 1962, pp. 25–26, 47–92.

92 Mao Tse-tung, *An Anthology of his Writings*, edited by Anne Fremantle, New York: New American Library of World Literature, 1962, p. 259

93 *Tulane Drama Review*, vol. 6, no. 1, September 1960, 18–25

94 For instances of contradictions in his political and sociological positions, see the chapters 'La política y Rubén' and 'Sociólogo y humanista' in Alejandro Reyes Huete's book *Darío en su prosa*, Granada, Nicaragua: Editorial Hospicio, 1960, pp. 179–226. For accounts of his changing views toward the United States, see the chapter entitled 'El águila norteamericana y Rubén Darío' in Antonio Oliver Belmás, *Este otro Rubén Darío*, Barcelona: Aedos, 1960, pp. 51–64 and José Agustín Balseiro, 'Rubén Darío y Estados

Unidos' in his *Seis estudios sobre Rubén Darío*, Madrid: Editorial Gredos, 1967, pp. 117–43.

95 In his article 'La imaginería oriental exotista en Rubén Darío,' *Homenaje a Rubén Darío*, Lima: Universidad Nacional Mayor de San Marcos, Instituto de Literatura, pp. 52–61. Estuardo Núñez is interested in these countries only as another area from which Darío draws his imagery.

96 See, for example, the second book of his 'La caravana pasa,' *Obras completas*, III, 677–742; 'La raza de Cham,' *Obras completas*, IV, 1387–94; and his essay 'Chinos y japoneses' which appeared in *La Razón* (Montevideo), 7 August 1894, where he expresses support for China against the aggressive designs of Japan, which seemed to him at that time to be losing its authentic identity to become the agent of Western attitudes. He writes: 'Si triunfáis vosotros, muy pronto la China interior y recóndita estará cruzada de ferrocarriles, y cerca de las pagodas de Budha se establecerán las oficinas de compañías industriales, *limited*, que hablarán lengua inglesa; y el Imperio celeste será con el tiempo una república demasiado terrenal. ¡Ah Japoneses! Los poetas están contra vosotros!' (*Páginas desconocidas de Rubén Darío*, I, edited by Roberto Ibáñez, Montevideo Biblioteca de Marcha, 1970, p. 46).

97 *De Marsella a Tokio*, Paris: Garnier Hermanos, 1906, p. viii

98 *Obras completas*, III, 343–54

CHAPTER THREE

1 *Obras desconocidas de Rubén Darío, escritas en Chile y no recogidas en ninguno de sus libros*, ed. Raúl Silva Castro, Santiago: Universidad de Chile, 1934, p. 201

2 Rubén Darío, *Obras completas*, II, 19–20

3 See Max Henríquez Ureña, *Breve historia del modernismo*, Mexico: Fondo de Cultura Económica, 1962, pp. 59–160

4 *Obras completas*, V, 1009

5 Ibid., 763

6 *Obras completas*, I, 206

7 *Obras completas*, IV, 875

8 *Obras completas*, III, 304–5

9 *Obras completas*, V, 859

10 For a comprehensive account of Darío's views of Modernism see Allen. W. Phillips, 'Rubén Darío y sus juicios sobre el modernismo,' *Revista Iberoamericana*, vol. 24, no. 47, January – June 1959, 41–64.

11 Pedro Henríquez Ureña, *Obra crítica*, edited by Emma Susana Speratti Piñero, Mexico: Fondo de Cultura Económica, 1960, p. 96. The essay first appeared in his *Ensayos críticos* (1905). For an excellent study of Pedro Henríquez Ureña as a critic of Darío see Ernesto Mejía Sánchez, *Cuestiones rubendarianas*, Madrid: Editorial Revista de Occidente, 1970, pp. 35–52.

12 For a discussion of the definitions of Modernism by some of its early critics such as Juan Valera, José Enrique Rodó, Rufino Blanco-Fombona, Francisco Contreras, Manuel Gálvez, Osvaldo Crispo Acosta, Manuel Machado, Isaac Goldberg, Erwin K. Mapes, Max and Pedro Henríquez Ureña, see Luis Monguió, 'Sobre la caracterización del Modernismo,' *Revista Iberoamericana*, vol. 7, no. 13, November 1943, 69–80. See also Juan Loveluck, 'Rubén Darío y el Modernismo en *La Biblioteca*,' *La Torre*, Año 15, nos. 55–6, January–June 1967, 229–51. For a comprehensive discussion of the critics' views of Modernism see Ned J. Davison, *The Concept of Modernism in Hispanic Criticism*, Boulder: Pruett Press, 1966.

13 Federico de Onís, *España en América*, Río Piedras: Ediciones de la Universidad de Puerto
    Rico, 1955, p. 176. In 1935 Juan Ramón Jiménez defined Modernism in similar broad
    terms when he wrote: 'El modernismo no fue solamente una tendencia literaria: el
    modernismo fue una tendencia general. Alcanzó a todo. Creo que el nombre vino de
    Alemania, donde se producía un movimiento reformador por los curas llamados moder-
    nista. Y aquí, en España, la gente nos puso ese nombre de modernistas por nuestra
    actitud. Porque lo que se llama modernismo no es cosa de escuela ni de forma, sino de
    actitud. Era el encuentro de nuevo con la belleza sepultada durante el siglo xix por un
    tono general de poesía burguesa. Eso es el modernismo: un gran movimiento de
    entusiasmo y libertad hacia la belleza' ("El modernismo," *La Voz*, 18 March 1935). The
    passage is quoted and endorsed by Ricardo Gullón in his introductory essay to Juan
    Ramón Jiménez's *El modernismo: notas de un curso* (1953), Mexico: Aguilar, 1962, p.
    17 and is reflected in the conceptual bases of Gullón's *Direcciones del modernismo*,
    Madrid: Editorial Gredos, 1963. Bernardo Gicovate in his 'El modernismo y su historia,'
    Hispanic Review, vol. 32, no. 2, July 1964, 217–26, has presented strong arguments for
    a distinction between the Hispanic literary Modernist movement and other movements
    that bear the denomination Modernist.
14 Federico de Onís, p. 619. The article, entitled 'Valoración,' first appeared in the *Revista
    Hispánica Moderna*, vol. 18, nos. 2–4, June–December 1952, 145–50.
15 Federico de Onís, *España en América*, p. 177
16 Ibid., p. 625
17 Ibid., p. 171
18 Enrique Díez-Canedo, *Juan Ramón Jiménez en su obra*, México: El Colegio de México,
    1944, p. 9
19 *Obra crítica*, p. 18, in the essay 'El modernismo en la poesía cubana' which first appeared
    in his *Ensayos críticos* (1905)
20 Juan Carlos Ghiano gives an excellent summary of the movement and of the terminology
    applied in its description in his article 'El modernismo entre América y España,' *Ramón
    M. del Valle-Inclán, 1866–1966*, La Plata: Universidad Nacional de la Plata, Facultad de
    Humanidades y Ciencias de la Educación, 1966, pp. 163–93.
21 Arturo Torres-Ríoseco, *Precursores del modernismo*, New York: Las Américas Publish-
    ing Co., 1963, p. 127. First edition, Madrid: Espasa Calpe, 1925
22 See the article 'Rubén Darío, poeta' in his *Crítica interna*, Madrid: Taurus, 1960, pp.
    163–209.
23 Fernando Alegría, 'Spanish American Poetry,' *Encyclopedia of Poetry and Poetics*,
    edited by Alex Preminger, Princeton: Princeton University Press, 1965, p. 795
24 Madrid: Editorial Gredos, 1969
25 Mexico: El Colegio de México, 1966
26 In addition to the exceptions already discussed, mention must be made of Vittorio
    Borghini, *Rubén Darío e il modernismo*, Genoa: Pubblicazioni Del' Istituto Univer-
    sitario di Magistero, 1955.
27 As is done by Raúl Silva Castro, for instance, in his article ' ¿Es posible definir el
    modernismo?' *Caudernos Americanos*, vol. 141, no. 3, July–August 1965, 172–9. In
    fact, the period suggested by Silva Castro is not greatly at odds with the view indicated by
    most of the literary historians who have written about the movement, i.e. that Moder-
    nism had its origins in the early 1880s, usually in 1882, and ended approximately with
    Darío's death in 1916. See, for example and for further references, Pedro Henríquez
    Ureña, *Literary Currents in Hispanic America*, Cambridge: Harvard University Press,
    1949, pp. 163–70; Luis Monguió, 'Sobre la caracterización del modernismo'; Ned J.
    Davison, *The Concept of Modernism*, pp. 13–15; and Mario Mendes Campos, *Ruben*

Dario e o Modernismo Hispano-Americano, Belo Horizonte: Publicações da Secretaria da Educação de Estado de Minas Gerais, 1968.

28 In the essay 'José Martí' from *Los raros, Obras completas*, II, 492

29 In the essay 'José Martí, poeta,' *Obras completas*, IV, 931

30 Ibid.

31 Osvaldo Bazil, 'La huella de Martí en Rubén Darío,' *Archivo José Martí*, no. 14, 1950, 481. A qualified reaction to Bazil's statement is Guillermo Díaz-Plaja's, who in his book *Modernismo frente a noventa y ocho*, Madrid: Espasa Calpe, 1951, p. 307, declares: 'Esta frase es verdad absoluta, en cuanto a la prosa.' The importance of Martí for Darío's work is also pointed out in Regino E. Boti's article, 'Martí en Darío.' *Cuba Contemporánea*, vol. 38, no. 146, February 1925, 112–24.

32 Ernesto Mejía Sánchez in a discreet article entitled 'El caso Martí-Whitman-Darío,' *Casa de las Américas*, no. 42, May–June 1967, 52–7, puts in doubt some of the influence on Darío attributed to Martí. Eugenio Florit in his article 'Modernist Prefigurement in the Early Work of Rubén Darío' (Translated by John Wilcox) *Rubén Darío Centennial Studies*, edited by Miguel González-Gerth and George D. Schade, Austin: University of Texas, 1970, pp. 31–47, suggests that Modernist elements were present in Darío's work before he knew Martí's writing.

33 I will discuss the question of influence in some detail later in this chapter. See González's article, 'Deslindes indeclinables,' *Casa de las Américas*, no. 42, May–June 1967, 36–51, where he makes statements like 'Nadie ha empleado tantos "ghost writers" en español como Darío' (p. 44).

34 Among these, see especially his *Notas en torno al modernismo*, Mexico: Universidad Nacional Autónoma de México. Dirección General de Publicaciones, 1958.

35 'Deslindes indeclinables,' *Casa de las Américas*, no. 42, May–June 1967, 50

36 *Sobre el Modernismo : Polémica y definición*, Mexico: Universidad Nacional Autónoma de México. Dirección General de Publicaciones, 1959

37 Caracas: Ediciones de la Biblioteca de la Universidad Central de Venezuela, 1970

38 Ibid., p. 9

39 See note 34 above.

40 I will return to these and other assessors of Darío's work in Chapter 6.

41 Jorge Luis Borges, 'Mensaje en honor de Rubén Darío,' *El Despertador Americano* (Mexico), vol. I, no. 2, May 1967, 9

42 Mario Benedetti, *Letras del continente mestizo*, Montevideo: Arca Editorial, 1967, pp. 31–2

43 See, for example, René Wellek's chapter on 'Literary History,' *Theory of Literature*, New York: Harcourt, Brace and Co., 1949, pp. 263–82.

44 See Santiago Argüello, *Modernismo y modernistas*, Guatemala: Tipografía Nacional, 1935, p. 43.

45 *Obras completas*, edited by Emir Rodríguez Monegal, Madrid: Aguilar, 1967, pp. 169–192

46 For a discussion of the difference between 'modernismo' and 'modernidad' see Raimundo Lida, 'Rubén y su herencia,' *La Torre*, Año 15, nos. 55–6, January–June 1967, 287–308.

47 Read at the Casa de la América Latina, Paris on 6 March 1967, and later published in *L/L*, Año 1, no. 2, April–December 1967, 15–32

48 *L/L*, Año 1, no. 2, April–December 1967, 17–18

49 Marinello had expressed this view in his *José Martí, escritor americano*, Mexico: Editorial Grijalbo, 1958.

50 'Rubén Darío: Meditación de centenario,' *L/L*, Año 1, no. 2, April–December, 1967, 19–20

51 Enrique Anderson Imbert, *La originalidad de Rubén Darío*, Buenos Aires: Centro Editor de América Latina, 1967, pp. 277–278

52 Rubén Darío, *Azul* ..., Valparaíso: Imprenta y Litografía Excelsior, 1888, pp. XLII–XLIII. For recent and detailed comments on Eduardo de la Barra's essay see Juan Loveluck's already-mentioned study 'Los primeros críticos de Darío,' *La Torre*, Año 15, nos. 55–6, January–June 1967, 217–28. Figueira examines Justo Sierra's prologue to Darío's *Pereg-rinaciones* (1901) and finds considerable similarity between de la Barra's and Sierra's views on Darío.

53 In Rubén Darío's, *Azul* ..., Guatemala: Imprenta de 'La Unión,' 1890, pp. VII–IX. Valera's 'Carta' appeared originally in *El Imparcial* (Madrid), 22 October 1888.

54 Ibid., p. xviii

55 Ibid., p. xxxiii

56 See my discussion of Rodó's essay in Chapter 2.

57 *Obras completas*, IV, 875–6

58 *Obras completas*, I, 60

59 Ibid., p. 24

60 Paris: Libraire Ancienne Honoré Champion, 1925

61 *Publications of the Modern Language Association of America*, vol. 49, no. 1, 1934, 310–26

62 Cambridge, Mass.: Harvard University Press, 1931

63 *Revista Americana de Buenos Aires*, vol. 36, no. 94, February 1932, 117–47

64 In Max Henríquez Ureña, *El retorno de los galeones y otros ensayos*, Mexico: Ediciones Galaxia y Ediciones de Andrea, 1963, pp. 7–57 (first edition, Madrid: 1930). For a recent study that stresses the Hispanic influence as the primary influence on Darío, see Antonio Oliver Belmás, 'El hispanismo mental de Rubén Darío,' *La Torre*, Año 15, nos. 55–6, January–June 1967, 195–202. For one that stresses the Spanish influence as decisive see Federico Carlos Sainz de Robles, 'El postizo afrancesamiento de Rubén Darío,' *La Torre*, Año 15, nos. 55–6, January–June 1967, 203–14. Concha Zardoya in her article 'Rubén Darío y "La poesía castellana,"' *Papeles de Son Armadans*, vol. 12, nos. 137–2, August–September 1967, pp. 229–71 deals with the influence of Spanish medieval poetry on Darío's formative period; Eleazar Huerta's, 'Perfiles de Rubén Darío,' *Atenea*, Año 44, nos. 415–16, January–June 1967, 133–46, emphasizes the influence of Berceo and Juan de Mena on Darío; and Rafael Soto Vergés, in 'Rubén y el neoclasicismo,' *Cuadernos Hispanoamericanos*, nos. 212–13, August–September 1967, 462–71, studies the influence of poets such as Jovellanos and Moratín on Darío's *Abrojos*.

65 *Revista Iberoamericana*, vol. 2, no. 4, November 1940, 401–17

66 *Rubén Darío y su creación poética*, La Plata: Universidad de la Plata, 1934

67 Avila: Editorial La Muralla, 1967

68 Mexico: Universidad Nacional Autónoma de México, 1962

69 'Las humanidades de Rubén Darío. Años de aprendizaje,' *Libro jubilar de Alfonso Reyes*, Mexico: Universidad Nacional Autónoma de México, 1956, pp. 243–63

70 (*Greco-Roman Mythology in his Stories and Poetry*), New York: Las Américas Publishing Company, 1963

71 *Libro jubilar de Alfonso Reyes*, Mexico: Universidad Nacional Autónoma de México, 1956, pp. 383–90

72 Fiore, p. 159

73 Ibid., p. 166

74 *Rubén Darío y la edad media*. (Una perspectiva poco conocida sobre la vida y obra del escritor.) Barcelona: Editorial Planeta, 1971

75 'Huellas épicas en la poesía de Rubén Darío,' *Revista de la Universidad de Madrid*, vol. 19, no. 75, 1970, 221–47

76 'Dante y Rubén Darío,' *Seminario-Archivo de Rubén Darío*, no. 10, 1965, 113–18

77 In his article 'Rubén Darío e Italia,' *Revista Iberoamericana*, vol. 33, no. 64, July–December 1967, 367–86

78 'Dante y Darío,' *Hispania*, vol. 40, no. 1, March 1957, 29–33

79 'Rubén Darío y la plasticidad,' *Atenea*, Año 44, nos. 415–16, January–June 1967, 193–208

80 'Rubén Darío y el siglo xv,' *Revue Hispanique*, vol. 50, no. 118, December 1920, 324–7. Also notable in this field is Alberto Forcadas, 'El romancero español, Lope de Vega, Góngora y Quevedo, y sus posibles resonancias en "Sonatina" de Rubén Darío,' *Quaderni Ibero-Americani*, no. 41, December 1972, 1–6

81 'El modelo estrófico de los "Layes, decires y canciones" de Rubén Darío,' *Revista de Filología Española*, vol. 19, no. 2, April–June 1932, 283–7

82 *Walt Whitman en Hispanoamérica*, Mexico: Studium, 1954, pp. 250–75

83 *Edgar Allan Poe in Hispanic Literature*, New York: Instituto de las Españas en los Estados Unidos, 1934, pp. 165–210

84 *Seis estudios sobre Rubén Darío*, Madrid: Editorial Gredos, 1967, pp. 103–43

85 *Rubén Darío y su época*, Bogotá: Sociedad Editora de los Andes, 1967, pp. 62–85

86 See Dieter Reichardt, 'Rubén Darío y Alemania,' *Papeles* (Caracas), no. 4, May–July 1967, 173–82. Concerning the influence of Wagner see Erika Lorenz, *Rubén Darío 'bajo el divino imperio de la música.' Estudio sobre la significación de un principio estético*, translated by Fidel Coloma González, Managua: Ediciones 'Lengua,' 1960; and Balseiro, *Seis estudios*, pp. 57–71.

87 Amado Alonso's article first appeared in *La Nación* (Buenos Aires), 25 September 1932 and it has been reprinted in several journals as well as in his book, *Materia y forma en poesía*, Madrid: Editorial Gredos, 1955, pp. 381–97; second edition, Madrid: Gredos, 1960, pp. 301–13. The article also appeared in *Estudios sobre Rubén Darío*, edited by Ernesto Mejía Sánchez, Mexico: Fondo de Cultura Económica, 1968, pp. 368–79. I quote from this publication, p. 372.

88 Michelangelo, *Rime*, Florence: Renascimento del Libro, 1944, p. 109

89 *Estudios sobre Rubén Darío*, edited by Ernesto Mejía Sánchez, p. 370

90 *Rubén Darío y su creación poética*, La Plata: Universidad de La Plata, 1934, p. 284

91 'La poesía "Lo fatal" de Rubén Darío,' *Revista de Educación* (Buenos Aires), Año 4, no. 2, Feb. 1959, 348–56. (This article is taken from the 1954 edition of Marasso's book, *Rubén Darío y su creación poética*, Buenos Aires: Kapelusz.)

92 *Rubén Darío y su creación poética*, La Plata: Universidad de la Plata, 1934, p. 278

93 *Revista del Profesorado* (Buenos Aires), March–June 1940, 39–46

94 Ibid., 42

95 Ibid.

96 Ibid.

97 In his article 'Anotaciones de un lector para una fuente más de "Lo fatal" de Rubén Darío,' *Estudios* (Madrid), Año 20, no. 65, April–June 1964, 325–6

98 *Asomante*, vol. 23, no. 2, April–June 1967, 44–9

99 His interpretation of the poem approximates that later arrived at by Enrique Anderson Imbert in his book *La originalidad de Rubén Darío*, Buenos Aires: Centro Editor de América Latina, 1967, pp. 141–8.

100 *Selected Prose*, edited by John Hayward, Harmondsworth: Penguin Books, 1959, p. 23
101 For two examples of such useful studies see Eduardo Zepeda-Henríquez's study, 'Los motivos,' in Julio Ycaza Tigerino and Eduardo Zepeda-Henríquez, *Estudio de la poética de Rubén Darío*, Managua: Comisión Nacional del Centenario, 1967, pp. 313–22; and Homero Castillo, 'Caupolicán en el modernismo de Darío,' *Revista Iberoamericana*, vol. 19, no. 37, October 1953, 111–18.
102 For further discussion of this point, see my article 'Concerning the Question of Influence,' *Hispania*, vol. 55, no. 2, May 1972, 340–2.
103 *Otras inquisiciones*, Buenos Aires: Emecé, 1960, p. 148

CHAPTER FOUR

1 *Inter America*, vol. 8, no. 1, October 1924, 29–38
2 *América y el pensamiento poético de Rubén Darío*, San José: Editorial Costa Rica, 1967, p. 17
3 *Rubén Darío y su intuición del mundo*, San Salvador: Editorial Universitaria de El Salvador, p. 55
4 In Rubén Darío, *Obras completas*, v, Madrid: Afrodisio Aguado, 1953, pp. 10–11
5 *Inspiration and Poetry*, London: Macmillan & Co., 1955
6 Particularly in his 'Preface to Shakespeare,' *Johnson on Shakespeare*, edited by Walter Raleigh, London: Oxford University Press, 1925, pp. 25–30
7 Especially in his *Biographia Literaria*, London: George Bell & Sons, 1894
8 Ibid. p. 145
9 See especially his *Science and Poetry*, London: Kegan Paul, 1926, pp. 55–67.
10 'Apolo o de la literatura,' *La experiencia literaria*, *Obras completas de Alfonso Reyes*, xiv, edited by Ernesto Mejía Sánchez, Mexico: Fondo de Cultura Económica, 1962, p. 83. He gave this definition of literature previously in his essay 'La vida y la obra,' *Tres puntos de exegética literaria*, *Obras completas de Alfonso Reyes*, xiv, edited by Ernesto Mejía Sánchez, Mexico: Fondo de Cultura Económica, 1962, p. 265.
11 *Selected Essays 1917–1932*, New York: Harcourt, Brace, 1932, pp. 115–16
12 See for a work informed by this notion, Mario Valdés, *Death in the Literature of Unamuno*, Urbana: University of Illinois Press, 1962.
13 See the chapter entitled 'Literature and Ideas' in René Wellek and Austin Warren, *Theory of Literature*, New York: Harcourt, Brace, 1948, pp. 107–23.
14 Buenos Aires: Editorial Losada, 1948
15 I quote from the second edition, Buenos Aires: Editorial Losada, 1957, pp. 47–8.
16 Ibid., p. 50
17 Ibid., p. 51
18 Alberto Carlos in his article *'El alba de oro* en "Canción de otoño en primavera,"' *Homenaje a Rubén Darío* (1867–1967), edited by Aníbal Sánchez Reulet, Los Angeles: Centro Latinoamericano, Universidad de California, Los Angeles, pp. 82–9, disagrees with Salinas's interpretation of the last line of Darío's poem and shows a different quality of eroticism in the poem. Also, Ricardo Gullón in his article 'Rubén Darío y el erotismo,' *Papeles de Son Armadans*, vol. 12, nos. 137–8, August–September 1967, pp. 143–58, suggests a different significance of eroticism in Darío than that observed by Salinas. Where the latter sees love ending in eroticism, Gullón suggests that eroticism for Darío is part of a transforming, almost mystical process. Gullón's view of transcendental eroticism is also put forward in his article, 'Pitagorismo y modernismo,' *Mundo Nuevo*, no. 7, January 1967, 22–32.

19 In his review of Salinas's *La poesía de Rubén Darío* in the *Nueva Revista de Filología Hispánica*, vol. 3, no. 1, January–March 1949, 91–3, Enrique Anderson Imbert seems to be more impressed by the extent of the dominance of the erotic theme in Darío's work (seen by Salinas) than he is in his *La originalidad de Rubén Darío*, Buenos Aires: Centro Editor de América Latina, 1967, pp. 88,180. He regrets in his review, however, that Salinas's work was not carried out chronologically, following the biography of the poet. Manuel Pedro González expresses the view, in his review of Salinas's book (*Hispanic Review*, vol. 17, no. 1, January 1949, pp. 260–3), that the emphasis placed by Salinas on the erotic theme subordinated unjustifiably other themes such as the love of art and the obsession with death.

20 See his rigorous exposition of the critical principle in his *Hacia una semblanza de Quevedo*, Santander: Editorial Bedia, 1969.

21 Catalina Tomás McNamee, *El pensamiento católico de Rubén Darío* (Extracto de la tesis doctoral del mismo título), Madrid: Facultad de Filosofía y Letras de la Universidad de Madrid, 1967, pp. 39–40

22 'El tema del alma en Rubén Darío,' *Atenea*, Año 44, nos. 415–16, January–June 1967, 39–62; and 'Rubén Darío ... huérfano esquife, árbol insigne, oscuro nido,' in Luis Oyarzún *et al.*, *Darío*, Santiago: Departamento de Extensión, Universidad de Chile, 1968, pp. 42–9

23 'El sentimiento religioso en la obra de Rubén Darío,' *La Torre*, Año 15, nos. 55–6, January–June 1967, 255–72

24 Julio Ycaza Tigerino and Eduardo Zepeda-Henríquez, *Estudio de la poética de Rubén Darío*, Managua: Comisión Nacional del Centenario, 1967, pp. 7–52

25 'Elementos religiosos en la poesía de Rubén Darío,' *Homenaje a Rubén Darío (1867–1967)*, ed. Aníbal Sánchez-Reulet, Los Angeles: Centro Latinoamericano, University of California, Los Angeles, 1940, pp. 139–48

26 'Principios cristianos en los cuentos de Rubén Darío,' *Revista Iberoamericana*, vol. 24, no. 47, January–June 1959, 28–39

27 '"Lo de dentro" en Rubén Darío,' *Hispania*, vol. 45, no. 4, December 1962, 651–7

28 In the chapter entitled 'Sincretismo religioso,' *La originalidad de Rubén Darío*, Buenos Aires: Centro Editor de América Latina, 1967, pp. 197–213

29 Ibid., p. 188

30 For a discussion which focuses on this aspect of Darío's work see Richard A. Cardwell, 'Darío and *El arte puro*: The Enigma of Life and the Beguilement of Art,' *Bulletin of Hispanic Studies*, vol. 47, 1970, 37–51. In this important article Cardwell succeeds in showing 'how intimately and paradoxically the beguilement of art, the creation of a timeless erotic myth, the enigma of life and the vanity of illusion are linked' (p. 38) and he suggests, therefore, that '*panerotismo* cannot be granted the total primacy Salinas gives it' (p. 38).

31 For a detailed study of this concept in Darío's poetry see Angel Luis Morales, *La angustia metafísica en la poesía de Rubén Darío*, Río Piedras: Biblioteca de Extramuros, Universidad de Puerto Rico, 1967.

32 *Estudio de la poética de Rubén Darío*, Managua: Comisión Nacional del Centenario, 1967, pp. 53–300

33 In his *La lección de Rubén Darío*, Madrid: Taurus, 1960

34 'La presencia negra en la obra de Rubén Darío,' *Revista Iberoamericana*, vol. 33, no. 64, July–December 1967, 395–417. Other writings of Darío not included in the *Obras completas* lend support to Jackson's view: for instance, the article 'El talento de los

negros,' *La Nación*, 28 January 1912, p. 6 and reprinted in *Escritos dispersos de Rubén Darío*, edited by Pedro Luis Barcia, La Plata: Facultad de Humanidades y Ciencias de Educación de la Universidad Nacional de la Plata, 1968, pp. 295–8. Darío's indication in his 'Palabras liminares,' to *Prosas profanas* that he might have been of partly African as well as Indian ancestry is confirmed by several of his biographers, as Jackson and Durand have pointed out, by Pedro Henríquez Ureña, Ricardo Rojas, and Leopoldo Lugones, for example. Darío's son, Rubén Darío Contreras has denied this with reasoning that is not convincing. Zulma Núñez in his article 'Rubén Darío recordado por su hijo,' *Argentina Libre*, 6 February 1941, p. 9, quotes Darío Contreras as saying 'Sus apellidos de García y Sarmiento son bien españoles ... Por otra parte, conozco el árbol genealógico de la familia y he comprobado que ninguno de sus componentes realizó matrimonio con nativos de color o indios.'

35 *La Négritude dans l'œuvre poétique de Rubén Darío*, Dakar: Centre de Hautes Etudes Afro-Ibero-Americaines de L'Université de Dakar, 1970
36 *Darío, Cernuda y otros temas poéticos*, Madrid: Editorial Nacional, 1969, p. 222
37 *Obras completas*, IV, Madrid: Afrodisio Aguado, 1955, pp. 1387–94
38 Carl E.W.L. Dahlström makes this distinction in his discussion of theme in his article, 'The Analysis of the Literary Situation,' *Publications of the Modern Language Association*, vol. 51, no. 3, September 1936, 872–89. His discussion forms the substance of the article on 'theme' in the *Dictionary of World Literary Terms*, edited by Joseph T. Shipley, Boston: The Writer, Inc., 1970, p. 333.
39 *Interpretación y análisis de la obra literaria*, Madrid: Editorial Gredos, 1958, p. 117
40 *A Glossary of Literary Terms*, New York: Rinehart and Co., 1957, pp. 53–4
41 *Rubén Darío: 'Bajo el divino imperio de la música,'* translated by Fidel Coloma González, Managua: Ediciones de la Academia Nicaragüense de la Lengua, 1960
42 See Kurt L. Levy's review of the original German edition (Hamburg: Cram de Gruyter, Ibero-Amerikanisches Forschungsinstitut, Hamburger Romanistische Studien, 1956) in *Modern Language Quarterly*, vol. 18, no. 3, September 1957, 266–7. Other notable works dealing with music in Darío's work are José Agustín Balseiro's already-mentioned 'Presencia de Wagner y casi ausencia de Debussy en la obra de Rubén Darío,' in his *Seis estudios sobre Rubén Darío*, Madrid: Editorial Gredos, 1967, pp. 57–72. For a study of musical effects in a specific poem, see Robert Avrett, 'Música y efectos melódicos en "Sinfonía en gris mayor,"' *Seminario-Archivo Rubén Darío*, no. 3, 1960, 33–7.
43 'Rubén Darío y la fuente,' *Asomante*, vol. 23, no. 1, January–March 1967, 7–14. A similar kind of study, dealing with the symbol Psiquis, is Enrique Rull, 'El símbolo de psique en la poesía de Rubén Darío,' *Revista de Literatura*, vol. 27, nos. 53–4, January–June 1965, 33–50.
44 *Comparative Literature Studies*, vol. 4, no. 4, December, 1967, 425–56
45 Ibid., 446
46 Dissertation, University of Michigan, 1969
47 Santiago de Chile: Editorial Universitaria, 1971
48 Ibid., p. 57
49 *Antología de la versificación rítmica*, San José: El Convivio, 1918; 'El endecasílabo castellano,' *Revista de Filología Española*, vol. 6, no. 2, April–June 1919, 132–157; *La versificación irregular en la poesía española*, Madrid: Publicaciones de la Revista de Filología Española, 1920.
50 'El modelo estrófico de los "Layes, decires y canciones" de Rubén Darío,' *Revista de Filología Española*, vol. 19, no. 4, October–December 1932, 421–2. This article rebuffs

José María de Cossío's statement (in an article with the same title and published in the same journal, vol. 19, no. 2, July–September 1932, 283–7) that Darío did not know Spanish literature well.

51 'La cantidad silábica en unos versos de Rubén Darío,' *Revista de Filología Española*, vol. 9, no. 1, January–March 1922, 1–29. See also his 'Fonología y pronunciación en las rimas de Rubén Darío' in his *Estudios de fonología española*, Syracuse: Syracuse University Press, 1946, pp. 178–90 and his 'Ritmo y armonía en los versos de Darío,' *La Torre*, Año 15, nos. 55–6, January–June 1967, 49–69

52 'Innovation and French Influence in the Metrics of Rubén Darío,' *Publications of the Modern Language Association of America*, vol. 49, no. 1, January 1934, 310–26; and 'Los primeros alejandrinos de Rubén Darío,' *Revista Hispánica Moderna*, vol. 1, no. 4, July 1935, 241–59.

53 'Los hexámetros castellanos y en particular los de Rubén Darío,' *Anales de la Universidad de Chile*, vol. 93, no. 18, April–June 1935, 5–90; and 'El verso que no cultivó Rubén Darío,' *Anales de la Universidad de Chile*, vol. 91 no. 12, October-December 33–61

54 'La función del alejandrino francés en el alejandrino español de Rubén Darío,' *Revista de Literatura*, vol. 4, no. 7, July–December 1953, 9–58. See also his study of the metrical system of the poem 'Urna votiva' in his article 'Un soneto de Rubén Darío,' *Seminario-Archivo Rubén Darío*, no. 1, 1961, 5–12.

55 'De la métrica en Rubén Darío, *Anales de la Universidad de Santo Domingo*, vol. 19, nos. 69–70, January–June 1954, 65–94

56 'La métrica en Rubén Darío,' Dissertation, University of Madrid, 1957

57 'La dislocación acentual en la poesía de Rubén Darío,' *Cuadernos Hispanoamericanos*, nos. 212–13, August–September 1967, 405–9. Oliver Belmás has also done important studies of Darío's versification in his *Este otro Rubén Darío*, Barcelona: Editorial Aedos, 1960, pp. 347–403.

58 Pedro Henríquez Ureña, 'Rubén Darío,' *Obra crítica*, edited by Emma Susana Speratti Piñero, Mexico: Fondo de Cultura Económica, 1960, p. 97. The essay was first published in 1905.

59 Ibid., p. 100

60 *Nueva Revista de Filología Hispánica*, vol. 13, nos. 3–4, July–December 1959, 345–51

61 'Desde Rubén,' *Asomante*, vol. 23, no. 2, April–June 1967, 7–21; and 'Notas al casticismo de Rubén,' *Revista Iberoamericana*, vol. 33, no. 64, July–December 1967, 333–58

62 'García Lorca y Darío,' *Asomante*, vol. 23, no. 2, April–June 1967, 22–31

63 'Rubén Darío y la gramática,' *Revista Nacional de Cultura*, vol. 3, no. 31, January–February 1942, 74–8

64 'Sobre el uso de los tiempos verbales en Rubén Darío,' *Revista Hispánica Moderna*, vol. 30, nos. 3–4, July–October 1964, 205–14

65 'Los americanismos en Rubén Darío,' *Papeles de Son Armadans*, vol. 12, nos. 137–8, August–September 1967, 191–6

66 'Rubén Darío: El hombre y su lenguaje,' *Papeles de Son Armadans*, vol. 12, nos. 137–8, August–September 1967, 287–304

67 For a study that deals with Darío's adaptation of French linguistic forms see Juan López-Morillas, 'El *Azul* de Rubén Darío. ¿Galicismo mental o lingüístico?' *Revista Hispánica Moderna*, vol. 10, no. 1, January 1944, 9–14.

68 Guatemala: Editorial Universitaria, 1966

CHAPTER FIVE

1 For a facsimile of the newspaper page bearing the second part of the article and for the complete article and a part of Darío's reply to it, see Diego Manuel Sequeira, *Rubén Darío criollo o raíz y médula de su creación poética*, Buenos Aires: Editorial Guillermo Kraft Ltd., 1945, pp. 156–69.
2 Ibid., p. 164
3 Ibid., p. 157
4 Ibid.
5 Ibid.
6 Ibid., pp. 157–8
7 Ibid., p. 159
8 Ibid.
9 Ibid.
10 See ibid., pp. 160, 163
11 Ibid., p. 164
12 *El Diario Nicaragüense*, no. 96, 29 October 1884
13 Darío, who characteristically remained silent in the face of foolish criticism, had no doubt forgotten about his reply to Contreras when he wrote in the 'Dilucidaciones' to *El canto errante* (1907): 'Tan solamente he contestado a la crítica tres veces, por la categoría de sus representantes, y porque mi natural orgullo juvenil, ¡entonces!, recibiera también flores de los sagitarios. Por lo demás, ellos se llamaban Max Nordau, Paul Groussac, Leopoldo Alas' (*Obras completas*, v, 952).
14 Matías Calandrelli, 'Prosas profanas y otros poemas de Rubén Darío,' *Revista de Derecho, Historia y Letras*, vol. 1, no. 1, October 1898, 519
15 Ibid.
16 Ibid., p. 521
17 Ibid.
18 *Revista de Derecho, Historia y Letras*, vol. 1, no. 2, November 1898, 54–69
19 Ibid., p. 57
20 Ibid., p. 64
21 Pedro Henríquez Ureña, 'Rubén Darío,' *Obra crítica*, edited by Emma Susana Speratti Piñero, Mexico: Fondo de Cultura Económica, 1960, p. 100
22 Ibid., p. 101
23 Rubén Darío, *Obras escogidas*, edited by Andrés González-Blanco, Madrid: Librería de los Sucesores de Hernando, 1910, I, 251
24 Ibid., pp. 276–7
25 Ibid., p. 291
26 Cf. Darío's own view of his method, expressed in his 'Historia de mis libros,' *Obras completas*, I, 201: 'En los versos seguía el mismo método que en la prosa: la aplicación de ciertas ventajas verbales de otras lenguas, en este caso principalmente del francés, al castellano. Abandono de las ordenaciones usuales, de los clisés consuetudinarios; atención a la melodía interior, que contribuye al éxito de la expresión rítmica; novedad en los adjetivos; estudio y fijeza del significado etimológico de cada vocablo; aplicación de la erudición oportuna, aristocracia léxica.'
27 Rubén Darío, *Cuentos completos*, edited by Ernesto Mejía Sánchez, Mexico: Fondo de Cultura Económica, 1950, pp. vii–lxvii
28 Ibid., p. lxv

29 'Rubén Darío and the Fantastic Element in Literature,' translated by Anne Bonner, *Rubén Darío Centennial Studies*, edited by Miguel González-Gerth and George D. Schade, Austin: University of Texas, 1970, pp. 97–117

30 In Luis Oyarzún *et al.*, *Darío*, Santiago: Universidad de Chile, Departamento de Extensión Universitaria, 1968, pp. 67–81

31 'Rubén Darío, prosista,' *La Torre*, Año 15, nos. 55 and 56, January–June 1967, 135–54

32 'En torno a las prosas de Rubén Darío,' *La Torre*, Año 15, nos. 55 and 56, January–June 1967, 155–77

33 *Darío en su prosa*, Granada, Nicaragua: Editorial Hospicio, 1960

34 'Análisis estilístico de la prosa dariana,' in Julio Ycaza Tigerino and Eduardo Zepeda-Henríquez, *Estudio de la poética de Rubén Darío*, Managua: Comisión Nacional del Centenario, 1967, pp. 417–40

35 'Rubén Darío, novelista,' in *Diez estudios sobre Rubén Darío*, edited by Juan Loveluck, Santiago: Empresa Editora Zig Zag, 1967, pp. 219–42

36 'El oro de Mallorca' Textos desconocidos y breve comentario sobre la novela autobiográfica de Darío,' *Revista Iberoamericana*, vol. 33, no. 64, July–December 1967, 444–92

37 'The Function of Irony in "El rey burgués," ' *Hispania*, vol. 49, no. 2, May 1966, 223–7

38 'Recursos narrativos en "El fardo," ' *Atenea*, Año 44, nos. 415–16, January–June 1967, 29–37

39 *Revista Iberoamericana*, vol. 33, no. 64, July–December 1967, 333–58

40 Ibid., pp. 352–3

41 *Insula*, Año 22, no. 248–9, July–August 1967, 11–12

42 Ibid., 11

43 Rubén Benítez, 'La celebración del amor en "Primaveral" de Darío: Voz poética y tono,' *Insula*, Año 22, nos. 248–9, July–August 1967, 6, 28

44 Rubén Benítez, 'La expresión de lo primitivo en "Estival" de Darío,' *Revista Iberoamericana*, vol. 33, no. 64, July–December 1967, 237–50

45 Eleazar Huerta, ' "Invernal" de Rubén Darío,' in Luis Oyarzún *et al.*, *Darío*, pp. 21–41

46 Homero Castillo, 'Caupolicán en el modernismo de Darío,' *Revista Iberoamericana*, vol. 19, no. 37, October–December 1953, 111–18

47 Rubén Benítez, 'La expresión de la frivolidad en "Era un aire suave ...," ' *Homenaje a Rubén Darío 1867–1967*, edited by Aníbal Sánchez Reulet, Los Angeles: Centro Latinoamericano, Universidad de California, Los Angeles, 1970, pp. 90–105

48 Arturo Echavarría, 'Estructura y sentido poético del "Coloquio de los centauros," ' *La Torre*, Año 17, no. 65, July–September 1969, 95–130

49 David Gershator, 'Rubén Darío's reflections on Manhattan: Two Poems,' *Romance Notes*, vol. 11, no. 1, Autumn 1967, 30–5

50 Allen W. Phillips, 'Sobre "Sinfonía en gris mayor" de Rubén Darío,' *Cuadernos Americanos*, vol. 113, no. 6, November–December 1960, 217–24; and Ann B. Darroch, 'Rubén Darío's "Sinfonía en gris mayor": A New Interpretation,' *Hispania*, vol. 53, no. 2, May 1970, 46–52

51 María Luisa Punte, 'El poema prólogo a *Cantos de vida y esperanza*,' *Rubén Darío: Estudios reunidos en conmemoración del centenario (1867–1967)*, edited by Juan Carlos Ghiano, La Plata: Universidad Nacional de la Plata, 1968, pp. 168–75

52 Antonio Pagés Larraya, 'Estructura y sentido en un soneto de Darío,' *Hispania*, vol. 53, no. 2, May 1970, 181–8

53 Antonio Pagés Larraya, 'Revelación y mito en un soneto de Darío,' *Revista Iberoamericana*, vol. 35, no. 69, September–December 1969, 441–58

54 Enrique Anderson Imbert, *La originalidad de Rubén Darío*, Buenos Aires: Centro Editor de América Latina, pp. 141–7; and M.P. Predmore, 'A Stylistic Analysis of "Lo fatal," ' *Hispanic Review*, vol. 39, no. 4, October 1971, 433–8; and Eduardo Zepeda-Henríquez, 'El proceso de la creación poética en Darío,' in Julio Ycaza Tigerino and Eduardo Zepeda-Henríquez, *Estudio de la poética de Rubén Darío*, Managua: Comisión Nacional del Centenario, 1967, pp. 306–11

55 Julio Ycaza Tigerino, *Los nocturnos de Rubén Darío y otros ensayos*, Managua: Imprenta Granada, 1954; Bernardo Gicovate, 'Lectura de un poema de Darío. Reflexiones sobre la originalidad,' *Asomante*, vol. 23, no. 1, January–March 1967, 38–42

56 Joaquina Navarro, 'Ritmo y sentido en "Canción de otoño en primavera," ' *Thesaurus*, vol. 24, no. 3, September–December 1969, 408–16; and Alberto Carlos, 'El alba de oro en "Canción de otoño en primavera," ' in *Homenaje a Rubén Darío*, edited by Aníbal Sánchez Reulet, Los Angeles: Centro Latinoamericano, University of California, Los Angeles, 1970, pp. 82–9

57 See David Gershator, 'Rubén Darío's Reflections on Manhattan: Two Poems,' *Romance Notes*, vol. 11, no. 1, Autumn 1967, 30–5.

58 All these have been studied by Zepeda-Henríquez in Julio Ycaza Tigerino and Eduardo Zepeda-Henríquez, *Estudio de la poética de Rubén Darío*, pp. 313–44, 383–416.

59 *Rubén Darío y su creación poética*, Buenos Aires: Biblioteca Nuevo, 1946, pp. 73–108.

60 *Rubén Darío y el mito de centauro*, Buenos Aires: Casa Editora Coni, 1961

61 'El motivo del centauro y la universalidad de Rubén Darío,' *La Torre*, Año 15, nos. 55–6, January–June 1967, 71–97. Durand's paper was read as a part of the program to celebrate Darío's centenary in Managua from 15–22 January 1967.

62 Ibid., p. 83

63 Ibid.

64 See for a case in point my study of a Neruda poem, ' "Poema xx": A Structural Approach,' *Romance Notes*, vol. 11, no. 3, Spring 1970, 507–17.

65 Even though, by avoiding the kind of comparative study of 'Lo fatal' carried out by Alonso, he makes observations about the poem, particularly about the versification, that long needed to be made.

66 'A Stylistic Analysis of "Lo fatal," ' *Hispanic Review*, vol. 39, no. 4, October 1971, 434

67 'Hipótesis cuadricontinental,' *Casa de las Américas*, Año 7, no. 42, May–June 1967, 59–67

68 See his notes to his various editions of Darío's *Poesías completas*.

69 'Variantes en un poema de Rubén Darío: "La tragedia del toro," ' *Revista Iberoamericana*, vol. 25, no. 49, January–March 1960, 153–61

70 'Rubén Darío and the Hispanic Society: The Holograph Manuscript of " ¡Pax!," ' *Hispanic Review*, vol. 35, no. 1, January 1967, 1–42

71 *An Analytical Index of the Complete Poetical Works of Rubén Darío*, Washington, D.C.: Microcard Editions, 1970

72 Some problems affecting methods of analysis such as I have been describing were examined recently by Wallace Martin in his article 'The Hermeneutic Circle and the Art of Interpretation,' *Comparative Literature*, vol. 24, no. 2, Spring 1972, 97–117. Martin feels particularly concerned about the circularity of arguments employed by several theorists of interpretation, a circularity which arises from the fact that meaning and value are shown in terms of individual poems and are derived from the relationship between what Martin finds to be analysable parts and an intuited whole. One must demur at the concept of the intuited whole. It is surely possible and desirable for the view

of the whole to be not intuited but formed by the demonstrated harmonizing of the analysed parts. At the same time it is sometimes the case that an analysed part can be shown not to function usefully in terms of the overall structure of the work. One problem facing Martin and anyone who is preoccupied with theory is the striking lack of demonstration some theorists give of their theories in the field of practical criticism. Another problem is the disparity between theory and demonstration. This can be noticed, for instance, in the disparity between W.K. Wimsatt's rigorously argued essay 'Explication as Criticism' in his *The Verbal Icon*, Lexington: University of Kentucky Press, 1954, pp. 235–52, and his inclusion in his edited book *Explication as Criticism*, New York: Columbia University Press, 1963, where the essay is republished, of such an essay as David V. Erdman's 'Blake; the Historical Approach,' pp. 147–63. Also, certain analyses of literary works, carried out in great detail by theorists whose primary interests are not literary, come to seem from the literary point of view to be tied to an external interest and to be carried out in indiscriminate detail. See, for example, Roman Jakobson and Claude Lévi-Strauss, '"Les Chats" de Charles Baudelaire,' *L'Homme*, vol. 2, no. 1, January–April 1962, 5–21, and the rectifying response this study elicited from Michael Riffaterre, 'Describing Poetic Structures: Two Approaches to Baudelaire's "Les Chats,"' *Structuralism*, *Yale French Studies*, nos. 36–7, October 1966, 200–42.

73 The text used is taken from *Cuentos completos de Rubén Darío*, edited by Ernesto Mejía Sánchez, Mexico: Fondo de Cultura Económica, 1950, pp. 79–85. The page references in the text are to this edition. The story was first published in *La Libertad Electoral* (Santiago de Chile), 9 June 1888. Later in that year it formed part of Darío's first edition of *Azul* ... and it has been included in all subsequent editions.

74 Jorge Luis Borges, *Ficciones*, Buenos Aires: Emecé Editores, 1969, pp. 13–34. For a work in which Darío merges historical reality and the fantastic to superb effect, see his little known story entitled 'Huitzilopotchtli,' in *Páginas desconocidas de Rubén Darío*, edited by Roberto Ibáñez, Montevideo: Biblioteca de Marcha, 1970, pp. 220–4.

75 The text of the poem used for this study has been taken from Rubén Darío, *Poesías completas*, edited by Alfonso Méndez Plancarte, Madrid: Aguilar, 1967, p. 535. This study was published in *Revista Iberoamericana*, vol. 33, no. 64, July–December 1967, 251–8, and is reprinted here with the permission of the editor of that journal.

76 I use poet to refer to the narrative voice in the poem.

77 In the notes to his edition of *Poesías completas*, p. 1179, Méndez Plancarte gives lines published in the original version of 1889 in *Repertorio Salvadoreño* which were later changed in the 1890 version.

78 In the poem 'El hombre invisible' which introduces his *Odas elementales*, in *Obras completas*, Buenos Aires: Editorial Losada, 1962, p. 936

79 *La poesía de Rubén Darío*, Buenos Aires: Editorial Losada, 1948

80 Ibid., p. 57

81 Andrés González-Blanco, *Rubén Darío: Obras escogidas*, Madrid: Librería de los Sucesores de Hernando, 1910, 1, 324. In his book *Rubén Darío: su vida y su obra*, Barcelona: Editorial Agencia Mundial de Librería, 1930, p. 175, he declares that the metre is a 'combinación no muy feliz del heptasílabo y el decasílabo.' For favourable comment on the rhythm of the sonnet see Gerardo Diego, 'Ritmo y espíritu en Rubén Darío,' *Cuadernos Hispanoamericanos*, nos. 212–13, August–September 1967, 247–64.

82 Darío was inaccurate in his comments on the metre of the poem when he wrote in his *Historia de mis libros* of the poem's 'versos de quince sílabas.' *Obras completas*, 1, Madrid: Afrodisio Aguado, 1950, 203.

83 The text of the poem used for this study has been taken from *Poesías completas*, pp. 639–41.

84 The opinions expressed of the poem have not, of course, all been favourable. Jorge Luis Borges, 'Mensaje en honor de Rubén Darío,' *El Despertar Americano*, vol. 1, no. 2, May 1967, 9, expressed the view that 'A Roosevelt' is one of Darío's forgettable poems; and Peter H. Goldsmith the editor of *Inter America* intervened in a discussion of the poem by C. Rangel Baez, 'The Poetry of Ideas in Darío and Nervo,' *Inter America*, vol. 8, no. 1, October 1924, 29–38, to describe the poem in a note (pp. 33–4) as 'one of the cleverest, and at the same time one of the silliest, of Darío's pieces, since it is a sprightly résumé of all the vulgar prejudice, cheap misinformation, puerile bombast and perverse hostility of spirit of certain types of quasi-Latins of America and Europe.'

85 The opinion of the United States implicit in this poem coincides with the opinions Darío had expressed prior to its composition. See with regard to this José Agustín Balseiro, 'Arieles y Calibanes,' in his *Seis estudios sobre Rubén Darío*, Madrid: Editorial Gredos, 1967, pp. 117–31. In the second edition of *Azul ...* (1890) Darío had stressed the materialistic values of the United States in his sonnet to Walt Whitman by beginning the poem with the verse: 'En su país de hierro vive el gran viejo.' In his article 'El triunfo de Calibán' published in *El Tiempo* (Buenos Aires), 20 May 1898, Darío developed the theory he had enunciated in *Los raros* (1896) of the correspondence between the United States and Caliban. For this reason and because of the emphasis Darío placed on the indigenous element in Spanish America, the influence of Rodó in the formulation of his attitude towards the United States does not seem to be as significant as is usually supposed.

86 In a different context, in his *Viaje a Nicaragua* (*Obras completas*, III, 1047), Darío wrote 'No iban a América los conquistadores a civilizar, sino a ganar tierras y oro.'

87 Its effect is nevertheless somewhat diminished since 'vive' appears earlier in the stanza.

88 Andrés González-Blanco, *Rubén Darío: Obras escogidas*, Madrid: Librería de los Sucesores de Hernando, 1910, 1, 377; and Pedro Salinas, *La poesía de Rubén Darío*, Buenos Aires: Editorial Losada, 1957, pp. 236–7, have commented on the emphatic effect of the assonance in 'o' in the final word 'Dios.'

89 During this period Darío expressed, in prose, the view that he had given of Roosevelt in his poem of 1904. In 'Dilucidaciones,' *Canto errante* (1907), he calls Roosevelt 'terrible cazador' (*Obras completas*, V, 945); and three years later, in his essay 'Roosevelt en París,' *Obras completas*, II, 671–9, he refers to him as 'gran cazador' (p. 671) and 'Nemrod' (p. 673). When this article first appeared, José Santos Zelaya wrote to Darío: 'Creo conveniente mandar a todas partes el número del *Paris Journal* en que se publica su artículo, para que sea conocido y se vea el patriotismo de usted y lo malparado que queda el ex-Presidente Roosevelt' (Alberto Ghiraldo, *El archivo de Rubén Darío*, Santiago de Chile: Editorial Bolívar, 1940, p. 236).

90 *Obras completas*, II, 1005

91 *Poesías completas*, p. 747

92 Ibid., p. 546

93 For theories concerning Darío's use of the indigenous in this and in other poems see Luis Monguió, 'El origen de unos versos de "A Roosevelt,"' *Hispania*, vol. 38, no. 3, September 1955, 424–5; and José Juan Arrom, 'El oro, la pluma y la piedra preciosa,' *Hispania*, vol. 50, no. 4, December 1967, 971–81.

94 For a study of the contemporary relevance of 'A Roosevelt' see Aurora de Albornoz, '''A

Roosevelt" un poema muy actual de Rubén Darío, *'Cuadernos Americanos*, vol. 107, no. 4, September–December 1961, 255–8.

95 *Poesías completas*, p. 628

CHAPTER SIX

1 Octavio Paz, *Cuadrivio*, Mexico: Editorial Joaquín Mortiz, pp. 9–65
2 Cecil Maurice Bowra *et al.*, *Rubén Darío en Oxford*, Managua: Academia Nicaragüense de la Lengua, 1966. Bowra's translated contribution to this book was published originally in his *Inspiration and Poetry*, London: Macmillan & Co., 1955, pp. 242–64.
3 'Nueva evaluación de Rubén Darío,' *La Torre*, Año 15, nos. 55–6, January–June 1967, 121–31
4 'Rubén y su herencia,' *La Torre*, Año 15, nos. 55–6, January–June 1967, 287–308
5 'Consideraciones polémicas acerca de la vigencia y actualidad de Rubén Darío.' *Repertorio Centroamericano* (San José), Año 3, nos. 7–8, May 1967, 6–19
6 Paz, p. 13
7 Ibid.
8 Ibid., p. 30
9 See Chapter 4 of this book.
10 Paz, p. 56
11 See Chapter 4 of this book.
12 Paz, p. 58
13 *Rubén Darío en Oxford*, p. 51. Bowra might also have written too hastily on the poetry of Pablo Neruda in his book *Poetry and Politics 1900–1960*, Cambridge: Cambridge University Press, 1966, pp. 132–6, where he emphasizes the primitive nature of what he regards as Neruda's uneven production. His only bibliographical reference to Neruda's poetry is Ben Belitt's book of poor translations, *Selected Poems of Pablo Neruda*, New York: Grove Press, 1961.
14 *Inspiration and Poetry*, London: Macmillan & Co., 1955, p. 253
15 Ibid., p. 255
16 Ibid.
17 Ibid., p. 242
18 'Experimento en Rubén Darío,' *Rubén Darío en Oxford*, pp. 57–77
19 *Darío, Cernuda y otros temas poéticos*, Madrid: Editora Nacional, 1969, pp. 13–143
20 *Rubén Darío en Oxford*, pp. 81–112
21 Saúl Yurkievich expanded on this idea in his article, 'Rubén Darío, precursor de la vanguardia,' *Memoria del xv Congreso del Instituto Internacional de Literatura Iberoamericana*, Lima: Universidad Nacional Mayor de San Marcos, Dirección Universitaria de Biblioteca y Publicaciones, 1972, pp. 117–31.
22 'Rubén Darío y la crítica,' *Hispania*, vol. 14, no. 1, February 1931, 99–106
23 'Nueva evaluación,' p. 131
24 'Rubén Darío,' *El Fígaro* (Havana), 16 February 1916
25 Madrid: Editorial América, 1916
26 Ibid., pp. 143–5. Similar views were later presented in books by Vicente Marrero Suárez, *Nuestro Rubén*, Madrid: Ediciones Cultura Hispánica, 1970, and by Guillermo de Torre, *Vigencia de Rubén Darío y otras páginas*, Madrid: Ediciones Guadarrama, 1969. See too with regard to Spain's indebtedness, Ricardo Gullón, 'Rubén Darío, España y los españoles,' *Asomante*, vol. 23, no. 1, January–March 1967, 15–23.

27 Manuel y Antonio Machado, *Obras completas*, Madrid: Editorial Plenitud, 1962, pp.
   851–952
28 *Antología poética*, Madrid: Editorial Magisterio Español, 1968, pp. 105–6
29 *Los heraldos negros*, Buenos Aires: Editorial Losada, 1961, p. 88
30 Federico García Lorca, *Obras completas*, Madrid: Aguilar, 1962, pp. 1717–21
31 *Homenaje a Rubén Darío (1867–1967)*, Los Angeles: Centro Latinoamericano, University of California, Los Angeles, 1970, pp. 296–298
32 *Obras completas de Vicente Huidobro*, edited by Braulio Arenas, Santiago de Chile: Editorial Zig Zag, 1964, I, 728
33 'Carta,' *La Estafeta Literaria*, nos. 360–1, 14 January 1967, 41
34 *La Torre*, Año 15, nos. 55–6, January–June 1967, 308

APPENDIX

1 Brief studies devoted to the subject are the prologue by Emilio Abreu Gómez to his anthology *Rubén Darío: crítico literario*, Washington: Unión Panamericana, 1951, pp. 11–16; Roxana Gardes, 'Lo raro en *Los raros*,' *Rubén Darío: Estudios reunidos en conmemoración del centenario (1867–1967)*, edited by Juan Carlos Ghiano, La Plata: Universidad Nacional de la Plata, 1968, pp. 179–92; Ludwig Schrader, 'Rubén Darío, crítico literario en *Los raros*,' *El ensayo y la crítica en Hispanoamérica*, Memoria del XIV Congreso Internacional de Literatura Iberoamericana, edited by Kurt L. Levy and Keith Ellis, Toronto, 1970, pp. 95–9; and María Salgado, 'El retrato como crítica literaria en *Los raros*,' *Romance Notes*, vol. 11, no. 1, Autumn 1969, 30–5. Other mention is made of it in some of the comprehensive studies of Darío's work, such as Enrique Anderson Imbert, *La originalidad de Rubén Darío*, Buenos Aires: Centro Editor de América Latina, 1967, pp. 69–74, 149–56, and Jaime Torres Bodet, *Rubén Darío: abismo y cima*, Mexico: Universidad Nacional Autónoma de Mexico, 1966, pp. 194–200.
2 For two recent studies of Darío's literary manifestos, as they relate to his creative work, see Raúl H. Castagnino, '"No soy más que un hombre de arte,"' *Rubén Darío: Estudios reunidos en conmemoración del centenario (1867–1967)*, pp. 128–37. Reyna Suárez Wilson's, 'Los prólogos de Darío,' appears in the same work, pp. 138–67.
3 Rubén Darío, *Obras completas*, V, Madrid: Afrodisio Aguado, 1953, 761
4 Ibid.
5 Ibid., 955–6
6 *Obras completas*, I, 413
7 Ibid.
8 *Obras completas*, V, 960
9 *Obras completas*, I, 419
10 See Marinello's 'Rubén Darío: Meditación de centenario,' *L/L*, Año 1, no. 2, April–December 1967, 32
11 *Obras completas*, IV, 933
12 *Obras completas*, I, 691
13 Ibid., 694
14 *Obras completas*, II, 440. The work in question, by Isidore Lucien Ducasse who was born in Montevideo in 1846 and who used the pseudonym of Comte de Lautréamont, was printed in 1869. Its violent tone caused its Belgian publisher to refuse to distribute it for fear of prosecution. It finally appeared in 1890 in a limited edition and remained virtually unknown until the nineteen twenties when the Surrealists discovered it and found it

exemplary. Cf. Gaston Bachelard, *Lautréamont*, Paris: J. Corti, 1939. Darío claimed to be one of 'un reducidísimo grupo de iniciados' who in 1896 knew this work, and he introduced it to Spanish America in this essay, warning young writers against its extremes. Publio González-Rodas, 'Rubén Darío y el conde de Lautréamont,' *Revista Iberoamericana*, vol. 37, no. 75, April–June 1971, 375–89, and Sidonia C. Taupin, '¿Había leído Darío a Lautréamont cuando lo incluyó en *Los raros*?' *Comparative Literature*, vol. 11, no. 2, Spring 1959, 165–70, have made the case that, although Darío had read about Lautréamont before he wrote about him, he had not read his work directly.

15 *Obras completas*, v, 860
16 *Obras completas*, ii, 245–518
17 *Obras completas*, iii, 13–374
18 *Obras completas*, i, 225–452
19 *Obras completas*, ii, 937–1032
20 Ibid., 783–936
21 *Obras completas*, i, 625–734
22 *Obras completas*, ii, 491–2
23 Mexico: Servicio de Informaciones Alemanas [n.d.]
24 *Obras completas*, ii, 1005
25 Ibid., 1006
26 *Obras completas*, iii, 325
27 *Obras completas*, iv, 738–9
28 *Obras completas*, i, 228
29 *Obras completas*, ii, 149–244
30 In Alberto Ghiraldo, *El archivo de Rubén Darío*, Santiago de Chile: Editorial Bolívar, 1940, p. 106
31 *Obras completas*, iv, 745–66
32 *Obras completas*, ii, 587–99
33 *Obras completas*, ii, 587
34 Ibid., 590
35 *Obras completas*, i, 15–178
36 *Obras completas*, iii, 258–65
37 *Obras completas*, iv, 837–41
38 Ibid., 839
39 Darío's article appeared first in *El Tiempo* (Buenos Aires), 12 May 1896.
40 *Obras completas*, iii, 326
41 Ibid., 328–9
42 Ibid., 331
43 Ibid.
44 *Obras completas*, v, 860
45 Ibid., 956
46 *Obras completas*, ii, 493–518
47 Ibid., 857
48 Ibid., 941–58
49 *Obras completas*, ii, 992
50 Ibid., 505
51 *Obras completas*, v, 960
52 Ibid., 957–8

53 Ibid., 947
54 *Obras completas*, I, 118
55 Ibid., 955
56 *Obras completas*, I, 499
57 *Obras completas*, III, 328
58 *Poesías completas*, p. 628
59 Torres Bodet, p. 196
60 *Obras completas*, I, 229
61 This definition coincides with Darío's explanation of 'lo raro' in his essay 'Los colores del estandarte' (IV, 872–82) where he writes 'lo raro es lo contrario de lo normal, … los cánones del arte moderno no nos señalan más derroteros que el amor absoluto a la belleza clara, simbólica o arcana – y el desenvolvimiento y manifestación de la personalidad. Sé tú mismo: esa es la regla' (*Obras completas*, IV, 880).

Index

UNIVERSITY OF TORONTO ROMANCE SERIES

This book
was designed by
ANTJE LINGNER
under the direction of
ALLAN FLEMING
University of
Toronto
Press

Lightning Source UK Ltd.
Milton Keynes UK
UKHW010000210722
406167UK00001B/242